A tale of two gardens

ELSPETH THOMPSON

The Sunday Telegraph Urban Gardener

CASSELL
ILLUSTRATED

For Frank

First published in Great Britain in 2003 by Cassell Illustrated,
a Member of Octopus Publishing Group Limited
2-4 Heron Quays, London E14 4JP

Copyright © 2003 Elspeth Thompson

Illustrated by Toby Morrison

Distributed in the United States of America by
Sterling Publishing Co., Inc.,
387 Park Avenue South, New York, NY 10016-8810

A CIP catalogue record for this book is available from the British Library.

ISBN 1 84403 100 4

Contents

Introduction

This is a tale of two gardens – or three, if you count the unruly south London allotments where I've grown my own organic fruit and vegetables for the past seven years. The first garden was created on a small square of bare concrete in Brixton, south London; the second on windswept shingle on the south coast – and the allotments are just a stone's throw from the traffic-choked south circular. None would be an obvious first choice for a garden – but I've always enjoyed a challenge, particularly that of helping nature gain a foothold in unpromising places. I was born in the country, and have had a recurring dream to return there for as long as I can remember, but all sorts of reasons – including love and work – have so far kept me in town. And it's in the city, where nature is too often edged out by tarmac, cars and buildings, that I've found gardening to be most necessary – for both my own state of mind and that of my surroundings. I love the way a single silver birch tree can soften the relentless lines of a sixties office block; a front garden liven up an entire street; some daffodils bring colour to a cheerless council estate. Flowers look even more beautiful against a backdrop of unremitting grey.

When we bought our London house back in 1996, the size of the garden – just 20 x 20 feet and hemmed in by buildings – nearly put me off. But for someone whose gardening, however keen, had so far been confined to window ledges, balconies and roof terraces, it was definitely a move in the right direction. The longer I looked, the more I could see that the high white brick walls and the privacy they afforded could become the backdrop for the intimate outdoor room I'd often dreamed of. Several years on, after a lot of hard work, a few mistakes (I'll never have a wall built in the wrong place again) and hassles with builders, it is a quiet leafy haven that gives pleasure all year round and is home to all sorts of wildlife, including a pair of nesting blue tits. Far from feeling compromised, I've learned to embrace the challenges of gardening in the city, and have become passionate about green spaces in gritty urban areas – from Newcastle to New York – where their presence always feels so vital.

True, I did carry on dreaming of that garden in the country, and looking back through these columns, I'm amazed at how consistently I held a vision of a house by the sea. That dream became reality in the summer of 2000 when, in the course of research for an article, I stumbled upon the magical place that soon became the second garden in this story. From the moment I saw it, I loved it. For a city gardener used to cramped shady spaces, a long cycle-ride to the allotment and raising seedlings in the back of an ancient VW camper van, this garden with its big skies and proper greenhouse and vegetable garden right outside the back door was sheer heaven. And only a couple of minutes walk away was a beautiful deserted beach where we could walk the dog for miles with only seagulls for company. We rented the house for a year, and fell in love with the area for ever.

I don't think I could live without a garden now. Reading over the columns while gathering them together for this book, I'm struck by what a struggle gardening can be – in those years when spring never comes and the slugs get the cream of the crop. Sometimes I wonder: why do gardeners never give up? For me, I guess, it's that the rewards always outweigh the setbacks, however tough it gets. Those allotments that began as a way to get some extra space soon became a way of life. They have given me so much over the years: open soil and big skies in the heart of the city; a source of delicious fresh food that is not sprayed with pesticides fifteen times and carted half way across the country before it gets to my door; and a place to learn – by trial and frequent error and from the example and advice of others more knowledgeable than myself. They have also given me a taste of self-sufficiency that won't go away, no matter where I live. Tending plants and growing my own food has become a lifeline in a world that often seems to have lost its way. It's easy to feel helpless in the face of the destruction of our environment, the spread of genetically-modified crops and the extinction of so many species. Somehow, doing what I can in my own little patch helps me feel more hopeful. And beauty, whether in plants, places or people, is its own reward. I hope I shall continue to gain more joy than is feasible from a bowl of fragrant white narcissi on my desk, the first peas of summer swelling in their pods, and the scent of home-grown basil being torn into a salad.

I've been inordinately lucky in being able to combine gardening with one of my other great loves, writing. A journalist for many years, I'd long nurtured a dream to write about gardening, but assumed it would have to wait until I had a big garden in the country and knew a whole lot more – as that is how the "proper" garden writers did it. Nonetheless, my weekly Urban Gardener column in *The Sunday Telegraph* Magazine began back in 1996, and I shall always be grateful to the editors for their faith in the idea that a column written by a keen but inexperienced gardener, faced with the challenges of gardening in the city, might strike a chord with readers in a similar position. And to judge from the addresses of the many who write in with comments, encouragement and the occasional correction, it is by no means only urban gardeners who have to cope with slugs, snails, shade and lack of space.

Most of the columns are set in one of my own gardens, taking the form of a gardening journal here in London, at the seaside or the allotment. Sometimes holidays or other trips take them further afield. Wherever I travel, I'm always on the look out for others who garden in seemingly inauspicious places. I'm frequently moved and inspired by these "gardeners against the odds", who create places of beauty and magic where previously there was none – amid the peeling stucco facades of balconies in Havana; in the poorest neighbourhoods in New York; on small strips of rooftop from Chinatown to Chelsea and on sun-baked sand and shingle. The column gives me a chance to pass on the stories of these gardeners, along with some of their wisdom. Most of the gardening knowledge I have has been learned from other people, and I like to contribute in this way to the endless swapping of tips and advice that has been circulating among gardeners for centuries. Though I've learned a lot over the years, I'm certainly no expert still – as regular readers of the column will know. But there's always something to learn – and, with luck, a laugh or two to be had – from even the most embarrassing mistakes. I've realized, from a writer's point of view, that it's often the catastrophes that make the best copy; after all, who really wants to know when everything in your garden's rosy? On that note, I do feel obliged to warn readers against following too blithely in my footsteps. Often, I'll write about an idea in its early stages, buzzing with the enthusiasm and blind hope of the optimistic amateur. But if you follow the story and read on, a few columns down the line you'll find out what actually happened. Still, as we all know, this is how gardening so often works in real life...

This book does form a story of sorts, and the columns are arranged chronologically in the order in which they were first published. But they won't read like the chapters in a normal narrative book. Newspaper readership may be intermittent, and its memories short, and the columnist is obliged to re-set the scene for those who may have missed, or forgotten, previous instalments. So I apologize in advance for an inevitable degree of repetition. And I hope that the index, suppliers, nurseries, books and places mentioned will make the book useful, to experienced gardeners and novices alike.

A Tale of Two Gardens ends with another new garden in the making. We have recently bought our own little house by the sea, with a substantial garden, just down the track from the one we used to rent. We won't be moving to the country full-time – or at least not yet. I've realized I'm not ready; I would miss my friends too much, and the art galleries and restaurants, and the view of London, all lit up, from Waterloo Bridge at night. (Not for nothing do Clarkey and Simon, the old friends with whom I share the allotments, nick-name me the "urbane gardener"....) I would also miss this little garden and all it stands for: a breathing space for nature in the midst of the city. I love to wander out in the morning with a cup of coffee, and sit there for a moment while the city kick-starts itself into life in the distance. Whatever the weather, there is always something to thrill me – raindrops on nasturtium leaves, the first ripe tomatoes, a new flush of morning glories. So I'll still be an urban gardener, if only part-time. As I did during the year we spent commuting between London and the country, I hope I shall enjoy having two gardens again, and that the contrast between them will only add to the pleasure. The best news about the new place is that it actually has soil! Having made one garden on bare concrete and tended another built on shingle, it seems high time to indulge myself with some of the real stuff. The fact that most of that soil's currently hidden beneath a tangle of brambles, weeds and Russian vine, and littered with decades of debris, doesn't dismay me in the slightest. The thought of creating another new garden is just too exciting. But that's another story....

Brixton, April 2003

ACKNOWLEDGEMENTS

Huge thanks go to the following people who helped to make this book happen: Lucy Tuck and Rebecca Tyrrel, the editors at *The Sunday Telegraph* Magazine who first had faith in the idea of the Urban Gardener column and have encouraged me ever since; the other staff there, especially Elfreda Pownall, Lucy Bannell, Sophie Murray and Jenny Brown, who have helped in more ways than I can say; Camilla Stoddart and all the team at Cassell Illustrated; Melanie Eclare, Polly Farquharson, and Jonathan Buckley for their photographs; Toby Morrison for his spirited illustrations; and my wonderful agent, Jane Turnbull.

I want to thank all of the many gardeners all over the world who have welcomed me into their homes and shared their stories; especially Michael Crosby-Jones for letting me loose in his seaside house and garden for one of the happiest years of my life. Thanks to all my family and friends – not least for taking all those surplus beans and marrows off my hands; to Michael (Clarkey) Clark and Simon Steele, for being the best friends a gardening girl could have; and, of course, to my husband, Frank Wilson, for taking my mind off the slugs and bindweed and making me laugh more than anyone I know.

1999

FLOWERS IN FOCUS

The house is full of budding, sprouting things. For the past few weeks, the desk where I write has been strewn with jars and vases of catkins and spring flowers coming into bud. The last bowls of hyacinths and 'Paper White' narcissi, bought as bulbs last autumn and staggered to bloom from Christmas on, are just about over. But there are huge branches of pussy willow and forsythia on the mantelpieces, and jugs of daffodils and frilly scented 'Cheerfulness' on the kitchen table. I love the fresh, unaffected shapes and colours of these early spring things.

I've always liked to have flowers to look at while I work. When gazing into space in search of the right word, it is good to have something beautiful for the eye to alight on. And having flowers in constant, close proximity, you really do *look* at them. Right now I have some catkins – lovely, lemon, lambstail hazel catkins – in front of me. When freshly picked, each tassel is tightly articulated; after a few days tiny feathery flowers sprout between each segment, and the catkins become looser, paler, powdery things that blow puffs of yellow dust if disturbed. Observing them closely is a totally different experience to seeing them on the tree. In the open, it is the total effect one appreciates – the way the tassles, like strands of thick pale wool draped artlessly over the branches, lend a delicate vertical element to the hovering lateral twigs. To come across catkins while walking in a wood is such a thrill – I love the first sight of them from a distance, almost luminous among the other bare trees. You might stop and pass a couple through your fingers, but not for very long. You'd never scrutinize them in the wild as I am now, sitting at my desk.

It's the same with the other twigs and cuttings in front of me: *Viburnum tinus*, with its clusters of tiny tight pink buds opening into clouds of white stars, and the fuzzy chartreuse flowers of *Cornus mas*. A member of the dogwood family, *Cornus mas* becomes a fine spreading tree of 7.6m (25ft) or more. Its moment comes in early spring, when the bare branches are flushed with a yellowy haze as round olive-green buds burst into clusters of acid-lime flowers. I have admired the effect from afar in our local park, but this is the first year I've snapped off a twig (taken from part of the tree that looked as if it might need thinning) and taken it home to watch the spectacle close-to. The buds are tinged with bronzy red, as is so much early green growth, if you look. As they burst, the tiny tips of the flower buds poke through – at first a dull lime green, but lightening as they open until the first starry stamens emerge, bright canary yellow and as delicate as the hairs on a Venus flytrap. Since the buds appear in groups of three to seven, the massed blooms – each in itself a spray of spiky stars – make a pom-pom featuring every possible shade of lime and yellow. This is what gives the tree that lovely fuzzy appearance from a distance.

All plants, of course, have this dual appeal – the fabulous detail that can be caught in sharp focus and the blurry overall effect that relies more on outline, texture and movement. Appreciating a garden, we move constantly from one way of looking to the other, like a camera zooming in on a single bloom or seed head and then panning out to place it in its wider context. Sometimes we get "stuck" in one mode or another, as Mirabel Osler wittily observes in her book *A Breath from Elsewhere: Musings on Gardens* (Bloomsbury £7.99). Dividing garden visitors into "crouchers" and "gapers", she despairs at the former, who "move through a garden at a stoop: naming, gasping, hooraying, admiring or coveting" individual plants while missing the subtler, more atmospheric pleasures of the garden as a whole, but also pokes gentle fun at those who "saunter, smiling and sighing" at the wider picture, only to trip (sometimes literally) over the finer details at their feet. I'm sure I've done both in my time. But right now I'm having my cake and eating it. The forsythia at my allotment that so badly needed reshaping has been given a more graceful and open silhouette – while the prunings, just knobbly bare branches when cut, are bursting into bloom before my eyes.

14 March 1999

A CEILING FOR AN OUTDOOR ROOM

Sorting out the retaining wall at the back of our little town garden has given the place – and me – a new lease of gardening life. Instead of sitting at the kitchen windows wondering *what* I can do with the awkward sunken space outside – one friend suggested turning it into a jacuzzi – I'm out there every morning, tidying up the beds, checking on the spikes of bulbs that are poking through and organizing the layout for later in the year.

My original plans for the tiny walled garden to be a proper "outdoor room" are finally coming to fruition. The backdrop of ivies and other climbing plants now winds its way right up the white trellised walls like leafy wallpaper. There's even a token ceiling in the form of five wires, stretched from the top of the back wall and sloping up to just below my study window, along which tendrils of ivy and clematis are beginning to twirl. In a month or two they should be like leafy ropes laden with the pinkish-white flowers of *Clematis montana*. We've wound some outdoor fairy lights up around the walls and along the wires, too – by summer I hope the effect will be more star-studded bower than Greek taverna.

The effect of all this is quite magical. It has totally transformed the feel of the garden and made it an enclosed, romantic space. The five wires – about 1.2m (4ft) apart – will give a little dappled shade come high summer, when the deck can become a baking sun-trap, and help screen us from overlooking buildings. They also provide some much-needed greenery in the foreground – for the first time since our neighbour's wonderful robinia tree was chopped down last autumn, I'm not aware of its absence. In time, we can hang lanterns, crystals and bird-feeders on the outer edges.

Treating the garden as an "outdoor room" has become almost commonplace – but it is all too easy to forget about the "roof". You can enclose the space on three or four sides; you can put an interesting surface on the floor, and add furniture, lighting, sculpture. Yet in a garden, you always have to remember that the ceiling is the sky. On the plus side, this extra height means you can get away with spectacularly bold effects – over-sized pots, large-scale furniture and plants have room to "breathe". But unless some attempt is made to address the transition from garden to sky, it can feel like sitting in a lidless box. You need almost to "sculpt" the space above you – and just adding these few wires has created the enclosing impression of rafters in a roof, while still letting through plenty of light and air.

In a larger garden you might try doing this in just in one area – in a corner that's struck by the midday sun, or a terrace where you often eat. One of the loveliest outdoor meals I've had is in a garden in Tangier, beneath an arching bower of passion flowers, jasmine and vines. The paved area outside the house was enclosed by a low wall with a flowerbed built in to the middle, in which the climbers were planted and a series of painted metal arches set deep enough to support the plants. Candle lanterns hung from the apex of the arches, and threw shifting shadows over the cloth. As we ate, seated on curly metal 1950s chairs, the city and sea below were framed by leaves and flowers, and the scent of jasmine hung in the air.

21 March 1999

BALCONY GARDENS IN HAVANA

Walking the streets of Havana, Cuba, on a recent holiday, my eyes were fixed on the storey above street level. Much of the life of that extraordinary city seems to take place on its balconies – and each one tells a different story. On famous old streets such as the wide, tree-lined Prado, the balconies are like large outdoor rooms. Once-grand *loggias* with cake-icing curlicues and ornate metal grilles, now beginning to crumble, are crammed with the detritus of life lived on the bread-line: rusty bicycles, rickety old chairs and outdoor standpipes, from which nursing mothers draw water. In the early morning, very old people shuffle out to take the air and smoke the first of many fat cigars in the watery sunshine: one woman who must have been in her eighties would appear in psychedelic clothing and patent leather boots, with a huge *Cohiba* permanently between her lips, and peer out from behind a chipped chandelier and a menagerie of cats and colourful caged songbirds.

Further into the Old Town, where many of the buildings are being renovated as Castro's government turns to tourism to fill the gap left by Russian funding, some of the older, 18th-century buildings have smart wooden balconies and verandas, freshly painted in bright blue, green or brown. There are glimpses into shady interior courtyards, where strings of orchid-like white blooms drop down from the trellised roof and peacocks strut in the shadows. Many doorways have ornate fanlights filled with red, bright blue, orange and green glass, which throw lozenges of coloured light across floors and walls.

Havana has few private gardens in the conventional sense, but every inch of outdoor space has its fringe of plants and flowers, often displayed in ingenious ways. One balcony was crammed with succulent plants: they covered the back wall, where the pots hung in diamond patterns from brackets in the plaster, and sprawled down from the front railings like a

living curtain. Another had air plants growing up all the uprights – epiphytic plants (which don't need soil) thrive in the hot, humid atmosphere and attach themselves to every hospitable surface – even the telegraph lines are bristling with them. Containers range from hand-painted terracotta for some of the more well-to-do houses to old plastic dustbins and other make-shift contraptions in the poorer areas. Decades of strict trade embargos have made the Cubans loth to throw anything away: the lengths of old plastic drainpipe, split along the side, filled with soil and hung horizontally with crude metal brackets along the front of some of the balconies, were remi-niscent of some of the home-spun structures at my allotments back home. And the aloes that grew in them (used throughout the Caribbean to rub on cuts and sunburn) were certainly thriving.

Cuba's greatest inspiration for city gardeners elsewhere, though, has to lie in its use of colour. On one house, the paintwork was painted brightest cobalt blue against paler blue and petrol walls, with other areas and furni-ture picked out in turquoise. These closely-related shades of blue and aqua created a surprisingly good backdrop for the dark glossy green leaves of palms and vine-like creepers. I have often fantasized about a blue garden, with the walls painted in different shades, and glazed ceramic pots of aga-panthus, delphiniums, cerinthes and other bright blue flowers. Another building was painted Neapolitan ice-cream shades of pale pink, cream, brown and blue, with the ironwork in acid lime. Other combinations that worked well with foliage included pea-green and turquoise (striped around the doors of Ernest Hemingway's favourite bar, the Bodeguita del Medio; turquoise with two shades of lilac; and strong mid-blue gloss paintwork against ochre walls. Now that summer is coming and our gardens and outdoor spaces, even in Britain, will be functioning once more as outdoor rooms, it could be time to get out the paintbrush. My rickety old cricket chairs will be painted the same greyish purple of the doors and window frames – and who knows? I might even repaint our deck.

28 March 1999

SOWING FOR SUMMER

Seed-sowing panic set in when I returned from our honeymoon. The bene-fits of three weeks away were nearly lost as I scrabbled about in the cellar looking for empty seed trays, pots and propagators, and searched in vain for the seed orders I had scribbled out (but, of course, neglected to send off) in the weeks before the wedding. Usually by now, every windowsill in the house – not to mention my ancient VW campervan, which is commandeered as a mobile greenhouse in spring) is fringed with green as hundreds of seedlings sprout into life: this summer's crops already on the way. Still, there are advantages in being a bit tardy.

Often, tempted by the photographs and descriptions in the catalogues, I end up with a huge pile of seed packets – enough to stock a large country estate rather than the 6 x 6m (20 x 20ft) back garden and couple of allotments that are my lot. (It's a good idea to share seed orders with a friend – particularly one who has a greenhouse.) This year, ordering by phone rather than by post seemed to restrain me – especially as, this late in the day, some things had sold out. Rather than going blindly for new vegetable varieties (20 types of squash, as I remember, last year – practically all of which succumbed to slugs), I disciplined myself to tried and tested favourites from The Organic Gardening Catalogue (01932 253666/www.organiccatalog.com) and just a handful of unknowns. Ferme de Sainte Marthe, a new company based in France, specializes in rare and forgotten vegetable varieties, including a vast range of squashes – I managed, with difficulty, to contain my order to six (they are now distributed by The Organic Gardening Catalogue). As for flowers, I went for a few things I love and which can be hard to find as plants (*Nicotiana sylvestris*, a dark maroon-black sweetpea called 'Midnight' from Thompson and Morgan (01473 688821) and the gorgeous bluey bracts and purple flowers of *Cerinthe major* 'Purpurascens' – as well as such staples as cosmos and morning glory. Any gaps will be filled with self-seeded love-in-a-mist, Californian poppies, pot marigolds and other annuals – nasturtiums and sunflowers – that I know can soon be sown straight into the soil and will make up for lost time.

This new, pared-down approach is not only cheaper but also more realistic until the day I have a greenhouse of my own and a bit more space to play with. I must say it is something of a relief to have a manageable number of pots and trays to look after; the pressure of all those little lives to nurture sometimes seems overwhelming. There is a crucial time with seedlings – when their roots start to emerge from the bottom of pots or plugs – when they must be either planted out or potted on into larger pots. The former is often not feasible if it's still early in the year and the ground is cold or wet; the latter means more work, more pots and more space. Dither about and, as I've learned to my cost in the past, the plants' growth is checked by the delay. I'm hoping that I have avoided some of this hassle by sowing later – even if I have to wait a little longer for the plants to fruit and flower.

The truth is that, unless you're super-organized, with a heated greenhouse and a lot of time on your hands, sowing too much too early can be counter-productive. The only things that really need a head start under cover are those that simply won't germinate without heat, or annuals which need more weeks of warmth than the average British summer can provide if they are to produce a good crop (tomatoes, for instance). So if, like me, you are late this year with your sowing – don't despair. Raise a few packets of tender favourites under cover, but for the rest, why not wait a few more weeks until the soil's ripe for direct sowing outside? The plants will soon catch up with those transplanted from inside – sow in small batches and cover with sawn-off plastic bottle cloches to get them off to a good start and protect from late frost and slugs. Plants, just like human beings, don't take kindly to too much shunting about, and I've often got the best results from being patient with those left to grow where they were sown.

11 April 1999
TOPPING UP THE POTS

In order to organize our tiny back garden for a summer of outdoor suppers and sitting in the sun, something had to be done about the builders' bags of soil still standing around after the alterations to the back retaining wall. Just cutting into a curved brick wall to make it square – an area that takes up no more than a square yard in the garden – had liberated huge amounts of topsoil, too heavy to move far and too good to waste. Time for some major re-potting.

All plants grown in containers, whether indoors or out, benefit from re-potting every two years or so. This gives rootbound plants some room to make a surge of spring growth, and also offers a chance to replace tired old soil with a fresh nutrient-packed supply. With any luck, you can also get rid of diseases and infestations at the same time. Sometimes removing just the top 6–8in (15–20cm) of soil will do; this year, because of all this lovely spare topsoil, I decided to replace the lot. The discovery of some dreaded vine weevil beetles in some of my pots last summer means I shall be on the alert for their fat white grubs around the roots. Although I treated the entire garden in autumn with nematodes from Green Gardener (01603 715096), you can never be sure how many of the grubs may have slipped through the net and are gorging themselves on the roots of your prize plants. Replacing the soil and checking all the roots in spring is the only sure-fire way to get shot of them. I covered the wooden deck with newspaper and began the first of many afternoons' work, freeing plants from their surrounding soil, working through the roots gently but firmly, and tipping the old soil in the containers into a pile which, once checked for weevils or worse, could be scattered on the surface of the large flower bed. (Any containing weevils should be bagged up and disposed of).

You have to work quickly, as you don't want your plants to dry out or suffer too much upheaval. I sank the bare-rooted specimens into a bath of dilute liquid seaweed feed before plunging them back in their pots and refilling with pristine fresh soil – the equivalent for plants, I'd like to think, of slipping between freshly-ironed linen sheets after a lovely long bath.

Inspired by the Irish garden writer Helen Dillon in her collection of writings *Helen Dillon on Gardening* (Town House Dublin, £10.99), I mixed six parts of the garden topsoil with two parts damp peat-substitute (coir or garden compost) and two parts horticultural sand. For the best results with summer flowering containers, she recommends the mixture used at Powys Castle in Wales, which is renowned for its excellent containers – one bucket Shamrock potting compost, half a bucket of garden compost and a quarter bucket of coarse grit. If you're still concerned about vine weevils, Levington now manufactures a special "Plant Protection" compost impregnated with "Intercept" insecticide, which kills vine weevil larvae and also controls aphids (while claiming not to harm beneficial insects such as ladybirds, bees and lacewings). Or for the natural alternative, order nematodes from Green Gardener, who will deliver twice yearly in April and August – the best times for treatment.

Before going anywhere near the soil, however, you need to ensure you've got good drainage. I've learned the importance of this the hard way and now never fail to put pieces of broken crockery over the holes in the bottom of the pot (*never* succumb to the temptation to plant straight into a pot without holes) and then fill with gravel for at least 3–4in (7.5–10cm) (more for larger pots). Then even if you should overwater or (more likely in this country) the pots are subjected to lengthy downpours), the roots won't get waterlogged and rot, causing the plant to die.

The last of our surplus topsoil was reserved for some lovely new pots and tubs we'd been given as wedding presents. Another friend's present is to be a couple of small trees to go in large containers in the front garden. I hope to report soon on their ceremonial planting.

11 April 1999

CREAM OF THE WINTER CROPS

Last year, as I frequently moaned in print, was not the best year for allotment crops. But such crops as there were have proved to be long-lasting. There seems to have been less of a gap this year between the last of the overwintering vegetables and this year's sowings. We have only recently enjoyed the last of the brussels sprouts; I was tempted to pull them up in late January, as they didn't seem to be doing anything, but since then, all the tight little buttons beneath the cabbagey heads have matured into tasty sprouts. The variety, 'Peer Gynt', which was recommended for its long season, has certainly lived up to its reputation. This year we're trying 'Falstaff', a purply-red variety which is said to have a good flavour (from The Organic Gardening Catalogue 01932 253666).

We are also appreciating this year's purple sprouting broccoli. Its young shoots, with a frill of young leaves attached, are delicious steamed, or dipped, like asparagus, into a mustardy hollandaise sauce. This is one of my all-time favourite allotment vegetables – well worth the ten months it takes from sowing to harvest, both for its beauty (that subtle combination of dark blue-green leaves and purply florets is heart-stopping, especially with a sprinkling of raindrops) and its fresh home-grown taste (eat your heart out, expensive, non-organic supermarket varieties). It is now time to think about sowing *this* year's brassicas – in drills 1cm (0.3in) deep for thinning out in early summer. Cover the seedlings with netting or else, as I found out the year before last, the birds will have the lot.

We unearthed still more jerusalem artichokes in the patch we were trying to clear for this year's peas – some rather slug-nibbled, but enough for a last lot of delicious soup. Following Christopher Lloyd's advice in his excellent book, *Gardener Cook* (Frances Lincoln £20) I now add two thirds of their weight in carrots, which not only makes for a beautiful colour and flavour but also, in his own words, has "a quietening influence" – not for nothing have these vegetables been nicknamed "fartichokes" in our household. It's worth keeping some of the tubers back for planting in rows 46cm (18in) apart and 15cm (6in) deep – you can do this about now, using shop-bought tubers if you've none of your own. As it's so hard to eradicate the plants from an area, it's best to leave a patch of artichokes in situ – we started out by rotating them with other crops and now find seedlings sprouting up everywhere. Our plants provide a screen against the Territorial Army depot next door, with morning glory and sweetpeas weaving in and out of the long stalks.

One of the best surprises over winter was the red Italian chicory (radicchio) that popped up among one of the 'Saladisi' salad leaf mixtures. In the course of a few weeks, long after most of the other leaves had bolted, what had looked like a rather leathery, red-streaked lettuce had transformed itself into a deep magenta beauty with crinkled, glossy leaves that added a certain bitter glamour to our salads. The colour remains brightest when the weather is cold, but it can apparently be cropped till May if it hasn't bolted by then. ('Palla Rossa' – the variety used in the mixture – is a red-leaved chicory that doesn't require forcing and is available in this mixture or on its own from The Organic Gardening Catalogue.)

Right the way through winter, we've been able to pick enough leaves off the two rows of perpetual spinach to make risottos and pasta sauces. *Beta vulgaris* is actually a type of beetroot with a very small root, and is often grown instead of true spinach because it is slower to bolt. This year I may have a go at the real thing, easily distinguishable by its darker, crinkly leaves and rich flavour – it needs well-manured, moist ground and has to be grown in large quantities to make for proper helpings ('Bloomsdale','Sigmaleaf' and 'Symphony' are said to be bolt-resistant).

We've already planted several rows of new potatoes ('Sharpe's Express', which will be ready in June), a bed of red onions and two more of shallots. How exciting to think of this summer's crops already on their way.

WEIRD AND WONDERFUL SQUASHES

Courgettes and squashes are some of the easiest and most productive vegetables to grow. Provided there is enough late summer sun, they should romp happily all over your vegetable patch and oblige with copious crops well into autumn. Just a few plants of each are enough to feed a family. The first year at the allotment I proudly planted out 12 courgette seedlings – they all flourished and I was giving away courgettes (some swollen into mini-marrows) until the first frosts. And each year, a single pumpkin plant, interspersed with self-sown nasturtiums, sprawls lazily across the bed allocated to it and often sets its fruit among a neighbouring crop. I let it have its way as I like a touch of wantonness in the late summer garden.

This year, we may well be overrun with the things, provided we can stave off the slugs that devoured half last year's crops while I was away on holiday. I've just received my order of seeds from some of the companies specializing in unusual or "heritage" vegetables, including an intriguing selection of squashes and courgettes. A few weeks ago I mentioned "Ferme de Sainte Marthe" – a new organic company run by a French couple from their farm in Montfort L'Amaury, and distributed in the UK by Chase Organics (01932 266630). Their catalogue is a beautifully-illustrated and informative affair including (alongside 34 types of tomato, ten types of cucumber, white aubergines and strawberry spinach, with its juicy scarlet fruits) an incredible 57 varieties of pumpkin, squash and (inedible) gourd. There are blue squashes, loofah squashes, squashes shaped like Turks' turbans, squashes shaped like huge warty black rugby balls, and squashes doubled over on themselves like trombones. There are large white pumpkins, small striped pumpkins and jack-o'-lantern pumpkins, not to mention technicolour gourds, which can be dried and made into bottles, bowls and plates. You can choose climbing squashes that can be grown over frames or arches (*Lageneria longissima* has fruits up to a metre long) and squashes whose flesh tastes of chestnuts ('Squash Potimarron'), of nutmeg ('Sugarpumpkin of Berry') and of almonds ('Lady Godiva'). Thanks to the evocative names, luscious colour photos and descriptions, I succumbed to a good half-dozen types, including butternut squashes (for my favourite risotto), the rare 'Olive squash' (said to have "orange flesh of the most exceptional quality") and the 'Spaghetti squash', which is cooked whole and cut open to reveal stringy innards which look exactly like a plate of spaghetti.

For courgettes, try Simpson's Seeds (01985 845004), a family-run business that specializes in unusual and old-fashioned tomatoes. Of the eight varieties on offer this year, one has yellow fruits ('Goldrush'), two are round ('Tondo di Chiaro di Nizza' and 'Triple Five') and one is a gorgeous dark bluey-green ('Zucchini' – recommended for early crops). Simpson's has also sent me trial seeds of a bi-coloured courgette called 'Zephyr' – half green and half yellow – which should be available next year. Or, for some seriously unusual vegetables, Future Foods in Somerset (01398 361347) combs the world for weird and wonderful varieties, including squashes named (honest) 'Achocca Fat Baby', 'Hairy Melon', 'Lady's Slipper' and the 'Snake Gourd'.

Squashes, pumpkins and courgettes can either be sown indoors in small pots and planted out when the risk of frost has passed, or direct into the soil from May onwards, protected by a cloche (sawn-off 2-litre/^{1}/$_2$-gallon plastic bottles do the job nicely). Prepare the ground for courgettes by making mounds of soil mixed with well-rotted manure at least 0.6m (2ft) apart, with a circular "moat" to retain water around the base. Pumpkins and squashes enjoy similar treatment, with larger piles and more space between, but this year we've decided to go for the traditional custom of growing them on a glorified compost heap. The huge mound of soil from the pond excavation has been banked up with prunings and the remains of last year's crops to make a semi-circular raised bed from which I hope the fruits and tendrils will dangle in a decorative fashion. We've been burying our kitchen waste in pockets spaced evenly across the surface in preparation for sowing next month. Here's to a squash-filled summer!

2 May 1999

PEST PARADISE

Our little back garden is now known as Pest Paradise. A small walled garden in London's mild microclimate is a haven for every baddie in the book, and owing to the almost total lack of frost this year, many of them have overwintered in alarming numbers. Like much of the country, we have been inundated with greenfly. I returned from holiday to find my climbing rose, all the euphorbias and the tubs of tulips bristling with them, and have been out every morning with the soft-soap spray ever since. The experience has reminded me how much of gardening is about looking. The friend who very kindly kept the pots and borders watered while we were away had not been

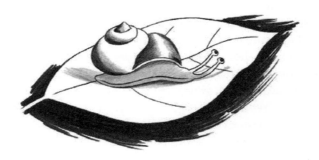

alerted to look for them: I had thought it was too early to worry. But I know I am not the only one to have been taken unawares.

Soft soap is a good organic insecticide (Phostrogen makes one that has a dose dispenser to help achieve the right concentration). It contains natural fatty acids that break down the casings of greenfly, blackfly, whitefly, mealy bugs and scale insects. I seem to have knocked the problem on the head now, but the new shoots on my roses were so smothered that I chose to prune them off. New growth is now returning, but if I miss a day or two's spraying, the aphids are back with a vengeance. Part of the problem must be our neighbour's rose bush, which is crawling with them.

Neighbours can be a real pest themselves when it comes to infestations – particularly in town gardens. No matter how well you may get on with the people, their horticultural problems are likely to leap the garden wall. This flummoxed me when I tried to work out how to deal with our dreaded vine weevils. These, too, are proving a real problem in urban gardens this spring – partly, again, because of the warmer winter, and partly due to the recent banning of chemicals that once helped control them. The increased popularity of container gardening has also been held responsible – the weevils' favourite habitat is pots, tubs and window boxes, where the larvae kill plants by feasting on their roots unseen. The official organic remedy is to replace the soil of every affected plant – I'd encountered some of the 1cm- (0.3in-) long cream coloured larvae with brown heads while re-potting my tub-grown plants last month. But if your neighbour has the problem and the weevils are simply going to march over from next door to lay their eggs (each vine weevil can lay up to 1,500 eggs in the course of a single season and they can travel long distances in search of the perfect home), all your labour will be in vain. Having spent the best part of a week re-potting, I couldn't stomach the thought of doing it all over again.

So that, I am afraid, is how I came to find myself in my local garden centre bulk-buying the sort of chemicals I have spent most of my gardening life avoiding (Sybol, if you're interested, is said to be effective against vine weevil larvae, as is Armillatox). "It's the only way," said the shop owner, "If you zap them now you'll save yourself problems later on when the larvae pupate and hatch into adults and the cycle starts all over again." He threw in a systemic insecticide for the greenfly (which is watered on to the plant and makes its way up through the sap to poison the pests) and some slug pellets for good measure. I felt like a traitor handing over the money, but told myself I was going to have to be cruel to be kind. And I can't afford to replace many more plants.

When I got home I unpacked my battery of weapons on the kitchen table and stared at them. When it came to it, I couldn't bring myself to use them. They are now propped on a chair by the french windows, as a warning to the garden as to what's on its way should it fail to sort itself out.

The Henry Doubleday Research Association (one of the principal national organizations for organic gardening) operates an advice service on how to deal with pests and diseases without harming other wildlife. Non-members should write to HDRA, Ryton Organic Gardens, Coventry CV8 3LG; members can telephone 02476 303517. Annual membership (which also includes a quarterly magazine, free entry to many gardens throughout the country and a 10 per cent discount off items in The Organic Gardening Catalogue) costs £18.50 for individuals, £22 for families and £12 concessions.

9 May 1999

COMMUNING WITH PLANTS

Last October I sat in a circle of people in a large room in Scotland, attempting to communicate with the soul of a cyclamen. After we had sat for several minutes in silent meditation round the little potted plant, people started "sharing". Our impressions were remarkably similar: lightness, innocence, beauty, quiet surprise. Cynics might surmise that these musings were suggested by the physical appearance of the plant rather than contact with any deeper, hidden presence. But, according to Dorothy Maclean, who led the week-long workshop entitled, "God, Humanity and Nature", there is no contradiction involved. Like some Hindu teachings, Ms Maclean holds that "form follows Divine function" – and that every different physical form on earth is an illustration of a divine idea in the mind of God. She therefore believes that everything has a divine "message" to impart to humans, whether this is received as words or, as she experiences it, as a deeper communion with its "essence".

I had come to the right place to learn more about the possibilities of communication with the plant world. The Findhorn Foundation on the east coast of Scotland first hit the headlines in the Sixties, when the Soil Association investigated claims that 60lb cabbages were being grown in the sandy soil of a scruffy old caravan site. They found a group of three friends – Eileen and Peter Caddy and Dorothy Maclean – who were meditating in their vegetable garden and playing classical music to the plants. In one of her meditations, Dorothy experienced a mystical contact with the spirit of the garden pea. Peter, the practical "man of action" of the group, gave her lists of questions to ask the different plant spirits or "devas" and their gardening followed Dorothy's guidance to the letter. When word spread of the experiment – and its spectacular results – visitors flocked from the ends of the earth, and an alternative community was born.

Today, there are no more giant cabbages at Findhorn, and Dorothy Maclean has moved to America – though she lectures and holds workshops all over the world. But the community in Scotland still practices a unique style of gardening, attempting to "tune in" to the plants during a brief meditation before starting work, and leaving space for contemplation. We were encouraged to work in silence, becoming aware of all aspects of the plants we were dealing with – their physical appearance, their growth patterns and particular energies. When pruning or transplanting, we learned to ask silent permission of the plant – to give warning of the disruption and explain our reasons. When harvesting, we were to offer mute thanks. Even the tools were to be thanked after use, by brushing them carefully clean and hanging them on their appointed hooks.

The week was a fascinating, peaceful experience, and offered me lots of food for thought. Like many gardeners, I talk to my plants and have enjoyed a special connection with certain loved specimens. Ever since reading *The Secret Life of Plants* by Peter Tompkins and Christopher Bird (Harper & Row, £11.25) – where I first read about Findhorn back in the early Eighties – I have been intrigued by the notion of deepening the relationship between humans and plants. The book contains reports of scientific experiments where a dracaena plant wired up to the electrodes of a lie detector appeared to respond clearly to friendly or hostile *intentions* – not just actions – of humans towards it. When the scientist *thought* about burning one of his plant's leaves, the needle on the graph swung wildly; when loving thoughts were sent – even from a distance of several hundred miles – the reaction was clearly positive. More recent experiments, backed up by research by the British scientist, Rupert Sheldrake, do seem to suggest that plants flourish in an atmosphere of active goodwill and cooperation. And at the Perelandra Center for Nature Research in Virginia, America, Michaelle Small Wright publishes books and papers and sells soil balancing kits that are the fruits of her conscious cooperation with the nature kingdom.

I hope to touch again on this aspect of gardening in the future and would be grateful to hear from readers who have had interesting experiences.

The Findhorn Foundation, The Park, Forres IV36 3TZ, Scotland (01309 672288); Perelandra Center for Nature Research, PO Box 3603, Warrenton, VA 20188, USA. *Choices of Love* by Dorothy Maclean (Lindisfarne Books, £11.95).

16 May 1999

PLANTING A NEW TREE

I've spent much of the past month travelling up and down the country interviewing people about trees for a series of features on Radio 4 (*Tree Stories*, which begins today at 2.45pm). Predictably, perhaps, talking to people who are passionate about trees has made me long to have some more around our house. We already have one tree in our tiny 20x20ft back garden – a *Prunus* x *subhirtella* 'Autumnalis', which has pinkish-white flowers on bare black branches from November to April and has only just substituted fully-fledged leaves for blossom. But when a friend offered to buy us a tree as a wedding present, I wondered if we could squeeze in one more. The corner of the garden opposite to the *Prunus* could do with a strong upright – I've thought of weaving a rose around a column, or installing a tall wicker teepee for sweetpeas. Why not go the whole hog and plant a tree?

Trees in small gardens make people nervous. What if they take over? Will their roots invade the walls? Would the entire area be plunged into shade? But then I remembered the gardening writer Mirabel Osler, whose narrow town garden in Ludlow is host to no fewer than 37 trees which she has trimmed and trussed into wonderful shapes. "Don't you worry about the trees growing too big for the space?" I asked her. "Not at all!" she laughed. "I'm in my seventies, so I shan't be around. Somebody else can deal with it!" Lighten up, I told myself. We'll probably have moved by the time our new tree grows to a tricky size – with any luck taking it with us to a larger garden, where it can grow old in style. So – which tree to choose?

In a very small garden you want either a tree with a compact, vertical habit, or a feathery, branching one that will not form too dense a canopy. After considering a rowan (too wild – I associate them with the Highlands), a Japanese acer (too red) or even a *Robinia pseudoacacia* to replace the one the neighbours chopped down, I settled on one of my other favourite trees. I'd first seen *Cercis siliquastrum* in our local park and was captivated by the maroon and magenta buds which appear in clusters all along the bare branches before bronzy, heart-shaped leaves emerge. Having tracked it down in the "Trees/Small/Pink" section in my *RHS Encyclopaedia of Plants and Flowers* (Dorling Kindersley, £35), I was heartened to discover it has a maximum height of 7.6m (25ft) and can tolerate light shade – just what I was after. Added to which, one of its common names is "The Love Tree", making it absolutely perfect for a wedding present.

One sunny Saturday last month we made a trip down to a nursery in Kent where I'd tracked down a 1.8m (6ft) specimen via the *RHS Plantfinder* (Dorling Kindersley, £12.99). It was planted immediately we got back, in a large hole about three times as wide as the rootball, with well-rotted stable manure dug into the base and bonemeal sprinkled around the sides. Planting a tree is a two-person job. I crouched down to unravel the roots, spreading them as gently as I could across the base of the hole, while Frank held the trunk and stake in position, jiggling them every so often to settle them in place. The displaced soil (also mixed with manure) was then shovelled back in and firmed down to the original level before watering well and mulching the surface with compost mixed with cocoa bark. The deep magenta blossoms are the perfect foil for the clouds of *Clematis montana* behind it and the pointy pink buds of jasmine just coming into flower, while the bronzy leaves are complemented by the phormiums, heucheras and bronze fennel growing nearby. The autumn leaves turn yellow, which will stand out well against the backdrop of dark ivy. As we stood back to admire our work, I thought how fascinating it would be to plant a lot of trees one day. Once they are planted, all you have to do is watch them grow – give or take the odd bout of pruning. And I couldn't help wondering where this little tree's graceful branches might end up spreading one day.

23 May 1999

READ ALL ABOUT IT

May is a wonderful time for gardeners. There is all the promise of summer with none of the disappointment of the wet, slug-filled Junes and Julys that have been our lot in recent years. There is the excitement of sowing seeds, buying plants, planning visits to other gardens and suppers out of doors. And there is all that hope – that *this* will be the year when we solve the slug problem, grow the perfect roses, time the lettuces and runner beans so that they aren't all ready at once.

I am certainly optimistic. The warm weather at the beginning of the month meant I was gardening for days on end, with only the lengthening shadows to tell me how long I'd been at it. For the first time ever, I actually feel on top of the allotment, with all 18 raised beds repaired and in cultivation, and scarcely a weed in sight. The first year, we got rid of the thistles, which used to pop up in all the beds, just by pulling them up with their tap roots intact. The second year saw the bindweed brought down to manageable levels in most areas: pinching off the snakey purple tips whenever they poke through the soil seems to weaken the plant over time, and we comb the beds for the white roots while digging. It is only the ground elder that is still a major problem – and that's only in one corner and along a border, where our neighbour has let it get out of control. I'm proud to say we resisted the temptation to use weedkillers, even when it seemed to be a seductive solution to the problem. (On one occasion I had to be physically restrained from running to the shop to get some.) Hoeing between the rows is the traditional way to keep weeds down among vegetables but in raised beds, where you can plant and sow closer together, in blocks rather than rows, weeding can be a rather finicky affair – at least until the leaves of the crops have grown big enough to shut out the light. So I was interested to learn of a new (to me) method of growing through newspaper, which acts as a mulch, keeping in the moisture and cutting down on weeds.

I came across this on a recent trip to Wales, where I met Brian Macdonald, who is restoring the two walled kitchen gardens at Maes-y-Neuadd hotel and restaurant, near Harlech. Mr Macdonald raises his beans, courgettes and salad crops under glass and then, when the plants are an inch or two high and ready to plant out, pokes them through holes in sheets of newspaper (five or six layers thick) which he has laid out to cover the soil in his beds. Watering well before and after laying the paper keeps the soil moist and the paper from blowing away – and you can weight it down with a further mulch of compost or grass clippings. As the paper gradually decomposes, the nutrients filter down into the soil with no weeding or digging. I am using this method with some of my beans and sweetcorn this year, and have also experimented with direct sowing into a narrow gap between two lots of newspapers, with the folded sides facing the furrow.

As for the slugs and snails, which caused me nightmares and cost me a lot of crops over the past two summers, I have developed a two-pronged attack. One is our new pond. I am hoping to encourage lots of frogs and toads to come and feast on our slimy friends. The other is grit – and lots of it. Quite understandably, slugs and snails do not like the feel of sharp, uneven surfaces on their soft underbellies, and can be deterred from even approaching your plants by a barrier of something sharp and gritty around the edges of the beds or surrounding the plants themselves. There is a special preparation in the shops which not only has a gritty texture, it also contains a naturally absorbent mineral which dries out the mucus produced by slugs and snails and claims to "stop them in their tracks". Completely environmentally friendly, "New Slug Stoppa" can be dug into the soil at the end of the season to improve structure. The only snag is it's expensive (ring LC Solutions on 01525 279555 for prices and stockists) and needs to be renewed regularly.

In the absence, so far, of frogs and toads, I am putting all my faith and hope in grit: I've even doubled up with strips of coarse sandpaper staple-gunned round the edges of the raised beds containing vulnerable plants such as lettuce and courgettes. This might seem like paranoid overkill, but I can't help thinking that all those nice newspapers might make a lovely new home for a colony of slugs....

30 May 1999

THE PLEASURES OF PONDS

The pond is the most exciting thing to have happened at the allotment since I discovered you could eat raw peas in their pods. We finally finished lining, filling and planting it up last weekend and can talk of little else. In fact, I have become a pond bore. I think everybody should have one. They're so easy. Particularly if, like me, you're lucky enough to have someone else do the difficult digging bit.

For a wildlife pond (and this is what we are after, the most welcome wildlife being frogs and toads who will gorge themselves on our slugs) a minimum depth of 0.6m (2ft) is recommended to give creatures an ice-free place for hibernation. The sides should be shelved, to allow different depths of water for marginal plants, and at least one side must be gently sloping, to

enable animals to get in and out easily. A friend has offered us some tadpoles, and all sorts of creatures seem to be making a home in our new pond, too.

Initially, we were going to "puddle" the pond – that is, tread the clay-like bottom down by foot in the hope that it would act as a natural liner. Our end of the allotment site is jolly waterlogged in wet weather and at one point we thought we might have discovered a spring. But as the weather got warmer, the water level in the roughly dug hole got lower and lower. We decided to line it, as it seemed irresponsible to encourage wildlife, only to have their home dry up in high summer. First went a thick layer of old newspapers, wetted down with a watering can, to stop stones or roots puncturing the rubber liner (you can use old carpet for this but it can be hard to manipulate). As an extra precaution we followed this with fluffy nylon fleece (the sort used to quilt unpleasant dressing gowns – about half the price of the stuff sold in pond shops and just as effective; John Lewis sells it in its haberdashery department). Then it was out with the liner, (a bargain in a sale), which we trod down into position with bare feet, trying to get rid of wrinkles and air bubbles. Empty of water and covered in shiny black plastic, it seemed hard to imagine how any wild creature would give this bald, artificial place a second look.

To fill the pond, we used a length of hosepipe as a syphon, plunging one end into the water tank several yards away. A syphon needs the tank end to be significantly higher than the other (which, happily, ours is) and a vacuum created in the pipe by sucking (which, happily, my friend Simon did – I stood by with the water and chewing gum to take the taste of the rank old water away). It took a good two hours to fill right up to the top, during which time we cut mats of turf from the edges of our paths to surround the pond, help hide the liner and knit it into the soil – this needs watering well in the early days to prevent it drying out and dying.

On our next visit we did some planting – oxygenating plants such as hornwort (*Ceratophyllum demersum*) and common pond weed in the middle, kingcups, marsh marigolds and flag irises around the edge (the labels tell you what depth of water they like). One day we might get a water lily. Till then, though, I'm completely mesmerized by the waterboatmen chasing to and fro and the changing patterns of the clouds reflected on the surface. I'm already trying to work out where we can incorporate a small pond into our already crowded back garden.

Not everybody shares my new enthusiasm, however. I was visiting some friends in their new house the other day and after dinner they took me outside (as people sometimes do) to see if I had any suggestions for the garden, which they had completely razed to the ground in a desire to create something new. "What about a pond?" I trilled with the true zeal of the convert. "That corner over there is crying out for one, and you could use that odd pile of stones as a surround." There was a silence before Niki replied: "That *was* a pond. We filled it in because we think they're boring."

6 June 1999

MIRROR, MIRROR ON THE WALL

Our tiny back garden has just doubled in size overnight. No, a wall did not fall down, nor has my neighbour made over his garden to me in a fit of beneficence. All I did was put up a mirror. The rear wall of the garden – the wall we look out on from the house – now has a 2m- (6ft-) square 'window' in the trellis, which appears to open on to another, secret, courtyard beyond. The effect is really quite magical. Not only is there an extremely convincing illusion of extra space; there also seems to be more light and movement in the garden. The plants immediately in front of the mirror – a small bamboo, a bronze *Phormium tenax*, a cardoon and a clump of *Euphorbia amygdaloides* var. *robbiae* 'Rubra' – suddenly look much larger, and sunlight bounces off their leaves and onto the mirror and back again until the entire border seems a-quiver with life. It's as if everything – ourselves included – has been given more room to breathe. A more tangible advantage is that we can now see the plants growing up the back wall of the house – a wisteria, a grapevine, several clematis, a passion flower and a golden hop – without even going outside. British weather being what it is, our enjoyment of the garden, even in summer, is often from the confines of the house, so extending the view in this way makes good sense,

Using mirrors is one of the most powerful ways to transform a small garden – or add a sense of intrigue to a larger one. But it's important to get it right, so experiment first with a freestanding mirror, noting its effects on light and space in different positions and at different times of day. Avoid placing a mirror directly opposite doors and windows – your own reflection staring back at you will shatter the illusion before it's even begun – and unless you want to turn your garden into a weird 'hall of mirrors', don't have two mirrors reflecting one another *ad infinitum*. A frame or, better still, a mock doorway, will strengthen the sense of a view into a phantom space beyond. Don't forget that the thickness of the arch itself will also be doubled by the mirror. Or you could go even more surreal: I once fell in love with a Parisian garden that had an old fireplace, complete with mirror above it and objects on the mantelpiece, built into one of the walls.

Mirrors give a good return for your money. When my regale lilies come up, it will look as if I'd bought double the number of bulbs. And by placing two large mirrors at right angles to one another you can create the effect of an instant large parterre with just a few box balls. A water feature would similarly be doubled in size – a formal rill running right up to a mirror "door" in the wall would be especially dramatic.

The improved light, though, is probably the most useful effect of installing a mirror – particularly in a small, shady urban space. Even though our mirror faces north-east, it has the morning sun and later in the day, lesser reflections off the other white-painted walls to work with. I am thinking of positioning one or two smaller mirrors to harness the afternoon sunshine, which plays on the back of the house. A metre-square mirror to one side of the french windows could bounce the late sun right back into the border; it might be enough to increase the range of plants that will be happy there. If we hang the mirror on a hinge, rather like an old-fashioned window frame, we could even control the direction of the light ourselves. The possibilities are endless.

To end on a practical note, mirrors are highly susceptible to damage outdoors, so sealing the back and edges is advisable. We painted on a couple of coats of yacht varnish, and used clear silicon bath sealant to attach it to its niche in the wall. 'Framing' the mirror in wood or waterproof tape will also prevent water seeping down inside and spoiling the silvering. One last thing: remember that you won't be the only one to be deceived by the illusion of space – don't place a mirror too high or in too open a spot, as there's a danger that birds might fly into it.

13 June 1999

KILLING SLUGS – THE NATURAL WAY

The other day I saw a song thrush at the allotment. It was perched on one of the big rocks by our new pond, smashing a large snail against the stone. I was happy to see the thrush – they are fast disappearing from our gardens and countryside – and even happier that we had resisted using slug pellets, which might harm the wildlife for whom our plentiful slugs and snails provide food. The temptation is often enormous, but even the 'eco-friendly' versions – which claim not to harm pets, worms and beneficial insects – can lead to as many problems as they solve. London, Wales and Bristol are apparently the slug hot spots of Britain, where frustrated gardeners are most likely to resort to pellets. As well as damaging the soil and other wildlife, pellets can end up making the problem worse.

A snail can lay up to 1,500 eggs in its lifetime, which are programmed to hatch in batches by a growth retardant enzyme present in the adults' slime. This ensures that there isn't a sudden mad competition for food. By killing all the adults we override this natural control and can actually create a snail population explosion. The other problem is that a substance in many pellets positively attracts slugs and snails to your garden – good news for the manufacturers of the products, but a nightmare for you.

The following are safe and organic methods of controlling slugs and snails; you may need to use a few in conjuction with one another.

* Make a barrier around beds, borders or plants themselves using very sharp grit (normal gravel is not sharp enough) or a new product called "New Slug Stoppa", which repels the creatures by absorbing the moisture in their slime (01525 279555 for stockists).
* Put coarse sandpaper or copper-backed tape (from Green Gardener 01603 715096) across the greenhouse entrance or around the rims of pots or raised beds.
* Encourage frogs and toads by making a pond or water feature.
* Sow a succession of lettuce seeds around treasured plants such as hostas. The slugs should be diverted by the sacrificial seedlings.
* Acquire a pet hedgehog. Send an sae marked 'hedgehog factsheet' (£1) to St Tiggywinkle's Wildlife Hospital, Aston Road. Haddenham, Bucks HP17 8AF (01844 292292).
* Use biological controls from Green Gardener (01603 715096) or Defenders (01233 813121). 'Nemaslug' and 'Slugsure' are natural parasites, or nematodes, that can be applied to the soil in a water drench. They stop the slugs feeding, so that they bury underground and die. Nematodes are only effective on slugs and very small snails, and have to be renewed every six to eight weeks.
* 'Slug pubs' (diluted beer in old yoghurt pots sunk into the soil) do work, but disposing of the drowned slugs may be messy, and other beneficial creatures may also meet a boozy death. Make sure to raise the rim slightly above soil level so that beetles don't stumble in.

Perhaps the best solution is the night-time patrol, armed with a torch and bucket. I've become familiar with the slugs' and snails' hiding places in my little London garden – behind the larger leaves of ivy, in snug corners of the trellis and on the lower, shaded stalks of large plants such as acanthus, arum lilies, macleaya and phormiums. Then all you have to do is decide what to do with them. The truly eco-minded take them to the countryside (though whether the countryside really wants our townie slugs and snails is doubtful). I toss mine up on to the flat-roofed building behind our house as an offering for the birds. No death is a kind death – but at least it's a natural one.

20 June 1999

SACRED GARDENS

In the Middle Ages, many churches had sacred gardens where the sacristan tended plants used in the liturgy – box and willow-palm for Palm Sunday, red roses and woodruff for Corpus Christi and holly and ivy for Christmas. The Reformation put paid to church decoration and, although the new legislation was often ignored, it became impossible for many churches to keep up these elaborate and costly gardens. Today, only a few such gardens survive, among them an informal wildflower garden at Stoneleigh churchyard in Warwickshire, a formal garden in the ruins of St Lawrence's, South Walsham in Norfolk, and a more recent garden of biblical plants in the grounds of St James's, Piccadilly.

The recently launched Sacred Land project (backed by the Worldwide Fund for Nature, English Heritage and Shell) aims to inspire and fund many more gardens with sacred or religious associations. Last month I visited one of the first gardens to be undertaken with the project's help – a tiny octagonal meditation garden within the burnt-out shell of Holy Trinity Church in Beckenham, south London. In 1993, the large Victorian church was gutted in a suspected arson attack. Rather than restore the ruins or rebuild from scratch, the congregation, led by its then-vicar, the Reverend Tony Rutherford, decided on an ambitious plan to construct a new modern building within the charred remains of the old. The chancel, where the former altar stood, was left open to the sky to become the site of a sacred garden.

The finished garden can be seen clearly from inside the church, through a window behind the newly positioned altar. Doorways on either side lead into a walled space with a small cobbled fountain in the middle and the original chancel windows, now devoid of glass, frame views of the church-yard trees and the sky beyond. Raised beds on the far side have seats incorporated into their walls, and there are benches for people to sit on and take in the atmosphere. Climbing roses, jasmine and several types of clematis have been planted up the walls to bloom throughout the year, together with a Virginia creeper (*Parthenocissus quinquefolia*) whose flaming autumn foliage will be a reminder of the fire from which the new garden sprang. Rutherford drew inspiration from gardens in Coventry Cathedral and Fountains Abbey in Yorkshire and the plans were developed with the help of Magali Nicole, the landscape architect for the Sacred Land project. "We had to start with the elements that were there," explains Nicole, "the rose window, the open sky and the colour of the stone."

The pair also made use of Francesca Greenoak's book *Wildlife in the Churchyard: The Plants and Animals of God's Acre* (Little Brown, 1993, sadly out of print) which lists plants with sacred associations including the medlar tree (*Mespilus germanica*), rosemary, monkshood, Madonna lily, pasque flower, angelica, Michaelmas daisy, Soloman's seal and Jacob's ladder, alongside the more predictable yew, holly, ivy and grapevine.

The new garden is not only for those who come for worship on a Sunday. Weddings can also be held there, and the beautifully rebuilt church is also home to children's and young people's groups, a day centre for the elderly and a community centre. There are plans to involve local people in planting and caring for the churchyard gardens. Sacred Land is also keen to work on non-Christian projects. It is currently working with a Buddhist centre in London, a new Hindu temple in the West Midlands and with Hindu and Muslim children at schools in Leicester and Nottingham. For further information contact Sacred Land on 0161 248 5731.

27 June 1999

FIRST FRUITS AND FLOWERS

That wonderful period of sampling the first new vegetables is underway. We picked the first broad beans recently from crimson-flowering plants sown last November, which have remained mercifully free from blackfly. The peas were next. They are so delicious, I'm glad I planted a second crop (peas can be sown as late as early summer). The 'cut and come again' lettuces at the allotment and in the old grape-treading vat in the garden are already keeping us in salads – mainly red and green 'Salad Bowl' and 'Black Seeded Simpson' (said to last a month longer than 'Salad Bowl') from Simpson's Seeds (01985 845004), with a few leaves of lovage, sorrel, parsley and marjoram chopped and thrown in. So long as you don't pull off more than half the leaves of a lettuce at a time (I try to keep to a third or a quarter of each plant), the leaves will replace themselves throughout the summer. A light mulch of grass clippings or compost around the plants keeps moisture in and weeds down (remember to water well before applying mulch).

Soon it will be time for the first runner beans. I am growing them up poles and wide-gauge plastic netting this year, interspersed with sweetpeas – a tip from the owner of an extremely well-tended garden near Harlech, who claims it helps with pollination. There are certainly a lot of buds on both beans and sweetpeas, so the prospects look good. Next it will be the turn of the courgettes, already flowering away in the large bed by the pond; and then the squashes and pumpkins in the huge mound (last year's compost heap topped with soil from the pond excavations, with pockets of well-rotted manure for the plants) on the other side of the water. They're still small, but I can't wait for them to sprawl across the bed and on to the paths, sending out spiralling tendrils every which way. There are some unusual types of different shapes and colours, so we are hoping for a good show. More by chance than design, many of the beds have self-seeded nasturtiums and love-in-a-mist around the edges, so it's looking pretty already.

The flowers have been a great success so far this year. The house has been full of them – huge, vibrant things from which colour emanates like an aura; they make shop-bought blooms look tired and artificial. After the tulips and daffodils, which kept us going from March to mid-May, the alliums took over – and now I can't think how I ever gardened without them. They are stunning in all their stages. First came the nectaroscordums (which used to be called *Allium siculum*), whose drooping umbels of bell-shaped flowers in shades of cream and milky green through to dirty pink and brown emerge, deliciously slowly, from pointed paper sheaths. Like all the flowering alliums, they keep on putting out buds from the centre, until they all turn parchment yellow and turn their heads to the sky. *A. hollandicum* 'Purple Sensation' is probably the best-known allium. Its dense drumstick heads of rich magenta performed well both at the allotment and among clouds of French and English lavender at the front of the house.

A. giganteum has similar blooms, but the buds, which look like miniature minarets, open much later. Most spectacular of all is *A. cristophii*, which develops from a cluster of slender stems into a quivering sphere of amethyst stars almost a foot across. Its only fault is that its shortish stems can make it awkwardly top-heavy. I have had a single bloom in a vase on my desk for the past few weeks and have watched it change daily, opening more and more flowers and shedding petals and seed pods till all that is left is a pale, papery skeleton not unlike the molecular models we used to create in chemistry lessons. If I were an artist, I should want to paint it.

All the above alliums can be ordered from De Jager (01622 831235) or Bloms Bulbs (01234 709099/www.blomsbulbs.com).

4 July 1999

THE CITY AT DAWN

On these bright summer mornings when the sun rises at 4.30 I often seem to wake up with the birds. Today, rather than lie in bed till a more respectable hour, I sat in the back garden for half an hour and then took my dog to the park. All gardens are magical at dawn – especially the public spaces, before the crowds come in to claim them. As I stole into the park through a gap in the fence, I felt as if I were entering a still, self-contained world. Setting off across the dew-wet grass was like diving into a swimming pool that has lain undisturbed all night. Everything was fresh and clean and new – and surprisingly full of life. The birds had been singing, the bees had been buzzing and the plants all photosynthesizing like mad long before even I'd been awake – and without the usual roar of traffic in the background, you could actually hear it all happening. I was reminded of another early midsummer morning long ago when I lived in Rome. Walking back from a party in the early hours, I suddenly realized I could hear the splashing of the city's many fountains – a sound usually drowned in the chaos of people and cars. There is something almost surreal about a silent, empty city.

It was the smells in the park that my dog, Rolf, was most excited about. He was even keener than usual to go sniffing about in the undergrowth, and traced a mad zig-zag across the grass – nose down, tail waving high – hot on the scent of a fox or a badger or some other creature whose tracks are normally covered by the time the dogs arrive. I followed him over to an old oak tree, and as he snuffled among its roots, I pressed my own face up against the bark. It was already warm in the early sun, and I swear I could *hear* the hundreds of creatures who must live in and on its branches – not just the pigeons coo-ing lazily overhead but also the insects and ants and infinitesimal life-forms that creep, crawl, bore or burrow up and down its trunk.

I stopped when I saw another dog-walker approaching. It seemed somehow strange to see another human being in this familiar, and yet all-too-unfamiliar world. Another fellow-explorer in this place that wild nature had claimed her own – just for a few hours. I wonder if he felt the same? We smiled a shy greeting before continuing on our way. Far away beyond the treetops I could see the City of London spread out in the heat haze, the felty grey silhouettes of the tower blocks with the sunlight glancing off them. A hot air balloon sailed in front of Canary Wharf. What a thrill it must be to be floating high above the sleeping city.

I made my way to the top of the hill to get a better view. For the past few years the council has let the grass grow long in this part of the park and mown a network of pathways across it. There is something wonderful about a narrow mown path between hip-high waving grass – it would look good on the outskirts of a garden, leading the way into a wood or the wilder land-scape beyond. Rolf plunged straight into the sea of grass. I could trace his progress by the wake of quivering plumes. Every so often his ears poked up against the sky – or his legs, as he enjoyed an ecstatic roll. Sometimes I think that dogs are the personification of joy. I, too, lay down on the path and enjoyed the smell and feel and sound of the grasses all around me. The traffic started to hum on Brixton Hill. Another half an hour and the magic would be broken as the day began for everyone else. I stared at the sky. A deep, even blue with not even a wisp of cloud. It was going to be another clear, hot day.

MAGENTA DIVINE

There were six new morning glory flowers out today in the bright blue pot by the back door. They were raised from a run-of-the-mill packet of seeds, in 7.5cm (3in) pots on a sunny windowsill as they are every spring, but this year's flowers seem exceptionally beautiful. Each bloom is of the usual, heart-stopping blue, but with a rib of rich magenta running in stripes from the centre. They are climbing up a late-flowering ceanothus, whose blossoms, now a faded slate blue, have been trained against the back wall of the house, and all around its bare trunk are the blue-tinged bracts and deep purply flowers of *Cerinthe major* 'Purpurascens'. This gorgeous annual seems suddenly to have become very fashionable. A lot of people I know are growing *Cerinthe* this year, raising it from seed as it's not often found in garden centres. But it's mysterious that it should have become popular only recently, as it is easy to grow and endlessly rewarding. The glaucous greyish leaves seem to become bluer the higher they grow up the stem, evolving into indigo bell-shaped bracts around the tiny nodding ultra-violet flowers. Pinching out the young plants several times encourages a crazy candelabra shape, with side shoots branching out at angles and the lower ones curving upwards from below. It looks great with my morning glories, but would have been equally well complemented by the filigree blue bracts and spiny leaves of the sea holly *Eryngium* x *oliverianum,* which was in this pot last year. Whatever happened to it? Perhaps I'll get them all together next year – thistly spikes would be the perfect textural contrast to the fleshy *Cerinthe* leaves, and the morning glories could weave a wayward path among them.

Purple plants have become a bit of an obsession for me this year. It began innocently enough, when I planted different types of lavender in galvanized pots and old dustbins around the front door, which was painted a rich, dark violet last summer. The rest of the paintwork is a duller, greyish mauve, which looks good with the grey-blue leaves of the lavender and the grey-green paint of the window-boxes. Different alliums have bloomed in succession, leaving their sculptural seedheads: the huge quivering heads of *Allium cristophii* have faded from lilac to silver and it's now the turn of *A. giganteum,* emerging from its tissue-like casing as a tight, purple ball. There's also a mound of the mauve cranesbill geranium, *G. wlassovianum* and some more of my lovely magenta-tinged morning glory.

The odd touch of magenta stops a purple garden from appearing dark and sullen – particularly when the sun's not on it. Some of my lavender is the lovely "butterfly" French variety *Lavandula stoechas,* which flowers a good month before the English types and is well on the magenta side of mauve. This has looked wonderful alongside the swelling buds of my regale lilies, which turn a deeper and deeper crimson before the huge, heavy pods split to reveal their creamy white insides. For me, waiting for lilies to open is one of the rites of high summer – I can't imagine being away at this time. (Actually, the only time I ever was, they came out bright yellow, which was a nasty shock – since then I've only bought bulbs from reliable sources.) Climbing around the door is an unusual clematis, 'Etoile Rose', which obligingly puts out curvy bell-shaped blooms of the same dark magenta from June to September, overlapping with the clear mauve 'Elsa Spath' for about a week. There's a wonderful clematis called 'Barbara Jackman' – rather larger-flowered than the clematis I normally prefer, but with purply-blue petals and a magenta bar – which might be a candidate to scramble among it all next summer, if the purple phase continues unabated.

The other good foil for purple is chartreuse or lime green but, again, you don't want to use too much. At the back of the house, the golden thyme and marjoram sing out against the purple aquarium gravel in my potted herb garden, while a golden hop is weaving its way among a vigorous grapevine and the purple-stemmed honeysuckle, *Lonicera periclymenum* 'Serotina'. Another couple of weeks and that gorgeous morning glory should be up there among them.

1 August 1999

SOS FOR STREET TREES

Last summer, I wrote about the tree opposite our house dying – probably as a result of damage caused by cable trenching gangs earlier in the year. As a bulging postbag confirmed, this is an all-too-familiar problem up and down the country. But few streets can have fared as badly as one I visited in Wolverhampton, which had been dug up no fewer than 57 times in the previous five years for "essential work" by utilities companies and highway authorities. The road, an avenue of mature trees that were planted at the same time as its Victorian houses were built, must have looked splendid until recently. But constant interference with the roots has left all the trees in a sad and sorry state. Lime leaves that should be like saucers are at least half their usual size and look limp and lifeless. Some of the other trees have branches without any leaves at all – and it looks as if whole sections of tree have already been cut out as a belated damage limitation policy. Many of the trunks are covered in a fringe of young sucker growth – a desperate sign that a tree is in trouble. The local authority is now aware of the situation, but it may be too late to save these trees. I felt like crying when I tried to imagine this once leafy street without its canopy of trees – nearly 100 years of selfless, graceful growth sacrificed so that some of us can watch more sport on television.

Trees not only soften the relentless urban landscape of buildings and cars; in these days of extreme and unpredictable weather they also provide shade in summer, shelter from harsh winds, and reduce the risk of flash floods by intercepting rainfall. Even more important, when our streets are so often choked with traffic, is their capacity to improve air quality, by filtering pollution, absorbing carbon monoxide and other poisonous gases and giving off oxygen for us to breathe. Streets with trees in them not only look better, they feel better, too. It is a shame we so often take our urban trees for granted until they fall under threat.

"Mean Streets to Green Streets" is a new campaign launched by *Gardening Which?* Magazine to raise people's awareness of urban trees and is designed to put pressure on government and local authorities to create a climate "in which neglect and abuse of trees is unthinkable". Its recent survey reveals that the "good practice guidelines" introduced in 1995 have failed to protect trees from damage by trenching gangs. Cable television is the worst offender (54 per cent of reported damage), followed by highways agencies (43 per cent) and water companies (39 per cent). In many cases, however, it is difficult to identify a single culprit, and "death by a thousand cuts" is to blame – the result of repeated digging around the trees until, irretrievably weakened, they succumb to disease or drought, or simply give up the ghost.

The "Blueprint for Trees", a list of recommendations presented to Alan Meale, the Under-Secretary of State for the Environment at this year's Chelsea Flower Show, demands not only more trees in our towns and cities but also the replacement of the voluntary guidelines with legal regulations and fines to protect trees from damage during digging work. Trenchless technology should be used wherever possible, and scanners employed to detect the presence of tree roots before work begins. Most crucially, local

authorities should have the power to insist on utilities coordinating their streetworks – which surely makes more sense for everyone. The aim is that these and the many other recommendations detailed in the "Blueprint for Trees" will be recognised in the forthcoming Urban White Paper. If you, too, feel strongly about the fate of urban trees, write to your MP demanding his or her support, or obtain more information by contacting *Gardening Which?* PO Box 44, Hertford X, SC14 1SH.

* PS: Still on the subject of trees, thanks to the many readers who wrote to inform me that *Cercis siliquastrum*, whose heart-shaped leaves and common name the 'Love Tree', had led me to think it an ideal choice for a wedding present is, of course, also known as the 'Judas Tree'. Oooops!

15 August 1999

WAYWARD BEAUTY

The allotment has entered its splendid late summer phase, when it lets itself go. For a short time each year, in early summer, I succumb to the illusion that I am in control there – that *this* will be the year when I will keep on top of the weeds and grow all my vegetables in nice straight rows. For a few weeks I actually believe it: as for the habitual smoker "giving up" for the seventeenth time or a natural clutterhead resolving to keep his desk tidy for ever, hope – not to mention smugness – springs eternal. I wrote from this state of mind a couple of months ago, and people remarked how envious they felt of my weed-free, trouble-free plot. Well, they can certainly relax now. Things are back to normal – by which I mean a degree of disorderly, yet extremely picturesque chaos.

I have to confess that I prefer it this way. There's a wild, wayward beauty about the place which makes it more exciting than the neater neighbouring plots. The first thing you notice is the enormous cardoon plants, shooting their thistly neon-violet flowers up into the sky. Perhaps this September we'll get around to trussing up the leaves around the stems to blanch them prior to cooking (they're supposed to taste like braised celery); perhaps, like last year, we'll just leave them as they are. Sunflowers and nasturtiums have self-seeded in between them, and among the purple-podded french beans in the opposite bed. The mix of violet flowers, dark purple pods and ochre and orange flowers is stunning. The other morning when I arrived, a heavy, hairy stem of borage, studded with star-like cobalt blue flowers, had flopped its way on to one side of the bed, bowed down by the overnight rain. I gathered some of the flowers, with a few sprigs of purply marjoram and lime green spurge, in a posy to take home.

My other favourite patch is the runner bean bed, where the poles and netting I set up back in June are completely covered with beans and sweetpeas. However many I pick of each, they always manage to replace themselves in my absence. The tip that to alternate runners with sweetpeas aids pollination has certainly paid off, and I shall do it again next year. The plants rise from a sprawling mound of nasturtiums – again self-seeded. Worried lest they compete for nutrients with the beans, I pulled out all those with roots inside the bed, but they have spread all over the soil all the same, which not only looks nice but keeps down the weeds. Once again, nature has come to a pretty good solution without me.

A slightly unruly plot is certainly full of surprises. There have been many times this summer when I've stumbled on an enormous courgette that I swear wasn't there a couple of days ago. It was probably hiding under the huge pumpkin leaves that have enveloped one corner of the plot. And along the south-facing fence, where we are nurturing climbing roses, various honeysuckles and a fruiting grapevine as a screen, what I'd assumed to be weed seedlings have turned out to be self-seeded teasels, furry grey mulleins and a fine crop of rocket.

Our new pond is partly to blame for the wildness. Somehow, sitting and staring into its waters, while dragonflies hover and waterboatmen skit and baby frogs hop all around, seems infinitely preferable to weeding. The pond has definitely lured more wildlife on to our plot; at times this summer, the whole place has seemed to be buzzing and fluttering and crawling with life. The other day I counted 15 types of insect just in the couple of square yards where I was sitting.

Woolly round the edges we may be, but we're in no danger of disqualification by the weed police. When the committee came round with their clip-boards the other day, they only seemed to notice the pond and the cardoons, which won us instant approval. Our neighbour, however, must have been threatened with the chop, as he made a lightning appearance last week to dowse his patch with weedkiller. His plot may now be tidy, but it's parched and brown and lifeless as a desert. If I were an insect – or a vegetable, for that matter – I know which side of the fence I'd prefer to live on.

22 August 1999

LAMBETH COUNTRY SHOW (Part I)

This year we finally plucked up courage to exhibit our vegetables at the Lambeth Country Show. Lambeth being one of London's grittiest inner city boroughs, the title is something of a contradiction in terms, but it is a wonderful event nonetheless. For one weekend in high summer, our local park is transformed into a cross between a traditional agricultural show, an enormous church fête and a magnificent, ear-splitting, spliff-toting Rasta jamboree.

The flower, fruit and vegetable displays tend to be dominated by one or two (male, middle-aged) names, but I remember thinking last year that, give or take the odd plate of perfectly trimmed and trussed onions, some of our own stuff might have an outsider's chance. So a week before this year's show I sent off for the schedule and regulations. These nearly put me off the whole idea. The 87 categories, which include hand knitting, chutney-making and the creation of "vegetable animals", seemed like a throwback to the 1950s, while the fruit and veg categories appeared to be written in a foreign language. What, for instance, did "Onions, from sets, dressed, 5 to be shown," mean? What was the difference between "Salading" and "Salad Vegetables" in Class 60? And could Class 59 ("Collection of 4 distinct kinds of vegetable (space allowed 60cm (2ft) x 60cm (2ft)), numbers to be staged as for Classes 43–56" include types of vegetables you were also showing in other classes?

All of a turmoil, I rang the Royal Horticultural Society (on whose code of rules such regulations are based) to ask for advice. I was faxed selected pages of the *Horticultural Show Handbook* (RHS, £7.95), the bible for that odd band of souls for whom showing their produce is a way of life. It didn't answer any of my questions, but it did contain advice on what the judges would be looking for in the various categories. Peas, for instance, should be "Large, fresh pods of a deep green with bloom intact, free from disease or pest damage and well-filled with tender seeds". I took it with me to the allotment early on Saturday morning, when I met Clarkey and Simon to decide which of our vegetables might be up to scratch.

We'd had high hopes for the courgettes, which have been putting out prolific numbers of glossy dark green and bright yellow fruits since early July. When watering on Thursday I'd earmarked five smallish ones, which I reckoned would have grown another couple of inches by the weekend. Wrong. They'd more than tripled in size, leaving nothing between the tiddlers and whopping great torpedoes. Several were on their way to Class 58 ("One table marrow"), but would need another week. Better luck with the peas, perhaps. Ten pods were required and we picked a good thirty from which to make the final selection. Great store is set by uniformity of size, so we whittled it down to ten plump pods, searching for signs of insect damage while trying to handle them as little as possible so as not to destroy their precious bloom. No sooner had we laid them out on the grass than the dog walked over them twice.

Several rows of potatoes ("Sharpe's Express" and "Aphrodite", a newish white variety recommended for baking and boiling) were dug in a bid to find four uniform tubers to enter under Class 43 ("Potatoes, white, 4 of any one variety"); there were a few that just *might* fulfill the judges' preference for "shapely, clean, clear-skinned tubers; eyes few and shallow". The red onions looked so pretty we thought we'd enter them, too, even if they weren't of prize-winning proportions. I was relieved to read that in Class 52 we could show them "as grown", without having to fiddle about with scissors and raffia.

Up at the Country Show, the atmosphere in the Floral Marquee was peaceful but industrious, as competitors put the final loving touches to their displays. With only half an hour till judging, we had no time to fuss over ours, laying out the peas in a straight line directly on the white cloth (much tutted over by one old-timer, who said they should really be in a circle) and arranging the potatoes and onions on kindly donated paper plates. As I snipped up the back of my programme with borrowed scissors to make labels detailing the varieties of vegetables shown (Old-Timer's tip number two), I felt rather like I used to feel at Brownies, when I never had the requisite thruppeny bit and length of string in my pockets. But before we knew it, an attendant was ushering us all out so that the judges could begin their rounds. To be continued....

29 August 1999

LAMBETH COUNTRY SHOW (Part II)

As the judges filed in with their clipboards, we left the Floral Marquee in a state of excitement mixed with trepidation. Not being old hands at showing produce, our preparations had been slapdash to say the least. While elderly gentlemen in cardigans shifted their beans and onions a quarter of an inch to the left or right (handed to them, I might add, by their wives, from cardboard boxes packed with damp tea-towels), we had fished about in carrier bags and cleaned our potatoes with spit and a hankie. Nor did we have any fancy display props. Had we known that others would come armed with smart square boards covered in black felt, or paper plates and doileys, we might have managed to rustle something up. As it was, the potatoes ("Class 43: Potatoes, white, 4 of any one variety") were hastily arranged on a paper plate begged from the cafe next door, while the red onions ("Class 52: Onions, 5 to be shown as grown"), really were "shown as grown", right down to the soil still clinging to the roots. As for our peas ("Class 51: Peas, 10 pods"), I couldn't get them to sit straight in a circle on a plate like the other entries, so I had lined them up in a row directly on the tablecloth. Would it matter? Presentation aside, I couldn't help thinking that they didn't look bad alongside the other entries. Two hours to go till the moment of truth.

We spent the time watching a parade of shire horses (fascinating to see them in all their folksy livery with the city skyline behind) and grazing the many ethnic food stalls. It was a perfect sunny day and the familiar landscape of our local park had been transformed into a surging sea of tents and people. At just before two, we made our way back to the main marquee. I was surprised at how nervous I felt. I saw it as soon as we entered the enclosure. A red sticker on the peas! We had won first prize! Exhibitors of prize vegetables rarely let out whoops of joy, but this one did – so loud that people turned to stare. And what did a yellow sticker mean? The potatoes and onions had won third prize! *What* a result!

As we shamelessly posed for photographs with each other in front of our displays, a few of the regulars came up to congratulate us. One even asked me how I had grown my peas – out of politeness, I suspect, as his own faultless selection of four carrots, four beetroot, four runner beans and four potatoes (entered under the "Collection of Vegetables" category) had been awarded "Best in Show".

The serious prizes, as usual, were divided between two names – Mr Lamothe, an elegant gentleman in his eighties who came over from Jamaica forty years ago and tends three allotments in South Norwood, and Mr Dare, whose perfectly trussed onions and 14 inch-long runner beans, grown in the back garden of his semi in Thornton Heath, were the envy of all. How did he do it? "I start picking a few days before the show," he told me. "I go round with a ruler twice a day, pick the beans that are 35.5cm (14in) and wrap them in a damp tea-towel and keep them in the fridge. And you can always stretch them up to half an inch or so on the day." He demonstrated – adding at least half an inch to one of his prize beans just by pulling. Another time I'll follow his advice and start picking my courgettes early.

Pleased to have some new faces on the scene, the kindly judges even invited us to exhibit at their next show in the autumn. Now that we have a few tricks of the trade up our sleeve, who knows? Some of the other categories look tempting, if only for their kitsch potential ("Class 70: Vegetable Animal – any animal, bird or insect – any combination of vegetables allowed", for instance. The winning entry was an owl, cleverly constructed using a globe artichoke for its body, shallots for eyes and a pair of green chilli peppers for its eyebrows). In all our excitement we forgot to collect our prize money – £1.50 for first prize, 75p for third. Still, we had a celebratory round of ice-creams all the same.

5 September 1999

TREES OF TIME AND PLACE

After a year of my "encouraging" letters, the council has finally removed the dead tree opposite our house and dug holes for a row of replacements. Planting should begin in a few weeks' time. According to a letter sent out to all residents, our new trees will probably be small ornamental species with an open canopy to avoid complaints of excessive shade or fears of root damage to buildings, but if there is room, the council is keen to plant larger trees. This is exciting. Looking at the row of stakes already in place on either side of the road, it is not hard to project into the future and see a leafy avenue, with new green leaves to admire in spring and dappled shadows on the tarmac in summer. In my mind's eye I picture the scene in two, ten, twenty-five and then a hundred year's time, when splendid mature trees, rather than houses or cars, will be the first thing anyone notices when turning into our street.

Trees have this effect of telescoping time. It works backwards as well as forwards. Who, in the presence of an ancient oak or towering redwood, has not found their mind filled with images of what the tree must have seen over the centuries; of how it came to be planted and what its original surroundings were? I've often tried to picture what Capability Brown's famous landscaping schemes looked like when they were just completed, and I guess the owners of the estates must have grown adept at looking into the future when they gazed out at the bald hills and saplings that had replaced their former parterres and terraces.

The American writer Jim Nollman writes sensitively on the imaginative power of trees in his excellent book, *Why We Garden: Cultivating a Sense of Place* (Henry Holt, $14 – available to order from Garden Books, 0207 792 0777). On impulse, at his local garden centre, he picks up a baby sequoia (redwood) tree just 0.6m (2ft) tall and plants it in his garden. Over the year that follows he becomes captivated by the tree, fantasizing about how his garden will be transformed as the sequoia matures. "What other processes of nature besides the growth of trees can so insistently cause us to envision a hundred or even a thousand years hence?" he asks. "The past, the present, and the future all seem jumbled together in one place in one moment, and through one entity.... The link with this tree in this place comes as close as I'll ever get to sensing a sacred grounding in nature." The sequoia reminds him of the questions scrawled by Gaugin on one of his Tahiti canvases: "Where do we come from? Where are we? Where are we going?"

The "Trees of Time and Place" campaign is urging us all to indulge in such fantasies as part of a practical millennium tree-planting project. The idea is to collect seed from a favourite tree and raise it in pots for planting out in the New Year. It's certainly a seductive scheme – I can imagine people travelling back to houses they used to live in, or forests where they spent childhood holidays, or even just choosing their favourite tree in their local park. We forget that these much-loved specimens won't be here for ever. The second Sunday in October has been designated "Seed Gathering Sunday", with hundreds of events planned throughout the country and advice on seed-gathering, sowing and aftercare on hand. If the trees are likely to grow too big for your own garden, they can contribute to a number of new "community forests" that aim to replenish Britain's diminishing tree cover.

I wonder which tree I shall choose. Shall it be the huge lime in our local park, whose branches billow like great sails in the summer sky? Or a weeping willow on a Sixties estate in Blackheath, underneath whose canopy a schoolfriend and I used to play unobserved? Or a noble old oak in the middle of a cornfield on the farm where I was born? It must have been one of the first trees I ever saw, and I like the idea of one of its offspring flourishing far into the future.

12 September 1999

IS GARDENING CONTAGIOUS?

The houses in our area have little in the way of front gardens: just a few feet between the building and the pavement. When we moved here three years ago, our pots and windowboxes were in the minority. But this summer, practically all of these cramped little strips are spilling over with flowers. It may be a sign of the much-hyped "gentrification" of this scruffy part of south London; or perhaps it's been inspired by the endless new gardening programmes on TV. Or could it be that gardening is contagious: spreading like a rash wherever enthusiasm takes root?

I find it fascinating to see what people do with these tiny spaces. The most successful are those where the front wall has been lowered, or replaced by a fence or railings. This not only makes the garden more visible; it also increases the light, and therefore the variety of plants one can grow. Picket fences are fun – especially if they're given a contemporary twist with a lick of bright paint or by using chunky reclaimed timber. Railings seem to lend themselves to plants that spill out in between the spokes – I'm thinking of lowering our 1.1m (3ft 6in) wall to a foot or so and replacing the rest with a purple fence or railings (to match the front door) and different types of lavender. The scent would be released as people brush past.

Many of the front gardens are that usual jaunty urban jumble of psyche-delic annuals – red pelargoniums next to purple striped petunias with a sprinkling of flaming african marigolds for good measure. But few can rival the house a few streets away, where the windows are only just visible through a curtain of climbers and hanging baskets. The front wall has small-leaved succulents and creeping plants crammed into every possible opening: cushions of white alyssum, crassulas and saxifrage sprout from mounds of soil piled precariously on top. Pots of petunias have been cemented to the gateposts: the pots themselves are coated with cement and encrusted with cockle and mussel shells. Other seashell planters have been wired to the uprights of the bay window and hanging baskets are strung around the door.

Startling and admirable though this may be, I confess to preferring more restrained schemes. Some of the most effective displays involve a single type of flower: a hedge of rosemary, for instance, or grasses set in gravel. Many of my neighbours have planted a single row of sunflowers that have reached 3m (10ft) or so, with dinner-plate sized blooms – one woman was complaining that she couldn't see the blooms from her downstairs windows. Tall plants seem to look good in long narrow plots – in one garden, a forest of pale lemon hollyhocks is stunning against a dark charcoal wall.

Here at our house I've been adding to my collection of old-fashioned dustbins, hip baths and buckets in which I have planted grey and silver-leaved plants such as lavender, helichrysum and artemesia and some purple-flowered clematis and geraniums. I'd never met anyone who shared my passion for these things till I visited another local garden that opens regularly to the public through the National Gardens Scheme. Its owner, Rosemary Lindsay, had a dozen or so such pots all planted with pinks – bright magenta ones, the raggedy white 'Mrs Sinkins' or 'Gran's Favourite', with its distinctive raspberry blotch. Like me, she enjoyed the association of grey-green leaves with weathered old metal, and found it was the perfect way to grow lime-loving pinks in her otherwise unhospitable garden. I might even try some myself.

They will certainly make a change from this year's experiment in our front garden: squashes and courgettes. The asphalt roof on top of the bay window is a mass of spiky leaves and wandering tendrils, with orange and ochre nasturtiums tumbling down between. We've had a fine crop of yellow courgettes, and a single 'Hungarian Blue' squash is maturing nicely. They need a lot of water, and the yields from pots are never as good as in the ground. But it has certainly been worth it, just for the bemused looks from people passing by.

19 September 1999

EARLY AUTUMN FAVOURITES

People moan about their gardens at this time of the year, but early autumn is when some of my favourite plants come into their own. They are not the blazing orange daisies and scarlet crocosmias of the traditional "hot" autumn borders. While I love all those sizzling colours – particularly when interspersed with some of the bolder perennial grasses such as *Stipa gigantea* or the bronzy *Pennisetum setaceum* 'Rubrum', these would be hard to accommodate in my small shady garden, with its quieter colour scheme of purple, bronze, lime green and white. Instead, I have found room for some longstanding favourites.

Japanese anemones were my best-loved flowers as a child. In the way that the childish aesthetic values artificiality higher than more subtle forms of natural beauty, I adored their waxy pale pink petals and button-like acid-yellow centres. They were the My Little Pony of the plant world – sugar-pink and plastic-looking, but robust enough to survive a few rounds of rough-and-tumble. In the intervening years, I've come to admire *Anemone japonica*'s more grown-up charms – its deeply divided trifoliate leaves, the beauty of the tight white spherical buds long before they open, and the way the flowers, particularly those of the single white varieties, can lighten up a dark corner of the garden when little else is in bloom. I put in three plants of the single white 'Honorine Jobert' earlier in the year and they are now a most welcome mass of flowers.

Daturas were the next flowers I fell in love with. Long ago, on holiday in Sicily, I was told that the scent of the pendant trumpet flowers was powerful enought to induce strange dreams and visions. In that particular village it was apparently a punishable offence to sleep beneath a datura tree in bloom – which of course, only made me determined to do it one day. Twenty years on, these daturas have been given the infuriatingly ugly name of *Brugmansia* – and I have yet to fulfil that particular dream. This could be the year, however, as the two tiny cuttings I was given last summer have grown into small trees with at least ten flowers on each. The white datura or angel's trumpet, *Brugmansia x candida,* is probably my favourite, but I was given the yellower form, 'Grand Marnier', whose flowers veer between peach and cream. Daturas are supposed to be brought inside during winter, which means keeping the plant at a manageable size. I chanced one of mine in this walled and usually frost-free garden last year and it survived – I'll do the same this winter but keep some fleece handy when a hard frost is forecast and take some cuttings just in case.

Nicotiana sylvestris – the tallest and most splendid of the tobacco plant family – can be grown from seed quite easily if you have a greenhouse. The leaves are a fantastic lime green, and the panicles of scented, tubular white flowers keep up a good display well into the autumn. The plant thrives in even quite deep shade, where it can grow up to 1.5m (5ft) tall, and the scent is wonderful on warm evenings. And where would I be without *Verbena bonariensis*? Another five footer, but with a spindly, "semi-transparent" habit, it can be placed at the front or middle of a border without hiding what's behind. The tiny clusters of clear mauve flowers, at the tips of fine, branching, square-sectioned stems, make a good contrast with all manner of other plants – mine are between a cardoon and a bronze phormium with a huge spray of the plume poppy, *Macleaya cordata*, bursting up behind.

Which brings me to my favourite plant of all. One of those herbaceous perennials that puts on such terrific growth in the single year it leaves you open-mouthed, Macleaya is also stunningly beautiful. As late as May I can be grubbing around at the back of the border looking for it, fearing that the slugs may have got it this year. Three months later the garden is full of its jigsaw-puzzle leaves and buff, grass-like plumes. Its only problem is it's terribly invasive – especially in rich soil and shade, which it has here in abundance. This year I killed some offshoots while moving them around, but there's still three times as much of the stuff as last year. If it carries on at this rate there won't be room for anything else in the garden at all.

26 September 1999

BLACKBERRY ICE-CREAM

For some reason, we have never grown fruit at the allotment. We inherited a large strawberry bed when we took over the second plot, but the plants must have been old ones – they stop fruiting after three years unless you peg out the baby runners into the soil and create new plants. Somehow, whenever strawberry season comes around (young plants need to be set out in early spring or summer), there is either not enough room, or I simply do not get round to buying any. Similarly, I have managed to miss planting raspberry canes in the autumn – even though raspberries are my absolute favourite fruit. Well, this is all about to change. We have decided to devote a third of the allotment to soft fruit.

It certainly makes sense. One of my guiding principles has always been to grow things that are a) delicious, b) hard to buy grown organically and c) expensive in the shops. It is now relatively easy to find organic vegetables, and top fruit such as apples, even in the supermarkets, but soft fruit seems to have fallen behind – possibly because it is delicate to transport. I also like growing things that are relatively undemanding – and fruit bushes, once established, really just get on with it. But for the best results you do have to prepare the soil in advance.

November onwards is the best time for planting raspberry canes and currant bushes, so now is an excellent opportunity to get ready. Practically all fruit except for gooseberries requires a fair bit of sun (strawberries need full sun and raspberries at least half a day), so choose a sunny patch of ground. Digging in plenty of well-rotted farmyard or horse manure will improve soil structure and drainage (whether your soil tends to clay or sand) as well as providing the nutrients to produce large juicy fruit. We have taken to buying fresh manure from the local riding stables and leaving it in the black plastic sacks for a good six months to rot down. Blackcurrants and raspberries benefit from advance dressings of manure; gooseberries, redcurrants and strawberries need less, as overfeeding produces too much leafy growth.

The other main task is to provide protection from birds, who will strip your plants bare as soon as fruit appears next year. You can buy ready-made fruit cages for around £100 but we made our own, using 21 2.4m (8ft) bamboo canes, (£7), two packets of plastic netting at £8.99 each and some rather nifty rubber ball joints (which took me back to school chemistry lessons) from a now-defunct mail order catalogue. I shall write about varieties of fruit and how to plant them in a couple of weeks.

In the meantime, all we have had this year is blackberries – even more than in previous years, since we began training the plants horizontally along the south-facing fence and pruning them back hard in the spring. I have been making lots of delicious blackberry ice-cream – from a recipe I learned as an au pair in Italy many years ago. It doesn't need an ice-cream maker and works equally well with other dark stewed fruit such as damsons. You need at least a pound of fruit, which has been washed and simmered for a few minutes with a little water and sugar to taste. Don't cook for too long – just enough to bring out the rich colour and thicken the syrup a little. Pass the fruit through a sieve to remove the pips (blackberries) or skins (damsons), helping it through with a wooden spoon, and leave to cool.

Whip up a pint (568ml) of whipping cream till it just stands up in soft peaks and pour in the fruit purée – you can mix it gently but thoroughly till it all takes on the same colour, but I prefer to swirl it lightly around to leave a ripple effect. Pour the whole lot into a 450g (1lb) loaf tin, which has been lined with cooking foil, and place in the freezer. After an hour or so give it a bit of a stir – but whipping the cream first seems to stop ice crystals forming, and if some of the liquid sinks to the bottom it just gives your ice-cream loaf a nice coloured top. The ice-cream needs about five hours to set and should be removed from the freezer half an hour before it's needed. Serve in thin slices with some stewed whole fruit poured over. It's one of the nicest, easiest and cheapest puddings there is!

3 October 1999

SUNFLOWERS, SQUASHES AND WINTER SALADS

I love these early autumn mornings at the allotment. When I got there the other day at about half past eight the dew was still heavy on the grass and everything was sparkling in the low light. As I moved among the beds, watering, pulling the odd weed and picking beans and tomatoes, my feet were soon soaked through my soft canvas shoes. But it felt magical. Perhaps because there won't be so many more of these mornings before winter sets in, I treasure them all the more, and still come down here quite often on my own during the week, even though all I seem to do is potter.

Usually at this time of the year I have the sense that everything will soon be shutting down for a rest, but this time the allotment seems still to have some surprises up its sleeve. I returned from a week in Devon to find that the sunflowers, by now at least 3.6m (12ft) tall, had finally burst into bloom. Last summer's sowings – three packets-full – were all devoured by slugs so it was a real joy to see the huge flowers silhouetted against a clear blue sky. I cut one to bring home, where it presides over the kitchen like a jolly yellow giant.

The squashes – a new experiment – are also coming up with the goods. For weeks now, the twelve or so plants (six different varieties) had yielded nothing except two enormous yellow fruits, two medium sized orange ones and an awful lot of leaves. The problem – or rather the joy – with squashes is that once they get going, their leaf production is so prolific that it's hard to see *what* is going on. On my last visit I had to wade through thigh-high leathery leaves, to discover a few new embryonic fruits in the middle of the patch. Among all the foliage and mad, spiralling tendrils, it was hard to trace them back to the parent plant – especially as my labelling system has gone seriously awry. I'm hoping the newest, whitish-grey spheres may grow into the 'Hungarian Blue' squash from the Ferme de Sainte Marthe catalogue, which has thick orange flesh inside its blue-grey exterior. And another new fruit – still only a few inches long – may be the pear-shaped butternut squash I sowed envisioning lots of lovely risotto. I hope there will be enough autumn sunshine for these latecomers to ripen.

We're still harvesting sweetcorn, the last courgettes and a few straggly runner beans. And the tomatoes, after a late start, seem to be going on for ever. They have been such good croppers that I haven't even minded the slugs getting some. Somehow, there seems to be enough for everyone. Now that the jerusalem artichokes have flowered, it won't be many more weeks before we are digging up the first tubers to mash with potatoes or make into soup. And it's good to see the purple sprouting broccoli and Brussels sprouts (a purple variety named 'Falstaff') coming along, protected from birds by the netting cage constructed when we planted out the seedlings in June.

This year I'm making another stab at winter salads. Good lettuce varieties for overwintering include "Imperial winter", "Winter density", "Unrivalled" and lamb's lettuce or Mache, whose delicious mild flavour I love – and I'm also trying mustard greens and "Mizuna", Japanese greens with spiky dandelion leaves and a peppery taste (from The Organic Gardening Catalogue 01932 253666).

I've sown some of these salads in rows outside and some in pots and trays in a nifty mini-greenhouse I found thrown out on the street. It is about 1.5 x 1.2 x 0.6m (5 x 4 x 2ft), with an aluminium frame, three slatted shelves and a clear plastic cover that operates rather like a roller blind. I've always yearned for a greenhouse, so until a larger garden comes my way, this will have to do. This year's squash and courgette seedlings were raised in it here at the allotment, but I'm taking it home to the back garden. In previous years the slugs or the frost have got the better of my attempts at winter salads, so I'm keen to keep a close eye on my precious crops.

10 October 1999

URBAN FRINGE

In old prints of Rome by Piranesi, buildings such as the Colosseum are often portrayed with plants and creepers sprouting from their crumbling ramparts. I often think how much better some of today's architecture, both ancient and modern, would look with a fringe of foliage to soften up all those straight lines. Royal Oak station – not normally a very prepossessing part of west London – is transformed at this time of year by the late-flowering buddleia that springs forth from every possible nook and cranny around the platforms. This is the point, just outside Paddington, where the Metropolitan line emerges above ground to join the overground trains heading west to Oxford and beyond. It's a supremely urban landscape, arranged in a series of parallel horizontal strips from the railway tracks to the platforms and graffiti-ridden retaining walls to the concrete sweep of the Westway overhead. Catch it at the right time and you can see tubes and trains sliding out in opposite directions while cars, buses and lorries zoom past in a blur above. A clever artist could paint an abstract of it.

What struck me the other day, though, as the train slid in from Bristol, was how well the place suited its mad urban fringe of purple flowers. Buddleia is renowned for its capacity to take root wherever it can find a crevice and a little water. At Royal Oak, it has managed to find footholds in cracks in the paving, along the tops of walls, in angles of the openwork metal bridges that span the different platforms, and even down among the tracks. Further out of the station itself, it is joined by that other lovely colonizer of urban decay – the pink spires of rosebay willowherb. I can truthfully say that even the graffiti – and it is of the more creative kind, sprayed in bold blocks of coloured lettering – looks good when glimpsed through a pink and purple haze. Lovers of these strange juxtapositions in which cities abound need look no further than this.

I mentioned Royal Oak to Sue Clifford, director of the arts and environmental charity, Common Ground, who champion such ordinary and yet extraordinary places in their "local distinctiveness" projects. She had noticed it herself – and something I couldn't appreciate from the train, the large number of birds and butterflies the plants were attracting. Ms Clifford said it gave her hope that one day even oaks, after which the station was named, might follow. Buddleia and rosebay willowherb are pioneer plants, she explained, among the first to put in a bid to reclaim derelict land for nature (as they did so famously on bomb sites during the Second World War). Left to their own devices, she said, it would only be ten or twenty years before young birch and then oak trees would be springing up, too.

Rather than indulge such romantic, post-apocalyptic visions, however, Common Ground has lots of positive and practical ideas to bring more greenery into our cities. Railway and overground tube stations in fact make prime locations – not just for the hanging baskets and "low maintenance" tubs that you see from time to time, but for imaginative, ecological planting that appeals to birds and insects as well as the human eye. At Taunton in Somerset, there have been efforts to persuade the local council to plant apple trees along the station platform. Apart from providing an eye-catching introduction to "cider country", the spring blossom and maturing fruit would attract wildlife – and passengers could even munch on an apple while waiting for a train. Some sheltered inner city stations could become home to even relatively tender plants – imagine espaliered peach and cherry trees or even grapevines trained to cover the graffiti on sunny, south-facing walls.

Common Ground's "Community Orchards" project – a campaign that aims to preserve Britain's dwindling number of existing orchards and create new ones – includes several schemes in cities. They range from just a few fruit trees in crowded city centres to the restoration of a neglected two-acre orchard on the northern fringe of Brighton and the creation of a new organic community orchard in Brockwell Park, south London. It's an inspiring vision: springtime in the city beneath clouds of white appleblossom and fruit ripening overhead in the autumn.

Apple Day, usually around 21 October, is Common Ground's tenth annual celebration of "apples, orchards and local distinctiveness". Since the first Apple Day in 1990, groups and individuals from all over the country organize all sorts of local events including tastings, tours of orchards, cider pressing, fruit sales and art, poetry and gardening workshops – on or around this date. For further information or a list of events send a stamped A4 sae to Common Ground, Gold Hill House, 21 High St, Shaftesbury, Dorset, SP7 8JE or visit their website at www.commonground.org.uk.

THE PLOT THICKENS…

The other day a fat padded envelope thudded through the letterbox. When I picked it up it rattled. Inside were ten or so small brown envelopes full of seed for next year's crops at the allotment. We're still harvesting the last of this year's beans, squashes and sweetcorn, but it's already time to start thinking about next spring, as I'm keen to try some overwintering vegetables. I pored over all the catalogues much more closely this year: a sure sign that I'm getting serious. When you first start growing vegetables, a pea is a pea is a pea – its most important characteristics being a) that it was grown by you and b) that it survived.

A few years down the line and I have all the warning signs of a potential vegetable bore: membership of the Henry Doubleday Research Association's 'Heritage Seed Library', which preserves rare and old-fashioned vegetable varieties for modern-day use; a telephone relationship with the owners of several rather obscure seed catalogues, and a tendency to wax lyrical about 'Pink Fir Apple' potatoes and 'Masterpiece Green Longpod' broad beans. Seed and bulb catalogues have long since overtaken cookery books as my preferred reading matter on these shockingly dark evenings when sometimes the only thing for it is to have an early bath and tuck myself up in bed. On the lookout for new winter/spring crops, I noted down 'Pilot' peas, an especially hardy variety which can be sown in the autumn to mature in late May. This is a round-seeded type; the wrinkled seeded peas, which are said to have a superior flavour, should be sown in March, when successive sowings will produce peas from late June until September. (This year's peas, which did us so proud in the Lambeth Country Show, were a 19th-century variety called 'Alderman'.)

'Futura' broad bean seed also went down on my order – organically raised seed that can be sown in November onwards for late May crops. My favourite 'Masterpiece Green Longpods', which produce 9 or 10 tasty beans per pod, can also be over-wintered. I'm trying autumn-sown onions for the first time, too. Organically-raised sets (small seed-bulbs) of 'Radar' can be planted in September and October for crops in June and July – it's said to have a "mild flavour and crunchy texture". Most onions are planted in early spring for a late summer harvest; last year's 'Red Baron' was a hit, and I shall try another red variety, such as the new 'Long Red Florence' or Red Brunswick' later on. What with the purple sprouting broccoli, purple brussels sprouts, spring cabbages and winter spinach and salads all growing away, the allotment will be a hive of activity compared to its usual sleepy winter self. All the above are available from The Organic Gardening Catalogue (01932 253666), which includes more and more organically raised seed every year.

Some of my other favourite catalogues include Simpson's Seeds (01985 845004), begun as a 'Tomato Grower's Club' to avoid EU restrictions on non-approved seeds. It now offers 100 types of potato and 104 types of tomato, many of which are organically produced. 'Future Foods' (write with sae to PO Box 1564, Wedmore, Somerset BS28 4DP (01398 361347) or visit their website on www.futurefoods.com) has by far the most bizarre yet tempting list, including rare and recommended varieties of vegetable from all over the world – Basque broad beans, Inca squashes and Chinese pumpkins as well as the pink-plumed calalloo greens grown in India and the Caribbean, and the gorgeous crimson-flowered broad beans I grew this year.

Jeremy Cherfas, who founded Future Foods, has co-authored a fascinating book about saving your own seed. I've saved rocket and radish seeds before, but reading *The Seed Savers' Handbook* (Grover Books, £12.95) made me enthusiastic to try traditional gathering and storing techniques that were used for centuries all over the world before the big seed companies stepped in to persuade us it was really necessary to buy all our seed new every year. As GM crops, which don't produce viable seed, threaten to throw the poorest farmers into total dependence on multinational seed suppliers, it seems an appropriate time to revive this age-old practice. Mr Cherfas' book, and the similarly useful *Seed to Seed* by Suzanne Ashworth (Seed Savers' Exchange, £15.95) can be ordered direct from Green Books (01803 863260). Or check out the Seed Savers' Network on the Internet (www.om.com.au/seedsave).

7 November 1999

BRIGHTENING UP THE BASEMENT

I have been thinking a lot about basement gardens and the particular problems they present. Regular readers of this column may remember that our own basement area, which opens off my husband's study and has steps leading up to the main garden, was the cause of something of a "turf war" last summer. I wanted it as a potting shed, but while I was away for a few days my husband appropriated it as an outdoor shower. I might not have objected had it been the type of outdoor shower I have occasionally encountered on trips to the tropics: smooth slate floor, water pouring from a bamboo funnel, screen of lush green plants glinting in the sunshine. Instead, it was just the head of the garden hose, which he had looped over a hook screwed into the underside of the deck, and would attach every morning to the kitchen tap upstairs. Difficulties in getting the temperature right, not to mention the total lack of privacy, did nothing to deter him, and my attempts to reclaim the area by lugging down sacks of manure and boxes of bonemeal resulted only in a damp and smelly mess.

Since then, we have happily arrived at the more conventional solution of installing a shower in the bathroom, so the basement area is once again up for grabs. It is difficult to know what to do with it. The part that is under cover (its roof is the decking of the garden above) would still make an excellent potting shed, but it would be nice to make something more decorative out of the remaining space – even if it's almost too small to turn round in. Many basement flats are presented with this problem: their only view is a vertical wall topped with iron railings just a few feet away from the window; it's dark, slightly damp, and nothing wants to grow in it. The obvious first step is to paint everything white, which we've already done – but where do you go from there?

I recently came across a basement garden that dealt with these drawbacks with great style and ingenuity. The area was only slightly larger than ours, and also had steps leading to a balcony above. The designer, Ruth Collier of Couture Gardens in London (020 7254 9462), a woman after my own heart, used a pair of mirrors in one corner to reflect more sunlight into the "well". As we did when we installed the large mirror that transformed tour garden, she found it vital to experiment with positions and angles until the effect was absolutely right. Mirrors maximize the effect of plants that are put in front of them: you don't need a lot to create a real urban jungle. Ms Collier wisely chose plants that positively enjoy shade, rather than merely tolerate it – a large tree fern at the foot of the stairs, and other ferns, hostas, trilliums, arum lilies and a chusan palm in pots or raised brick beds. I've learned the hard way that this is the only thing to do in deep shade; trying to get away with plants that prefer half- or dappled shade will only result in sulking plants, a sulking gardener, and several more trips to the garden centre.

The real *coup de force* in the garden Ms Collier designed, though, is the mural. On a side wall that can be seen clearly from both house and garden, an enormous arum lily snakes its way up two entire storeys. Painted in a clean, contemporary style, its sculptural shapes and restrained greens, whites and creams are the perfect complement for the simple, predominantly green garden below. It looks especially beautiful in spring, when the real arums are in bloom, but the joy of a mural is that it gives you a view all year round, even where there isn't one.

Will we have a mural in our basement? I'm torn between that idea, or the notion of a "hanging wall" of shade-loving plants in pots, dotted up and down the wall and cascading down the sides of the stairs. It has actually occurred to me that if I chose the right plants, they might even enjoy the daily dowsing that a shower of water might provide. My potting shed could retreat to the far end, where the ancient privy (now deceased) would make a great little store room. With some slate or slatted wood on the floor and plants all around, all we'd need to do is install a hot and cold water tap out here. And then we'd *both* be happy.

THE QUEEN'S FAVOURITE STRAWBERRY

I've had fun researching varieties for our new fruit garden at the allotment. Never having grown fruit before – not even so much as a strawberry – I was at a loss as to what to choose, and have been leafing through catalogues and looking at the plants on show in display gardens such as RHS Wisley. November onwards is the best time to buy and plant bush fruit such as raspberries, gooseberries and currants, so I've placed my order for enough plants to fill the top end of the plot.

Raspberries are my favourite fruit of all – I love everything about them, from their dull crimson colour to that perfect marriage of soft, felty texture and elusive, sharp-sweet taste. By all accounts, they seem very easy to grow, so why I haven't tried them before, I can't say. I've made up for lost time by ordering 30 canes – they can be placed just a hand's breadth apart, with 1.2m (4ft) between the rows, so they shouldn't take up *too* much space. To spread the crop from late June to October, I've chosen 'Glen Moy' (said to be the best early-fruiting variety, and lacking in spines), 'Malling Delight' (heavy cropping and disease-resistant, but hard to find), and the late-fruiting 'Autumn Bliss', which bears large flavoursome fruit from August till the end of October. You have to wait till the second year for good crops from summer-fruiting canes, but 'Autumn Bliss' should be cropping away heavily next year. There's also a yellow autumn type called 'Allgold' – but, call me old-fashioned, I'd sooner have a blue banana than a yellow raspberry.

My husband can't stand gooseberries, and I, too, have reservations dating back to the 'Pick Your Own' days of my childhood. Gooseberries were by far the easiest fruit to pick, and my sisters and I would fill basket upon basket, not realizing our reward would be relentless gooseberry puddings from the freezer for many months to come. This hasn't stopped me selecting a couple of bushes, though: 'Pax' is a new-ish red-fruited variety, which is vigorous, spineless and resistant to mildew, while 'Invicta', which has green berries, is a heavy cropper and also mildew-resistant – the yield is between 2.7–5.4kg (6–12lb) of fruit per bush. The key to growing big, sweet fruit is apparently rich, moist soil in partial shade – gooseberries hate hot, dry spots.

I don't know quite what I'll do with all the currants from my six new bushes (average yield 4.5–6.8kg [10–15lb] per bush). I love summer pudding, for which they are a vital ingredient, and can never get enough blackcurrant jam – but I also love the way they look on the bush, especially the pale, opalescent gleam of white-currants. I was recommended 'Ben Sarek' blackcurrants (a heavy-cropping, frost-resistant variety bred in Scotland), 'Redstart' and 'Junifer' redcurrants (the latter a new type giving a good yield of sweet early fruit immediately after planting), and both 'Blanka' and 'White Versailles' whitecurrants. All the above are available from Highfield Nurseries in Gloucestershire (01452 740266 for a mail order catalogue). Or make your own selection by browsing through the excellent chapters on fruit in Bob Flowerdew's *Organic Bible* (Kyle Cathie, £14.99) or Anna Pavord's *The New Kitchen Garden* (Dorling Kindersley, £9.99).

No fruit garden would be complete without strawberries, of course. I planted mine out in September (you can wait until spring, but plants established the previous autumn are reckoned to give greater yields). I bought them on a visit to Waterperry Gardens in Oxfordshire (01844 339226) – they were recently potted-on runners and I was impressed by how healthy they looked. Of the ten or so varieties for sale, I picked four, and took three plants of each – as many as I could happily take back on the train. It was only on the way home, reading *A Dream Fulfilled* (Merlin Books, £6.95), Ursula Maddy's entertaining history of Waterperry, that I realized I'd chosen probably the best place in the country to buy strawberries – and had hit on the best variety as well.

The principal of Waterperry's legendary horticulture college for women, Miss Beatrix Havergal, won 15 gold medals in 16 years for her hot-house strawberries at the Chelsea Flower Show in the Fifties and Sixties. 'Royal Sovereign', now relatively rare, but described as "the best dessert strawberry ever grown", was the variety repeatedly requested by the Queen on her private Monday visits to Chelsea. "The prospect of meeting the Queen and offering a sample Royal Sovereign – invariably accepted – added to the excitement and joy of the occasion," remembers Ms Maddy, an ex-student. "There was always the absorbing question as to what the Royals would do with their stalks. Prince Philip usually strode to the staging and flicked the stalk underneath, while the Queen's was rumoured to pass from hand to hand, lady-in-waiting to equerry and so on until it was lost."

19 December 1999

A CHRISTMAS BUSH

Last year I vowed not to have a traditional Christmas tree. I can never quite bring myself to buy a cut tree, and the allotment was turning into a retirement home for all our friends' discarded trees that we'd planted out and agreed to keep till the following Christmas. Trouble was, the friends would invariably forget about their old tree and buy a new one, or couldn't be bothered to come and collect it, or else decide that "it looks so happy in its new home it seems a shame to disturb it". Vegetable-growing space was fast giving way to a mini pension forest, and the last thing we needed was another tree. In the end, of course, I succumbed to pressure. My husband, who is a man of tradition about certain things, said that the smart clipped bay pyramid that I'd picked up at New Covent Garden Market just wasn't festive enough, even with little white fairy lights all over it. So I went back and got a little blue Norwegian spruce – more of a Christmas bush than a tree, really – and we covered that with winking white stars and everyone was happy.

When Christmas was over, I took the little tree down to the allotment, but left it in its red plastic pot, where it flourished. In my childhood, when we tried to keep our potted Christmas trees at the end of the garden, we often used to forget to water them, so that by midsummer all that was left was a bare ginger skeleton. But by putting this tree next to the thirsty pumpkin patch I ensured its survival. It even put on a good few inches of growth all the way round, sending out bright lime green brushes at the ends of all its branches, which in time turned the same grey-blue-green as the rest.

Both the bay tree and the not-so-little spruce have found their way back inside the house this winter, strewn with white fairy lights and topped with the usual homemade silver stars. We're holding a big family Christmas here this year, and with the house so full of people, I'm keen to keep the decorations festive but simple. I've raided my country friends' woods and hedges for hips and haws and other red berries, and bought huge tangles of trailing ivy from the flower market. The ivy twists into long thick 'ropes', bound with wire all along their length, so that berries and mistletoe and wisps of old man's beard can be tweaked in between. Thinner ropes are festooned around the room, stretching along surfaces or hanging like swags over fireplaces and picture frames, while a big fat one makes a great centrepiece running the length of a long table. You could lay a line of tea lights on either side, or secure some thick church candles at intervals among the greenery.

With all that dark glossy green and red, I like to have some white, and 'Paper White' narcissi are always a joy at this time of year. I grow them in shallow clear glass bowls, on a bed of pebbles or large pea shingle, cramming a layer of bulbs in as closely as I can and pouring in water to *just* below the bases. The mere presence of water is enough to stimulate root growth – leave bulbs sitting in water and they will rot, as I found out with my hyacinths last year. Keep the levels topped up and watch while green shoots turn to buds and then clouds of white flowers that fill a whole room with their scent. The whole process takes just four to five weeks and it's so easy that I did a few extra bowls as presents this year. In fact, the only difficult part was tracking down the pebbles. There seems to be a national shortage of those small Scottish beach pebbles you used to be able to buy in bags for a few pounds. The man at B&Q blamed it on the sudden popularity of water features. I blame Charlie Dimmock. It's a rather bizarre thought: Scotland's beaches growing emptier and emptier as our gardens grow ever stonier, and pebbles moving from north to south in a mysterious migration.

2000

COMPOST PREJUDICE

I have developed an alarming new prejudice. It shows how much my concerns have changed since my political, rad-fem youth. These days, my righteous wrath is reserved for those who don't keep compost heaps. I know that not everyone has the time, space or inclination to recycle their kitchen and garden waste, and clemency is granted to those who live in upper-floor flats. But I am amazed by the number of people with gardens far larger than my own, who still throw away their potato peelings and leave hedge prunings for the dustmen. With land-fill sites bursting at the seams and local councils offering discounts on ready-made bins, there is no excuse not to give compost-making a try.

True, it can seem daunting. Like many aspects of gardening, there is an air of science and mystique surrounding it, which can put off beginners. We may not get the perfect, chocolate-brown crumbs of the professionals at first, but the great thing about compost-making is that few attempts are irredeemable. It's usually a case of giving the pile another turn and getting the mix right by adding more wet or dry materials. And it's extremely satisfying when it works.

Whatever the size of your garden or allotment, you'll produce a fair amount of lawn mowings, hedge-clippings, prunings and weeds in the course of a year. The best way for these to rot down is layered (that is, making sure that lawn mowings are followed by a dose of more open, twiggier stuff, and vice versa) in a square slatted wooden bin, ideally with two compartments, so you can use one pile while you build up the other. Ritzy versions of these are sold through mail-order companies such as the Organic Gardening Catalogue (01932 253666) but my husband, who is by no means a DIY freak, knocked one up easily enough from some old lengths of wood. You can also add kitchen waste and newspaper to the pile; the Centre for Alternative Technology in Wales (01654 705950) has devised a 'lasagne' method using layers of cardboard and newspaper, with wetter, slime-prone waste such as lawn mowings and vegetable peelings in between.

In smaller gardens, where a large unsightly bin can't be screened behind a trellis or shed, it's possible to make a loose pile in a shady corner behind some tall-growing plants. It will rot down more slowly than in a protected bin, though I'd be careful with kitchen waste here as it might attract rats and foxes. In tiny gardens (or if your compost heap is far from the house or, like mine, at an allotment), a worm bin can be useful for recycling peelings, eggshells, coffee grounds, and so on. Not only is the whole smelly process hidden beneath a lid (I kept one on the balcony when I lived in a small flat with no ill effects); you get lots of lovely liquid feed into the bargain. Worm composting can be tricky but it's worth persevering. I thought I'd killed my worms last summer, but kept on adding to the pile anyway, and in the end

they came back. (The 'Can-o-Worms' composting kit is ideal for first-time compost makers. You don't have to touch the worms and harvesting the compost is easy (just lift out the finished tray). Each kit comes with 1000 worms and costs £88 from Wiggly Wigglers of Herefordshire (0800 216990/www.wigglywigglers.co.uk).)

An easy way to deal with kitchen waste (and in my experience, the easier something is, the more likely I am to do it) is to lay out a sheet or two of newspaper when peeling fruit and vegetables, and wrap the waste before adding it, paper and all, to the compost. The paper helps the balance of the mixture, as well as keeping things tidy. If you're preparing a lot of food, hang a plastic carrier bag over the back of a chair while you're working, adding paper parcels as you go, and take it outside when full. After a while, you'll notice that your regular dustbin fills more slowly. And you'll be turning something you would have thrown away into useful, ecologically-produced compost – which tests have proved to be the best growing medium for plants. So there you are. A slightly bossy start to the new millennium, but I hope it hits the spot. A happy and humus-filled gardening year to you all.

23 January 2000

THE TRANSFORMING POWER OF FROST

A harsh frost has put an end to a most unseasonable display of flowers in the back garden. Well into midwinter, nasturtiums continued to sprawl their way up and over a south-facing wall, while the daturas I raised from cuttings two summers ago put out 30 or more kamikaze blooms just before Christmas. They lasted a week before the frost turned those mad trumpet flowers into limp wet washing overnight. A few other things suffered, most notably a couple of potted pelargoniums hung high up the walls and a clump of arum lilies (*Zantedeschia aethiopica*), whose glossy dark green leaves are now bent double and lifeless. The arums made a comeback after last winter – and the thick mulch of compost I applied back in autumn should protect the crowns from permanent damage – but I fear that the foliage is done for. As for the daturas, who can tell? They are supposed to come indoors for the winter, but the plant that chanced it outside last year has grown too unwieldy to fit through the door. I do wish I'd taken some cuttings just in case. It's amazing how much new growth these alluring plants can put on in the course of a summer. As this tiny walled garden usually affords protection from all but the most severe weather, I'm really not accustomed to its effects. The view from the window is now droopy and depressing.

I sought consolation at the allotment, where the frost had worked the other way around, bringing magic and romance to what, at this time of year, can seem a banal and abandoned landscape. The grass, which had turned into a muddy mess, now crunched and glistened underfoot as I made my way down to our corner. The surface of the pond was puckered into geometric patterns – more than an inch of ice, I discovered, as I bashed a hole in it for birds and other wildlife. As I walked around our two plots, it became clear that there was more to wonder at than worry about. The scrolling silvery leaves of artichokes and cardoons looked even more beautiful with their spikes and curlicues outlined in sparkling white. We'd drawn the earth up around the stems for protection earlier in the autumn; if you live in an area prone to harsh frosts it's also a good idea to cover the crowns in straw, with an opening in the centre. Broccoli and brussels sprouts, not normally the most glamorous of vegetables, had undergone a transformation, their purple-tinged, frilly-edged leaves as beautiful as filigree brooches. The frost had also given extra definition to the architectural folds on the leaves of onions, leeks and garlic. And I was pleased to see the winter salad leaves – red and green mustard, mizuna and corn salad – had survived.

There was little work I could do – the earth really did stand, in the words of the carol, "hard as iron", making it impossible to plant garlic, or even dig up jerusalem artichoke roots for winter soup. So the dog and I went for a stroll around the deserted site, my fellow plot-holders all being sensibly tucked up at home with their seed catalogues. The tidy plots up at the far end, where the "old-timers" keep their raised beds edged with brick and grow beans up old-fashioned tee-pees, looked wonderful. Like the bones of a good garden, their organized aesthetic was given an extra edge by the frost. In many, the soil had already been prepared for next year – worked to a fine tilth and mounded high in the beds. It looked soft and crumbly beneath its dusting of white, but proved hard and impenetrable as rock. But even the disgraced and overgrown plots – soon, no doubt, to be requisitioned by our strict committee and handed on to new owners – looked stunning. Seed-heads on top of waist-high weeds sparkled like candied fruits, while strings of long-forgotten french beans looked weirdly sculptural. And –

surely the real litmus test of the transforming powers of frost – even the sheets of black plastic stretched across empty beds had become felty white carpets etched with a delicate criss-cross of fox prints.

30 January 2000

LETTERS FROM LORI

On these bleak midwinter days, when it sometimes seems as if nature has come to a standstill, I take solace in letters from my friend Lori in Florida. Since we met on a gardening course two years ago in Scotland, we have corresponded every few months, comparing notes on what's happening in our gardens and exchanging snaps and sketches. Like me, Lori has a small town garden – it surrounds the clapboard cottage her boyfriend built her at the end of his long narrow lawn. But the climate being what it is in Florida, we find ourselves occupied with diametrically opposing tasks at any given time of the year. The southernmost states of America can have summers so hot that many plants just sizzle up, so Lori's main sowing and planting season is during our autumn, when things here are just winding down. Now, when all I've got at the allotment is a sea of jerusalem artichokes, some rows of straggly salad and the purple sprouting broccoli that has yet to start to sprout, she is reaping her first harvest of runner beans, courgettes and tomatoes. I've just received a letter with photos of a 12m (40ft) avocado tree heavy with fruit and a loofah vine laden with what look like huge spotted cucumbers.

The hot moist weather means Lori can also grow flowers one would not attempt outside in London: showy birds of paradise and pink and green-

splattered caladiums, gloriosa lilies and a maroon-spotted variety of the Dutchman's pipe vine called *Aristolochia elegans*. She threads her flowers in among the vegetables, and dots multicoloured impatiens and anthemis in between. Compared to my dull and lifeless beds her garden must look like the Rio Carnival. When I read of clouds of butterflies feeding at the blooms of her yellow cassia tree, I can feel every one of the 4,500 miles that stretch between us.

But then, cupping my hands around my coffee mug for warmth, I venture outside for my daily potter in the garden – and of course there is a lot more happening than it might at first appear. The first bulbs are nosing up through the soil: the white tips of tulips and tiny fringed shoots of lilies; snowdrops and pushkinias beneath the winter-flowering cherry, and *Iris reticulata* around my tiny fig tree. In among the glossy new acanthus leaves is the strappy lime green foliage of seven or eight *Fritillaria persica* – I find their gorgeous spires of dusky purple blooms easier to integrate in a garden than the show-stopper clusters of the crown imperial fritillary. And up through the ground cover of different types of ivy and silver dead nettle are pushing the spear-like points – like perfect, dead-straight arrows – of *Arum italicum*, the ornamental cousin of our hedgerow lords-and-ladies.

There are flowers to be found, too – if you know where to look. This is hellebore time, and I do think these plants are responsible for some of the loveliest colours in the garden – at any time of year. *Helleborus argutifolius* and *H. foetidus* are bearing their beautiful clusters of pale milky green bells, while the purply hybrids have buds and flowers of a heavenly dirty dark rose-pink. This is the third year I've grown them in high containers, so you can better admire their downward-drooping flowers. The white potato vine *Solanum jasminoides* 'Album' has only just stopped putting out the tiny white stars that have studded the north and west walls since July, and the ceanothus is already in tight white bud. Even the herb bed is surprisingly lively – though I love it when the perennials die back to reveal its mulch of bright purple aquarium gravel. Despite repeated plunderings over Christmas, the rosemary is covered in felty white buds, and the golden and green marjoram are already making flat mats of new leaf. Self-sown seedlings of last year's favourite, *Cerinthe major* 'Purpurascens', are romping through the pots by the back door – I can't wait for another crop of those curious, peacock-blue bracts and bright violet flowers. So there is plenty to tell Lori after all, as I sit down by the window with my pen and writing paper.

6 February 2000

THE JOY OF SPUDS

When I acquired my allotment three years ago I decided not to bother with potatoes. They take up too much room, I reasoned. They are not attractive plants. And these days it is easy to find organic potatoes in the shops. But then my neighbour gave me his leftover Pink Fir Apples to plant, and I have never looked back. Nothing can compare with the sweet, slightly earthy flavour of a freshly dug, home-grown crop. They are undemanding and great fun – qualities as appealing in a vegetable as they are in a person. Harvesting potatoes – that moment when you plunge a fork into the soil beneath the fading foliage – always feels to me like digging for buried treasure. The haulm (stem) and leaves give no clue as to what is underground – whether your fork will come up laden with clusters of creamy, egg-shaped tubers, or will be scrabbling about for the few that the slugs or blight have left behind. Even without pests and diseases, yields can be unpredictable.

I have been quite content to take pot luck with my potatoes, simply setting them in the soil each spring, watering them when I remember, and earthing up around the emerging foliage to prevent light from penetrating to the tubers and turning them green and poisonous. But there are further steps one can take to encourage a bumper yield. Incorporating plenty of manure into the soil the previous autumn helps, as does watering heavily when the flowers appear. Bob Flowerdew, whose *Organic Bible* (Kyle Cathie, £19.99) is packed with useful advice, suggests adding wilted comfrey leaves to the bottom of the trench when planting, and mulching with straw mixed with grass clippings.

Now is the time to buy seed potatoes – they look like any other small potato, but have been raised for cropping and should be disease-free. The Organic Gardening Catalogue (01932 253666) claims to have each of the 30-odd varieties currently raised organically in Britain, while Simpson's (01985 845004) has 100 varieties, about a quarter of which are organic. The names are as romantic as those of apples or roses: the classic salad potato 'Belle de Fontenay' sounds desirable, as does 'Ballydoon' (prized in Ireland and eaten boiled with bacon and spring cabbage), 'Edzell Blue' with its bluish skin and tasty flesh, and 'Ulster Sceptre', a high-yielding waxy new potato. You usually have to buy a 2 or 3kg (4 or 6lb) bag of one variety, but The Organic Gardening Catalogue offers other options, including a 'Cook's Choice' of ten to 12 tubers of five or six different varieties. If you are keen to sample unusual varieties, nip along to one of the National Potato Days organized by HDRA, the organic organization, at Ryton Organic Gardens in Coventry (call 024 7630 3517 or visit website www.hdra.org.uk for details).

When you have your seed potatoes, they need to be 'chitted' or sprouted. Leave them in a single layer in trays or old egg boxes in a cool light room for about six weeks, until sturdy short green shoots appear. Plant out 'earlies' (early-maturing types that can be harvested as new potatoes from midsummer) a month before the last frost is expected, 10–13cm (4–5in) deep and a foot apart; 'second earlies' and 'maincrops' follow in succession from mid-spring, set slightly wider apart. You can even grow new potatoes on a balcony in a deep pot. Place 15cm (6in) of compost and manure in the base, set six or so seed potatoes on the surface and cover with another 15cm (6in) of potting compost. Water well, and add more compost to cover the shoots as they break through. Harvest in about three months – the yield will be small, but rewarding. Just think: if you plant a tub on 1 April, you could be celebrating Midsummer Day with a dish of the most delicious new potatoes ever.

PLANTING BY THE MOON

When I was in Italy last autumn, I enjoyed talking to Guido, the old gardener and estate manager at the house where I was staying. I was intrigued to find he used a system of planting and harvesting by the moon, which, he said, had been practised throughout Italy for centuries. All sowing and transplanting was carried out at full moon or during the few days beforehand. Harvest time depended on the crops and what they would be used for – those eaten fresh or used for juice should be picked when the moon was full, whereas those required for storage (potatoes, apples, even timber) were gathered at new moon. I resolved to do some research into lunar gardening on my return home.

I soon realized I had opened a huge can of worms on the outer horticultural fringe. "Loony gardening, that's what I call it," said my husband, as strange-looking books, charts, calendars and almanacs decorated with stylized stars and moons and astrological runes started arriving through the post. "You don't want to start getting into any of that weird stuff." But it wasn't just weird; it was multifarious. Guido's system is just one of a number of different practices, some of which seem to be as old as agriculture itself. Some recommend that root crops, where the part to be eaten develops below ground, be planted at new moon and all other crops at full moon. Some say you can sow everything at full or new moon. Others divide the plant world into categories that correspond to the four elements – earth (root vegetables), water (leafy crops such as cabbage and lettuce), air (flowers, including broccoli, cauliflower and globe artichokes) and fire (seeds and fruits) – and allocate planting days when the moon is in an astrological sign of that element.

Though such divisions will be familiar to those who have read Culpeper or Gerard's 1597 *Herball*, the most detailed charts of the past 100 years were refined under the auspices of Rudolf Steiner's school of Biodynamic farming. And though on the surface of things this system – with its mysterious 'preparations' involving herbs buried in animal horns – seems the weirdest of them all, it is the only one to offer any evidence to support its theories. In Germany in the Fifties and Seventies, Maria Thun

(who publishes an incomprehensibly translated calendar of her own) carried out strict trials using potatoes, which recorded a 30 per cent increase in yield for crops sown on "root days" compared with other sowings. And in this country, Reg Muntz, a market gardener from Sussex, and Colin Bishop, an amateur gardener and astrologer from Wales, have separately recorded increases of up to 50 per cent on sowings of beans, radishes and lettuce as well as potatoes. I rang Nick Kollerstrom, author of *Planting By the Moon* (Prospect Books, £9.99) to find out more.

Mr Kollerstrom is a science historian whose interest in the subject dates back to the Seventies, when he was working on a Biodynamic farm. At first sceptical, he was amazed at the evidence in favour of the system, and carried out his own research on the effects of the moon (including a fascinating paper on its effects on horse breeding, published in last month's *Equine Veterinary Journal*). Though he finds sowing around the full moon brings on faster germination, he has no evidence of a beneficial effect on the final yield. In areas prone to drought, such as the Mediterranean, where germination can be scanty, he thinks the evidence pointing to more moisture in the soil around full moon may account for their preference to sow at that time. In a further fascinating twist, he reveals that tests have found that peas and beans (a "seed/fire" crop) sown on a "leaf/water" day develop lots of strong leafy growth, but fewer pods than the smaller but higher-yielding plants sown at the more auspicious time.

Exciting experiential evidence or a load of old moonshine? In these days when scientists are prepared to acknowledge the effect of the moon on the weather and women's fertility, and that migrating birds may use the constellations to navigate by night, I'm prepared to give it a go. Steiner was, after all, the man who predicted the BSE crisis back in 1923. And some prestigious French vineyards have converted to Biodynamic methods, most notably Noel Pinguit's Le Haut Lieu, which has since won every award going. This year, I'll be conducting a little research of my own, and would be intrigued to hear from readers with experience in this field. I may be a crank, but I'm in good company.

Copies of Nick Kollerstrom's *Planting by the Moon* can be obtained from Prospect Books, Allaleigh House, Blackawton, Totnes, Devon TQ9 7DL (01803 712269). "Gardening by the Moon" posters based on this calendar are available from Permanent Publications (01730 823311).

27 February 2000

A LIVING WILLOW BOWER

I think I've finally found a way round my allotment committee's annoying rule banning members from having sheds. I'm going to make a 'living willow' structure, woven using live willow wands that are rooted in the soil. It won't provide the total shelter and privacy of a shed, but it should get round the regulations by being, technically, at least, a group of plants rather than a permanent building. I've seen living willow structures – simple fences, woven seats and bowers – in magazines and in a couple of community gardens. In winter the woven strands remain bare, so the beauty of the openwork construction can be clearly seen. In spring they begin to sprout: soft pussy-willow tufts at first, then catkins and finally leaves – until by midsummer the outline is obscured by jungly foliage. What I have in mind for the allotment is a roughly circular bower with a quarter segment cut out to make the opening – and a low bench seat round the interior wall of the leafy dome. I can picture myself sitting there in the summer, enjoying the cool shade and sense of enclosure, away from the eyes of the committee's Weed Police.

But I'd better get a move on. Living willow must be cut and worked between December and the end of March; by early spring the wands are sprouting so much they are difficult to weave, and by late winter many suppliers are running low on longer rods, because of the recent rise in popularity of this craft. This is why I am writing about this project before I've actually done it – to give those who are interested the time to get organized.

In spite of a Girl Guide Camper's Badge and a surprising aptitude for knots, or "lashing" as I seem to remember it was called, I decided it wasn't wise to embark on such an ambitious plan without some training. So I rang the RHS to try to get on a workshop run by Clare Wilks, one of the leading living willow experts in the country. Clare runs several courses from December till March, on which participants make a covered seat that they can take home and plant at the end of the day. The courses sell out within days of the dates being announced, and there was already a long waiting list, but I was invited to "sit in" on the class and watch the others at work.

I learned a great deal – from the many different types and colours of willow that can be used (dark purply brown, rich ochres, orange, olive and lime green) to the various weaving techniques. The basic principles are simple: the uprights, which will be the living part of the structure, are buried 30cm (1ft) deep and between 7.5cm (3in) and 30cm (1ft) apart in moist, weed-free soil (the course participants used special wooden frames with a ring of holes). These can then be bent and woven to form the rough shape you require (straight up for a fence or hurdle; curved and criss-crossed inwards for a shelter or bower) and bound with an in-and-out basketwork weave using slimmer wands of a contrasting colour. You can use string to secure the willow temporarily – it is very whippy and has a tendency to spring out of place – but the aim is that the weaving should support the finished structure, and the stems may eventually graft together. New growth can subsequently be pruned (which helps the original rods establish and keeps a clear design) or woven in diagonally upwards across the framework to increase the shade in summer. It all seemed hopelessly complicated at first, but by the end of the day almost everyone was standing back to admire their completed seat and wondering how to cram it into a hatchback.

Leafing through Clare's portfolio of towering cone plant supports, woven treehouse "nests" and intricate interconnected bowers, I tried hard to stop myself from getting too ambitious. I've measured my patch of ground and ordered my willow. But I think I might practise on a low enclosing fence for the pumpkin patch first.

Clare Wilks' Living Willow courses, in which participants make a woven covered seat to bring home, are held at RHS Wisley in Surrey (01483 224234) and English Hurdle in Somerset (01823 698418). Suppliers of willow wands for making living willow structures include English Hurdle (as above); Edgar Watson near Bristol (01934 838017) and Blagdon Gardens near Newcastle (0191 281 4771).

5 March 2000

WHEN IS 'ORGANIC' NOT ORGANIC?

When a friend asked me if I'd tried organic slug pellets the other day, I did a double-take. Was this some new product I hadn't heard about? It turned out she meant the ones that come in tubs labelled "eco-friendly", "for people who care about the environment" and "featuring pet-repellant". Such products, of course, are not "organic" at all. Anything containing a substance from which pets need protection is, *ipso facto*, going to be harmful to more than just slugs. Some slug pellets kill birds and other wildlife, and they all leave residues in the soil, which may harm earthworms and other organisms, eventually damaging the living structure of the soil. And the basis of organic gardening – indeed, of the organic movement as a whole – is healthy soil.

There has been a phenomenal explosion of interest in organic food and gardening over the past few years. When I began this column in 1996, it was

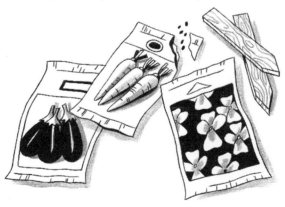

hard to find organic vegetables anywhere other than a health food shop; now the supermarkets are full of them. The Soil Association (0117 929 0661) and its sister association the Henry Doubleday Research Association (HDRA, 02476 303517) – which is geared to the smaller-scale organic gardener – have been so inundated with inquiries that they have had to employ extra staff and install new phone lines. The BSE crisis and GM food scares seem to have forged for good that crucial mental link between production methods and the food on our plates. But in spite of this welcome burst of enthusiasm, it seems there is still confusion about what the term "organic" actually means.

Growing organically involves a lot more than *not* using chemicals. When the Soil Association was formed in 1946 in response to farming's increasing reliance on artificial fertilizers and pesticides, the key concern of its founder, Lady Eve Balfour, was the renewal of living organic matter in the soil. Her groundbreaking book, *The Living Soil*, argued that it was the micro-organisms in the soil, which break down the humus and make its nutrients available to plants, that are the source of true, sustainable soil fertility. The HDRA leaflet entitled *Guidelines for Organic Gardening* (£1, telephone 02476 303517) lists the best ways of encouraging healthy soil in our gardens today.

Keeping the soil surface covered with protective vegetation or mulches helps prevent damage to soil organisms and structure from exposure to extreme temperatures, heavy rain and strong winds, and to reduce the washing out of nutrients. In a vegetable plot, the use of green manure crops over the winter months (for instance, mustard, grazing rye or fodder radish) is strongly favoured; ground cover plants in garden beds work just as well. Manure and compost added to the soil should be from reputable, preferably organic sources, and mineral fertilizers such as wood ash, seaweed and bone-meal should be regarded as supplements to, and not replacements for, the recycling of nutrients within the garden via the compost heap and careful growing practices. Crop rotation, for instance, should ensure that leafy crops requiring high levels of nitrogen should follow on from legumes such as peas and beans, whose root systems "fix" nitrogen in the soil.

Both HDRA and the Soil Association have been involved in heated debates as to whether to respond to recent developments and heighten their profiles by incorporating the word "organic" into their names. The Henry Doubleday Research Association nearly became the Organic Gardening Association, but eventually retained the name of the Quaker smallholder who had inspired its founder, Lawrence Hills. It is now to be known as "HDRA – the organic organization". Likewise, the Soil Association voted to keep Lady Balfour's original title in order to honour her fundamental concern, and the focus of the entire organic movement, on the state of the soil.

"'Feed the soil, not the plant' is one of organic gardening's great tenets," says Pauline Pears of the HDRA, who writes many of their useful leaflets on organic growing methods. "Then you shouldn't need so many extra products. Tests have proved that plants are healthier and less prone to pests and disease on a 'whole-food diet' of compost and other organic manures than on a 'fast food' diet of artificial fertilizers." And it costs less, too, in the long run. Advertising is constantly telling us we need to feed this or kill that, but adverts exist to sell products. Going organic doesn't mean changing your brand of slug pellet. It means changing your way of thinking.

12 March 2000

JEWEL-LIKE INTENSITY

Every gardener has his or her favourite colour for flowers. One of mine is chartreuse – that lovely, luminous lime that is neither yellow nor green, to which I have already devoted a column. Another, which has been much in my mind while filling out seed orders and planning for summer, is deep, plummy purple. Purple in the garden can veer towards blue or towards red, and it is the rich red-tinged shades, from mulberry to claret to aubergine, that I am particularly keen to encourage in my garden. I have them already, in the velvety faces of the darkest hellebores, in 'Queen of Night' and 'Black Swan' tulips, and in the dark brownish pink of regale lily buds before they open. It's there in the purply-red stems and flowers of *Euphorbia amygdaloides* var *robbiae* 'Rubra' and the smaller leafed *E. dulcis* 'Chamaeleon'. And the fritillary family supplies it in abundance, from the nodding snakeskin bells of *Fritillaria meleagris* to the exotic waxy spikes of *F. persica*. But there is room for more.

In a few months the little plants of *Geranium phaeum* that I put in last autumn should be showing dark maroon flowers – they thrive in shade, and the variety 'Samobor', which has a chocolate-blotched leaf to match, is particularly fetching. The darkest astrantia, 'Hadspen Blood' has been added alongside its white counterpart, *A. major*. Set against the backdrop of a large bronze phormium, with its strap-like metallic leaves, their papery pointy flowers seem even more delicate. And there should be lots of lovely dark sweetpeas up the sunny back wall of the house, where they thread in and out of a wisteria, grapevine and golden hop – as well as at my allotment, where I grow them in profusion for picking. 'Midnight' (rich burgundy) and 'Matucana' (bi-coloured dark purple and violet) are good dark varieties, available from Thompson & Morgan (01473 688821). I missed out on 'Midnight' last year, as all the seed catalogues had sold out, so this time I got my order in early.

The first young seedlings are doing well in my mini-greenhouse, but you can plant the seeds straight into the ground in March or April if you don't mind waiting till July for flowers. Sweetpeas like lots of organic matter, and mine did well alongside the runner beans last summer, in a deep trench dug in spring and lined with well-rotted manure and kitchen waste. The extra flowers seemed to help pollinate the beans – we certainly had a bumper crop – and the purple and scarlet flowers looked lovely together.

Combining deep plums and purples with other colours in the border needs some thought, however. They can be sombre shades, and a natural approach, and one in tune with the current fashion for bold associations would be to combine them with the contrasting acid yellows and lime greens of euphorbias, buplureum and dill. But the subdued opulence of these colours can be used to create areas of mystery and jewel-like intensity in the garden. Dark purply reds look good against the glaucous grey-blue foliage of plants such as macleaya, cardoons or *Melianthus major*, all of which I have in my garden. The double poppy, *Papaver somniferum*, with its petals of dark plum and finely-cut bluish leaves, contains this combination in one plant.

If you are brave enough, you can let the dark colours speak for themselves. In her highly entertaining book, *Gardening with Light and Colour* (Kyle Cathie, £19.99), Marylyn Abbott argues that dark areas with poor light do not need pale colours, but points of strong, rich colour, glowing against glossy green foliage as if from the depths of an open jewel box. She chooses ".... the colours from the varnished gloom of a baroque ecclesiastical painting, the magenta of a beretta, a red cloak, a purple sash...." for her transformation of the gloomy south borders at West Green House in Hampshire. "It all looks like a late summer Vatican meeting, especially when the dark purple flowers of *Penstemon* 'Burgundy' hang down gently, as though asleep through a long homily on a hot afternoon." This is all very well if you have acres in which to play with contrasting moods and effects, but in a little garden such as mine, I shall stick to a sprinkling of these colours, working with subtly contrasting leaf colours and textures in an attempt to add richness and depth.

19 March 2000

SCREAMIN' JAY'S LEGACY

The allotment is coming out of its winter dormancy and becoming interesting again. Our autumn sowings of early peas and broad beans are now a couple of inches high, and the second sowing, made last month, should soon be appearing. The winter-sown onions look good, and the rows of shallots are sporting spiky sprouts, like tufts of green hair. Best of all, I've picked the first tender shoots of purple sprouting broccoli. When the birds got our young plants a couple of years ago (I forgot to protect the seedlings) we really missed it. Purple sprouting broccoli is one of my favourite vegetables, and seems all the more delicious because there is nothing else to harvest for another month or two.

I've also been preparing the unused beds for new sowings, digging in well-rotted manure where the soil structure needs improving and elsewhere adding a dressing of 'Six X' – a powdered chicken manure said to have six times the nutrients of normal farmyard manure. But remember that some crops – especially root crops like carrots and parsnips – do not like manure in the soil. I'm keen to succeed with carrots this year. Previous attempts have failed, either due to carrot fly or to wet summers turning our soil to clay; carrots and parsnips like a loose, friable soil. I was going to dig in lots of sand – the standard practice when trying to lighten heavy soil – but the man in my local garden centre told me of a method his father used to swear by. Using a dibber, you prepare individual holes for each carrot, fill them with compost and sow a single seed in each – pelleted seeds make this task a lot less fiddly. The carrots can then push down their roots with ease, unimpeded by clay, stones and other obstacles that induce them either to give up the ghost or grow into candidates for a rude vegetable competition. This way, I've been able to slot the carrots in between my rows of onions – a good bit of companion planting as the strong smell of the onions confuses the carrot fly into searching elsewhere.

Turning a third of our allotment over to fruit this year means we have to allocate the remaining space with care, or there won't be room for all the potatoes quietly chitting in the spare room, not to mention the unusual salad seeds I bought in Tuscany last autumn. The salad can go where the broad beans grew last year – legumes 'fix' nitrogen in the soil and so a traditional crop rotation follows them with leaf vegetables.

The last two summers have taught me that you can't do enough to deter slugs and snails, particularly if, like me, you garden organically and can't resort to pellets. I've ordered my slug nematodes from Green Gardener (01603 715 096) but you can't use them till the soil is a constant 5°C (41°F); I've already seen some small black slugs around the broad beans. Bran is supposed to be a good deterrent – scattered around vulnerable plants it provides the creatures with a gourmet last supper, which then swells in their stomachs so they are unable to return to their hiding places. You can scoop them up the next morning as they lie in sated torpor.

I was recently provided with the ingredients of another old-fashioned remedy. Seventy or so squeezed grapefruit halves were added to the kitchen compost at the weekend (the result of a new cocktail devised by my husband to honour his recently departed hero, Screamin' Jay Hawkins, for whom he was holding an impromptu wake). Citrus peel is slow to break down in a compost heap and I was about to throw some away when I remembered you can turn the halves into traps. Slugs and snails use them as shelters, so you simply lay them on the soil, cut side down, and collect them up a few days later. When I'd finished, the allotment was dotted with yellow and orange circles, not unlike an installation by Martha Schwartz, the avant-garde American landscape designer, who once planted bagels in a Boston garden. So far, precisely two slugs have fallen for the trick. Oh well, at least it looks cheerful.

THE TROUBLE WITH DECKING

The more we turn our gardens into outside rooms, the more gardening becomes like housework. Decking and painted wood are all very stylish, but they are not as low-maintenance as all those TV programmes would have you believe. A light growth of moss or even mould can look attractive on old stone or brick, but the sharp contemporary lines of decking and concrete must be kept pristine for best effect. And, exposed to the elements all year round, outdoor paint is inevitably going to need re-touching and woodwork protecting much more frequently than it would inside. I was thinking about such matters, and more, as I gave my little garden its annual spring clean last weekend.

First I swept the upper and lower decks, shunting pots and containers just as you would furniture, to reach the forgotten leaves and spilt soil that had collected in the corners – the garden equivalent of fluff under the bed. I might as well have used the Hoover and made life easier. Then it was down on my hands and knees to scrub the deck with a stiff-bristled brush and a pan of weak bleach. The deck had secretly been trying to turn itself into a lawn by developing a light layer of bright green moss or algae that becomes slippery in wet weather. I wanted to get it clean in preparation for its annual spring wash of watered-down white paint. An hour and a half later I was utterly exhausted. Will there be a "decking back-lash" once others discover the hidden work involved?

There has been more cleaning up to do than usual this year, owing to the continued presence of the builders converting the warehouse that backs on to our garden into a flat. They are particularly messy workers and don't respond well to requests to cover my plants with dust sheets while they add more unwanted – and unapproved – layers of bricks to the party wall. We are contesting this increase in height. In spite of our site meeting with the

council planning officer two months ago, when he made clear to the architects the highest permissible limit for the wall, a further three lines of bricks have gone on regardless – which has had a considerable impact on all the tiny gardens that surround the warehouse. Photographs have been forwarded to the planning enforcement officer, who has asked that the wall be lowered, or amended drawings submitted for approval. Various neighbours have got involved now, many of whom are as annoyed about damage to their gardens as the height of the wall. Our plants are encrusted with cement mix, and our flowerbeds littered with chunks of old mortar and slops of cement. The builders broke a sculpture that was attached to the wall in one couple's garden, and flung the pieces down on their lawn. Another neighbour had a ten-year-old jasmine plant sawn down to a stump. To be fair, the builders have now offered to come in and clean up our gardens, but having seen the size of their boots and watched the way they deal with plants, I'd rather do it myself.

Cement is not hard to wash off if you get it while it's wet. I go out armed with the jet hose when the builders are packing up and squirt it right up into the climbers that cover the wall. Not only does this wash down the leaves, it dislodges dead foliage and over-wintering snails that have become lodged in the trellis – and if I'm lucky I might just catch the back of a builder's leg in the process. As for the beds, there's nothing like getting right in at close quarters to appreciate all the spring bulbs and seedlings and new growth on the perennials that are pushing through, in spite of all the mess. I picked off a large carrier bag of debris and then laid a mulch of dark compost around the plants to hide the remains and counteract any excess of lime from the cement. The garden looks sparkling and well-cared-for again. My only worry now is that if the council should press for the building to be lowered, we'll have to go through all this again....

2 April 2000

GOOD COMPANIONS

I touched on companion planting a few weeks ago, when I wrote about sowing my onions and carrots in alternative rows, in the hope that the smell of the onions would fool carrot flies – the cause behind many a failed crop of carrots – into looking elsewhere. Now that the soil is warming up for the major sowing and planting season, it seems a good time to expand on this effective, and often extremely decorative way of gardening.

Scent is one of the simplest ways in which companion planting works. Some strong-smelling plants such as onions, garlic, chives, chervil, dill, summer savory and French marigolds just confuse the pests, most of which rely on their sense of smell to home in on target plants. Scatter them among other crops and by paths and gates so their smell is released as you brush past. Other plants directly repel pests with their own odour: asters, autumn chrysanthemums, cosmos and coreopsis are particularly effective, and would make unexpected splashes of colour in the vegetable patch. *Limnanthes douglasii* (the 'poached egg plant') is one of many scented plants that act as a lure to beneficial insects such as hover-flies, whose larvae feed on aphids. Limnanthes looks lovely as an edging plant, or sown in rows between aphid-prone crops such as lettuce. Many scented flowers attract bees, which are useful pollinators for fruit and vegetables. This is no doubt why traditional cottage gardens, in which vegetables, fruit and flowers were mixed together in a glorious jumble, were so productive.

Simpler still is the physical protection that certain planting combinations provide. The summer shade from jerusalem artichokes is good for lettuce, while broad beans and spinach are a well-proven partnership. The beans provide shade for the spinach, which stops it bolting, while the spinach keeps the ground cool and covered around the beans, keeping down weeds and discouraging blackfly, which thrive on dry soil. In his *Organic Bible* (Kyle Cathie, £19.99), Bob Flowerdew recommends a combination of peas, potatoes and sweetcorn that I am keen to try this year. He has the peas in a row down the middle of a raised bed, with alternate sweetcorn and potato plants on each side. The peas provide shelter for the tender young corn shoots, and the potatoes keep the soil covered and moist which the sweet-corn and peas enjoy, while none shades out the others. In his experience, beds containing a mixture of these vegetables provide higher yields than when the crops are grown separately.

Other combinations seem more mysterious. Some plants exude substances below soil level which can help or hinder the growth of other plants. African marigolds (Tagetes) can be particularly helpful; their root secretions have been found to kill ground elder and bindweed, while also repelling certain pests. And garlic planted around roses is supposed to penetrate the entire plant, making its sap repulsive to aphids – I've tried this in the back garden with some success. But this principle also works the other way. Dandelions give out a pungent ethylene gas that can harm plants grown nearby, allowing the dandelions to colonize, and grass roots exude a substance that can stunt the growth of apple and pear trees.

Sometimes the recommendations seem almost the stuff of folklore or fairytales. For instance, I've heard that planting a single pumpkin in among your marrows will lead to treble the yield – but I'd be more likely to try it if I could be sure it would work with courgettes. I'm also intrigued by claims that borage interplanted with strawberries not only improves the yield and flavour of the fruit, but also helps prevent fungus and mould diseases. No one can tell me why this should work, but even if it doesn't, the combination of the starry sapphire flowers and scarlet fruit will look stunning.

Like so much in gardening, companion planting provides scope for experiment. If you have room for a "control" crop grown on its own in another bed, you can get a better idea of the effectiveness of a particular pairing. The crucial thing is not to overcrowd. Any benefits in terms of pest control and so on will be cancelled out if your plants are having to compete for space and nutrients.

9 April 2000

ASPARAGUS TIPS

It is testimony to my married-and-settled-down life that I have finally got round to planting some asparagus. Asparagus takes two to three years to produce a decent crop, so like many young(ish) urban types who don't know where they are likely to be in three years' time, I didn't bother with it when we first took on the allotment. Pity – I'd be harvesting a fantastic crop next month. How truly luxurious it would be to stroll in from the garden with a heap of fresh-picked, milky-green spears to cook for supper. Apart from its slowness to establish, and the fact that it takes up a lot of space, asparagus does well in my quick and easy "Worth growing your own?" questionnaire. It is expensive to buy in the shops but, after the initial outlay of £10–15 for the 20–30 crowns you'll need to be able to pick a decent meal at any one time, your own plants should keep on cropping for twenty years if left undisturbed. In addition, organic asparagus is hard to come by and deteriorates fast on the shelf; ideally, the pan should be steaming on the stove before you go to cut your spears.

Traditional asparagus beds are 1.2m (4ft) wide, giving room for two rows of plants and allowing easy access for weeding and cutting. They are a lovely sight in late summer, when billowing, fern-like leaves have taken over from the spears – the female plants carry small red berries. But the moment every asparagus lover waits for is the sight of those first purple-tinged shoots nudging through the soil in early May. I had in mind a long raised bed where we grew peas last year and sweetcorn the year before that. It was well-manured, so I just sprinkled some concentrated chicken manure and dug in a bag of sharp sand to improve the drainage – asparagus will not thrive on heavy soil. The crowns, whose long white roots make them look like straggly spiders, need to be spread out gently in the bottom of trenches dug 46cm (18in) deep with a ridge down the middle. The roots should be draped either side of the ridge so the plants are 46cm (18in) apart and the tiny pink buds 10cm (4in) below the suface when the trench is filled in. After that, they need very little care, except thorough weeding and mulching with manure or compost in the winter, when you also cut down the dead foliage.

Although you'll get the fattest spears in a plot devoted entirely to asparagus, it makes a good companion for tomatoes, as the tomato scent helps mask it from the asparagus beetle, while root secretions from asparagus kill a nematode that attacks tomato roots. Both like basil, so you could have the ingredients of a heavenly summer's cooking all in the same bed. In Italy they earth up the soil around the emerging stems to blanch them, but green asparagus has more flavour – so long as it's fresh. Then all you really need to do is steam it and serve with butter, vinaigrette or hollandaise sauce. The season for home-grown asparagus is so short you won't have time to tire of it simply cooked.

Such delights seemed rather a long way off to me, as I dug my trenches on a sunny day in March. If you can find two-year-old crowns you can enjoy a small harvest the year after planting, but year-old crowns (which I fear mine to be) require a further year of growth. Not one single spear must be picked during the first year, and only a few the following season. Only after three years can you pig out to your heart's content. As I carefully untangled the roots of my asparagus crowns and laid them on the soil, I couldn't help but be haunted by a memory of digging up something decidedly similar when we dug over the plot for the first time four years ago. Back then, anything with white roots was probably bindweed in my book, so we threw whatever we found away. I mustn't dwell on it. Better to dream of the pleasures to come – provided, of course, that we haven't moved house in the meantime.

30 April 2000

ECO PEST CONTROL

Lovely fresh spring growth is everywhere – but so, unfortunately, are the pests that love it, too. My morning walk around the back garden is peppered with excitement and anxiety in equal measure. Look! The climbing rose is covered in pink-tinged new leaves and buds – but just look at the greenfly all over them. The tulips are sending up fleshy grey-green leaves, but *what* is making all those holes? The first tiny fan-shaped lime-green leaves of *Alchemilla mollis* are appearing, and the geraniums I planted last autumn are quivering with fuzzy fresh growth, but what has happened to my *Verbena bonariensis*? And why do my heucheras, usually bushy with new bronze foliage at this time of year, look so spindly and sick?

As spring seems to arrive earlier each year, especially in London's already mild microclimate, so do the pests secure an earlier foothold. As well as aphids on the roses and hellebores, and in clusters on the growing tips of various climbers, I've been spotting small slugs, snails and caterpillars in the flowerbeds for a few weeks now. One of the advantages of a tiny garden such as this is that I now know exactly where the creepy-crawlies lurk, and can pick off a lot of them by hand if I'm vigilant. I've finally got used to squishing greenfly between my fingers, and slugs and snails get quick and easy death in a bucket of salt water that follows me around. Until the weather becomes reliably warmer (usually late April/May), this is the best organic method of dealing with early pests. Soft soap is useful for aphids, but can scorch young leaves if used too often or when the sun is out. Very soon, though, it will be warm enough to experiment with biological controls – natural predators that target the pests but leave other useful insects and soil micro-organisms unharmed.

Lacewing and ladybird larvae can be introduced to prey on aphids once the temperature reaches a constant 10°C (50°F). (If you have a greenhouse or conservatory, another natural predator called *Aphidius* (for small numbers of aphids spread throughout plants) or *Aphidoletes* (for large colonies on a few plants) can be used year-round.) Lacewing larvae arrive in a corrugated cardboard sandwich, and you simply tap them on to affected plants. A single lacewing larva eats more than 300 aphids, and will also feed on whitefly and other pests, so a pack of 200 (£9.99 from Green Gardener 01603 715096) must surely be worth a try. Ladybird larvae are more expensive (£9.99 for 25), but it is always lovely to have ladybirds in the garden. As the larvae are relatively large, you can actually watch them at work, which is rarely possible with other biological controls.

Slug nematodes are becoming more widely known and used. Once the soil temperature is higher than 5°C (41°F) you dilute the fluffy brownish paste containing the nematodes and water it on to the soil. It is less effective against snails, but Green Gardener, who sells packs of Nemaslug for £11.95 says its customers have reported some success. The mixture needs to be reapplied at six-weekly intervals throughout spring and summer, and Green Gardener offers a planned programme of three applications, sent out automatically at the appropriate time, for £35.85. I've watered the nematodes on my garden, and also down at the allotment, where slugs have been defying my traps and tucking into young broad bean and pea seedlings.

I was still rather puzzled by my sickly heucheras, so I carefully dug one up – a good idea if you can't see a likely culprit above ground. Its roots looked rather small for the size of plant, and my suspicions were confirmed when I saw a small curled white grub with a brown head at the bottom of the hole. The dreaded vine weevil, scourge of city gardeners everywhere, had struck again. Vine weevil grubs eat away at the root systems of plants unseen, before pupating at the end of April, so now is the ideal time to order the nematode control, which can be used outside when the soil temperature tops 12°C (56°F)

I'm more than ordinarily anxious about pests this year, as I'm going away for two weeks. Like many gardeners, I often holiday in winter, but we ended up delaying it this year. Still, Sicily will be full of almond blossom and wild flowers, and I'd be a very sad person if I spent the fortnight fretting about my plants back home.

PRETTY AS A PICTURE

I came back from holiday itching to get to work in the garden, but relentless wet weather put paid to my plans. Time and again I ended up sitting in the kitchen, doors closed against the cold, watching the rain beat down on the deck and splash off new leaves. Still, the garden does look lovely. It is poised – nearly ready to flesh out into full summer mode – and in spite of the glories of the tulips and lilies and roses still to come, I think I like it best as it is now. There is still a lot of that luminous fresh lime green – in the *Helleborus argutifolius* flowers still lingering on from winter, but most of all in the new crinkled leaves of ivy and honeysuckle, and in the strange, beautiful heads of euphorbias that have been nodding, slightly curled, for weeks and have only just raised and opened their clusters of acid yellow, red-flecked flowers.

The blossoms of the winter-flowering cherry, which first appeared in November, have finally given way to foliage, but above its branches, the buds and flowers of *Clematis montana* hang like huge swags in the sky, entwined around the wires I stretched from the rear wall to the back of the house. The pink-tinged one, *C*.var. *rubens,* opened first, and engulfed the entire wall in a cloud of shell-like blossom, while the white one, *grandiflora*, has lovely milky-green buds that are opening into slightly larger, pure white flowers. The tight pink pointed buds of jasmine will not be far behind. It's a sequence I look forward to all year. Sitting outside in the few moments of sun we had in late April, with the whole garden festooned in these mad ethereal blooms, I had the strange feeling of having been transported into a Fragonard paint-ing – which is quite something in the middle of Brixton.

The colours and textures in the large bed are finally coming together. It was only properly finished last year, and looked a bit patchy for much of the summer, in spite of my impatient tendency to over-plant. This time around, the plants that are happy in this mostly shady bed – the acanthus, hellebores, my bronze phormium and the euphorbias *E. mellifera*, *E. amygdaloides* var. *robbiae* and *E.characias* subsp. *wulfenii* – are bushing out well, providing an evergreen structure through which spring bulbs, and the fresh lime green growth of alchemilla, astrantias, aquilegias and geranium phaeum (both the white 'Alba' and dark maroon varieties) have begun to sprout.

I have enjoyed watching the tulips progress from tightly furled twists of glaucous grey-green to stately, sturdy plants whose dark purple buds ('Black Swan') and green-streaked white flowers ('Spring Green') just opening now, seem to float above the rest of the foliage. I've planted them in drifts – the dark ones near the phormium, in among the euphorbias, heucheras and hellebores, and the white ones over to the left, where a variegated ivy and silver-streaked lamiums bring some lightness to a particularly dark corner.

The lovely pale leaves of the dark-coloured tulips are the perfect match for the foliage of *Fritillaria persica*, one of the larger members of the fritillary family, with spiky leaves spiralling around a central stem from the top of which dark bell-shaped flowers, somewhere between chocolate brown and purple, hang from mid-April to mid-May. This same shade of green is echoed by the delicate, deep-cut leaves of *Melianthus major*, which is thriving in a spot where my datura succumbed to a punishing winter frost. I'd hankered after this plant for years, but the books say it needs sun, and the hot spots in this little garden were snapped up early. But on a visit to Architectural Plants in Sussex (01403 891772), I was told by the extremely knowledgeable and helpful staff there that they had a lot of success with it in shade. My 1.2m (4ft) plant seems to bear this out – it is putting out lots of new growth, the youngest leaves folded up like fans, their edges serrated, as if cut with a pair of pinking shears.

Among all this, the purply-grey paintwork I used for the doors and old slatted cricket chairs looks most harmonious. It is exactly the colour of the ceanothus buds that are just opening in front of the back door. For the next few weeks, as I look out of that window – rain or no – the garden will be glimpsed through a glorious blue blur.

21 May 2000

ALLOTMENT UPDATE

So much has happened at the allotment during the weeks when this column didn't appear that I feel the only way to fill you in is in the style of the "soap opera up-dates" published in various magazines, dealing with the different plot-lines in turn. Here goes:

* The allotment committee Weed Police eject a number of neglectful plot-holders, and a flurry of new activity from groups of twenty-somethings and couples with toddlers ensues as they attempt to tame their overgrown, weed-ridden plots. Once again, our neighbour survives the purge by dousing his plot in weedkiller at the eleventh hour and hasn't been seen since.

* Incessant rain reduces our two plots (at the bottom of a shallow slope) into a quagmire – after years of patiently improving the soil with sand and well-rotted manure, the autumn-sown broad bean patch looks more like a paddy field and the soil can be sliced like pâté. The pond, however, is thriving, with at least one large frog and swarms of fat tadpoles.

* After a slow start, the fruit patch looks set for a good summer. High anxiety while the new raspberry canes, cut to the ground on planting as per instructions, failed to sprout, but new shoots finally emerged in early April. Meanwhile, the cut-off tops which were stuck on impulse in the ground along the fence are a-fuzz with new leaves, so we have double the plants for our money. One currant bush seems to have died, the rest are covered in flowers, and the strawberries should fruit any minute. But the netting fruit

cage, mooted when the plants went in last autumn and much-discussed since, has yet to materialize. Will it be built in time, or will the first crops be lost to the birds?

* The allotment committee announce plans to move the water tank nearest us (already a fair walk with heavy watering cans) further away. The pipe is leaking below the ground and moving the tank is easier than digging down and repairing it. Elspeth complains, only to be told in no uncertain terms that contribution to general site upkeep instead of griping would be appreciated from those down at the far end. Smarting with anger and just a little guilt, Simon and Clarkey volunteer to dig a trench to expose the pipe so a plumber can come and fix it. Offer graciously accepted by committee – albeit with eyebrows raised. The trench is dug and it's Brownie points all round – until we have to be reminded to fill it back in again afterwards. But principles – not to mention our watering-can-carrying muscles – have been saved.

* Second sowings of peas, broad beans and carrots have gone in, along with all the potatoes (the favourite 'Pink Fir Apples' along with 'Aphrodite' and a selection called 'Cook's Choice' from the Organic Gardening Catalogue (01932 253666)). Spinach, salad greens and fennel have also been sown straight into the ground, with runner and french beans, tomatoes, sweet corn, courgettes and squashes (from the excellent all-organic Terre des Semences catalogue (01227 731815/www.terredesemences.com), burgeoning in small pots in the back of my VW camper-van-cum-greenhouse. More tomato seedlings (including 'Black Plum', 'Golden Cherry' and the desirable, deep red 'Chocodel') have been delivered from Simpson's Seeds (01985 845004).

* The Battle of the Slime continues; this year's weapons of choice being Nemaslug from Green Gardener (01603 715096) – a biological control that is mixed with water and poured on the soil and stops slugs eating, and good old "slug pubs" – plastic cups filled with cheap bitter and sunk into the soil that lure them to a boozy death. (The empty grapefruit skins, though eye-catching, did not attract the numbers of slugs we had hoped.)

* Hundreds of tulips – striped, frilled, fringed and parrot varieties in mad swirly colours – have been a joyful addition to the plot, providing some wonderful flower arrangements back home. Alliums of various kinds, pot marigolds, love-in-a-mist and self-sown cerinthes are now pushing up between the dying leaves.

* Star of the show, however, is the living willow bower. My attempt to get around the allotment committee's ban on sheds by planting and weaving a structure made from live willow seems to have come off and the uprights are now sprouting bright green leaves, making a dappled green dome. Trees are not allowed either, but these are just 3.6m (12ft) high wands stuck in the soil, watered well and woven with slimmer horizontal wands like an upturned basket. Will the bower survive the committee's eagle eyes or will it transgress some newly-unearthed by-law?

ALL CHANGE IN THE FRONT GARDEN

Work has at last begun on our tiny front garden. A nice New Zealander called Mark has been busy for the best part of a week, lowering the wall that borders the street, laying a stone path, making a space for bins at the far end (with its own separate entrance) and, most importantly, building a big raised bed where I can plant all the things that won't fit – or can't grow – around the back. I've been looking forward to getting this done. My dustbins full of lavender have been a cheering sight for a few years now, but the shade from the solid brick wall has made growing much else here hard. The remaining space has become dominated by rubbish awaiting collection or recycling and, of course, the hideous wheelie-bin. An attractive, well-planned front garden would raise the spirits on leaving or returning home, while also giving something back to the street. Or so I thought.

The trouble with building work is that things always get worse before they get better. By the end of the second day, most of the wall was in chunks all over the pavement, along with our rotten old gate and its posts and other debris. The new bed had been constructed, but didn't make sense visually without the new picket fence that will run along the front. Worse still, while the wall was still coming down the front gate, which is to be repositioned slightly off centre, looked as if it had been narrowed to less than 6.5m (2ft). No one, it seemed, could pass the house without passing comment or asking, in dubious tones, what was going on. Mrs Mills from over the road, who came to Brixton from Jamaica in the Fifties and knew the old woman who used to live in our house (and who probably had the wall built), shrieked with laughter and said I must be mad. In her view, a shabby front garden puts off potential burglars – I remember her warning against my pots of pelargoniums before we'd even renewed the peeling paintwork. And I had forgotten about Melvin. In his Eighties and also originally from the Caribbean, Melvin takes his constitutional walk twice a day along this very stretch of pavement. As he uses a stick and is slow on his feet, he knows all the front gardens better than the owners themselves, and often stops to

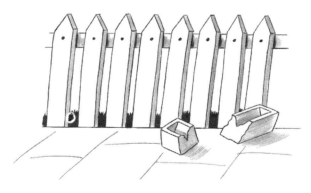

offer words of encouragement and advice to anyone carrying out work to the front of their property. "What on earth are you doing?" Melvin asked, when he saw all the mess. Mark and I explained while he stood there shaking his head. "But that's a perfectly good wall you took down there," he said. "A fence will rot in just a few years, but a wall – a wall is forever."

Suddenly, I felt almost ashamed. To re-model one's front garden in an area where (in spite of its much-hyped "gentrification") many residents don't have spare cash to throw around must seem hopelessly extravagant. And, far from beautifying the street, my new garden was not, it was clear, going to conform to my neighbours' idea of what makes a good garden. Melvin's front yard is the epitome of Caribbean good housekeeping: concrete floor painted cherry red and swept spotless every day, and high white wall given an annual coat of gloss. It looks, in fact, just like our back garden when we moved in. Neatness, not plants, is the priority. When I badgered the local authority into planting more trees in this street both Melvin and Mrs Mills told the council they didn't want one outside their own houses, thank you very much. "Too much mess with all those leaves to sweep up," Melvin told me.

The complaints didn't stop there. My husband is now insisting that my ancient sit-up-and-beg bike, which has been parked in the hall for years, is to be found a new home in the garden. But a shed would need planning permission, as does any structure more than 1m (3ft) high on land bordering the street. There's just about space for it up near the bins, but Mark isn't keen. On dear. Is *anyone* besides me going to like my new garden?

4 June 2000

AURICULAS AND SEMPERVIVUMS

As a contrast to all the big plants in my little garden (bamboos, acanthus, macleaya and *Melianthus major,* to name but a few), I like to keep some very small and intricate things in pots on tables, walls and ledges where they can be admired at close quarters. I have been indulging my passion for auriculas as far as I dare – seven little clay pots in total, that sit on the low table in the sunken area of the garden where people tend to congregate. Auriculas can become an obsession – the Victorians used to build elaborate tiered "theatres" in which to display them to their best advantage, while the garden designer and writer Mary Keen has converted an old outdoor privy to house her collection of 150 plants. In a garden my size you have to be restrained, which means hanging around the stands at the RHS spring shows like a lovelorn suitor, picking up first one little pot and then another, gazing into each tiny face with longing. I succumbed to the charms of three more this year – a beautiful clear mauve one with a yellow and white central eye called 'Lavender Lady'; 'Gizabroon', which has flowers of deepest black-red velvet with powdery pale grey leaves; and 'Hawkwood', which has that most covetable combination of dark red and pale grey-green around a yellow-ringed white eye. They're as beautiful as any painting – if rather more difficult to keep looking their best.

Unknown to me till now, my other auriculas, which have thrived and multiplied in their conical terracotta pots, producing healthy new offsets and masses of flowers, are alpine auriculas. These are much easier to grow than my tricksy thoroughbreds, which hate the wet weather we had for most of this spring; their roots rot, their colours bleed, like make-up running in the rain, and the desirable dusting of grey on their leaves is disturbed. And the minute the sun gets comfortably hot they wilt. Over- and under-watering prompts similarly sulky behaviour. After shunting them about the garden like aristocratic old invalids in wheelchairs, I have finally found the spot they like best – on a table beneath my autumn-flowering cherry tree, where the dappled shade provides shelter from extremes of sun and rain. Come winter, I may have to invest in one of those beautiful and expensive lantern cloches, under which they can huddle against the cold. (The alpines will be fine outside, and are hardy enough to plant in a border.) It will be well worth it if I can coax those heart-stopping flowers to bloom again next year.

In total contrast, my collection of sempervivums needs next to no attention. They are less showy, but to me just as beautiful as the auriculas, their tight little rosettes of leaves appearing in every possible shade and combination of green and maroon. I must have twenty or more different types. They all had names and labels to begin with, but as I'm making a garden not a plant museum, I wrote the names down in a book (now lost) and threw away the labels. All I know is that there are basically three different sorts – *Sempervivum arachnoideum* and its derivatives, which have spider's-web white threads strung between the points of the leaves; the more fleshy, web-less *S. tectorum* (or common houseleek); and the web-less but hairy *S. ciliosum*. Planted in well-drained, gritty soil (a 50:50 mixture of John Innes no 1 compost and horticultural grit is ideal), and protected against vine weevils (using nematodes or a chemically-treated compost such as Levington's) they should grow away quite happily, producing lots of satellite offspring around the central plants. They look good in a large, shallow bowl, and you can have great fun arranging them as the different colours go so wonderfully together. A top dressing of grit not only looks smart, it also helps deter slugs, who will nibble away at them, given half a chance. Traditionally, houseleeks were grown on rooftops to ward against lightning, witches and other terrors. To establish them on a shed or porch, wedge a few plantlets, with a small amount of soil, in a gap between tiles or timbers. You'll need to water once a week or so till they're established, but dead leaves and other debris will soon collect around the stems and store enough water to keep the plants alive.

11 June 2000

MULCHING MANIA

This is to be the summer of mulch down at the allotment, I have decided. The mulch urge has struck before now – I have made copious notes from books and admired the efforts of others – but you have to be organized to be a mulcher. For a start, you have to have something to mulch with. Mulch is a (usually) porous but light-proof layer that is added to the surface of the soil – it could be compost, it could be grass clippings, it could be black plastic or newspaper. Applied to a wet soil, mulches keep in moisture and keep down weeds. So they also keep your workload under control.

Now is usually the time when weeds get out of hand. The wet spring, followed by a few hot spells, means that chickweed and Good King Henry, not to mention bindweed and ground elder, are rampant – there are days when I swear I can *see* the bindweed snaking along, inch by inch, and many of the beds need constant hoeing. But in the mulched beds, all is miraculously neat. I was given a pile of grass clippings in early May, which were put to good use around the broad beans. It's no use mulching tiny seedlings – these were an autumn sowing, and already 15–20cm (6–8in) high. They are now nearly 1m (3ft), and the pods have set well – it's important that legumes don't dry out while the fruit is forming and swelling. My sister is going to save the clippings from her lawn, so I can put them round the peas and beans.

Straw was the obvious choice for mulching the new strawberry patch – it's a traditional method which looks pretty, and while low in nutrients, does a good job in keeping weeds down, allowing all the nutrients and moisture in the soil to go to producing fruit. I'm also hoping it will keep the slugs away from the fruit, though I fear that it may just provide them with yet another type of home. The raspberries are doing well, after a slow start, and it's exciting to see the clusters of green bead-like currants forming. Can't wait for that first home-grown summer pudding.

Hungry plants, such as raspberries, courgettes and pumpkins, benefit from a richer mulch of garden compost. I've a large bin full that needs to be forked through for larger stems and stalks that haven't rotted down, and added around the young plants after watering. This will also help improve the structure of our rather water-logged clay soil, as the worms drag choice fragments down below the surface to decompose them further. Leaf-mould makes another good mulch – lower in nutrients than compost, but excellent at improving soil structure. Almost everyone has a source of dead autumn leaves – from garden trees, the street or their local park – just empty them into a chicken-wire pen, or leave them in plastic sacks to rot down. The process takes about a year.

Mulches are a vital factor in the "no-dig" school of gardening. The appealing principle is this: that if you add a 5cm (2in) layer of compost, manure or leaf-mould to the surface every year, the soil will condition itself, building up a better structure than it would through digging. I had never seen this used convincingly until a recent visit to the excellent Ryton Organic Gardens near Coventry, home of the organic gardening association HDRA (024 7630 3517). One of the many inspiring demonstration plots is called the "No-Dig Garden" – and I was amazed to see peas, beans, salad crops and even potatoes flourishing in ground that has never been turned over in thirteen years. Mulch was used to clear grass and weeds the first year, and crops were planted out the following season. By the next year, the soil was ready for direct sowing. The only crop that requires special treatment is potatoes. These are planted in shallow holes so they are just level with the surface of the soil, which has been lightly manured in spring. Cover with a 10cm (4in) mulch of old hay or straw, and top up as the shoots show through. One load of grass clippings excludes the light and weights the straw down. Harvesting is easy – you just pull aside the mulch and there are your potatoes, nestling like eggs on the ground. This must surely be worth a try one year.

18 June 2000

BATTLE OF THE SLIME

I've had up to here with slugs. So far this year the slime-bags have eaten six young tomato plants, raised from seed, down to the bare stalks while they sat "hardening off" under the willow bower, prior to planting out in the soil; devoured any attempts at sowing a salad crop at the allotment, even with the added protection of Nemaslug nematodes (a biological control); nibbled the buds of my bearded irises the first year they showed signs of flowering; and penetrated the fruit cage to embark on what I mean to make a short-lived strawberry fest.

Drastic action is required. The trouble is that, since my allotment is a bike-ride away (fifteen minutes if I pedal fast), I can't be as vigilant as I am in my own garden, where I am out every evening or early morning with my "death bucket" of salt water, delivering my victims to a quick and watery death. In a small garden such as this, I know all their hiding places: the undersides of hellebore leaves, the innermost crux of acanthus or cardoon stems, or the cool shady side of pots. Snails meet the same fate – their favourite havens are where the trellis criss-crosses, or behind large ivy leaves. But, like most allotment holders who also work, I simply cannot make it down to the plot every day. Sadly, it has got to the stage where dread fills my heart on arrival. What will have vanished this time?

I have tried practically every method of slug protection possible, with some degree of success, it has to be said. There is no doubt that nematodes *do* keep the slug population down, but they have to be re-applied every six weeks throughout the summer, which can be expensive. Slug pubs are also effective, though you need an awful lot on a big plot like ours, and they have to be topped up and emptied regularly. Last year's big success, a grit-like product called "New Slug Stoppa", which dries out the creatures' slime on contact, stopping them quite literally in their tracks, is good for creating barriers around individual plants or beds. Again, it is expensive (01525 279555 for stockists), and you get through it fast as it is easily dislodged by watering or heavy rain.

Earlier this year, the newspapers reported a slug-eating robot invented by students at the University of the West of England, one that totters about the garden devouring slugs, fuelled by the gases emitted as their corpses are decomposed. I dreamed of borrowing it, but couldn't work out how you'd prevent it trampling on young plants. Another fantasy I've indulged in is that of a "slug moat" that would transform my raised beds into islands amid a slug-repelling – and irrigating – narrow ditches.

So I was intrigued and delighted to receive a press release about a new range of products called "Slurp!" which work on a scaled-down version of this very principle. Why didn't I think of it? Clear plastic troughs and rings are sunk in the soil around vulnerable plants and beds and filled with diluted beer – thus combining the "death-trap" element of the slug pub with a non-toxic barrier method. Sounds like a winner to me. Slurp! troughs and plant rings are available in garden centres (020 8420 2140 for stockists). They certainly seem worth a try – even if emptying them sounds onerous.

In the meantime, I've fallen back on skills honed during my *Blue-Peter*-watching youth, and have cut thirty or so plastic plant collars from empty two-litre (0.5-gallon) plastic bottles. Pushed into the soil around young plants or new-sown seeds, with at least 5cm (2in) showing above, these should deter slugs and snails, who will not want to expose their sensitive underbellies to the sharp-cut edge. I'm hoping that the collars will also work like mini-greenhouses to warm the soil, while also keeping foliage off the ground and directing water straight down to the roots. My right index finger is red and raw from endless snipping so it had jolly well better be worth it.

Three days later, and can you believe it? The first ripe strawberry – picked with much mouth-watering excitement – was completely hollow, save for a fat black slug. Two young courgette plants have been eaten, right down to the bare slimy stalks, and there's no sign of the other seed I sowed two weeks ago. Half my new runner bean plants have vanished, in spite of having been transplanted into protective plastic collars. I have had to buy new plants, and surrounded the replacements with "Slug Stoppa". Are slugs becoming more intelligent? Or have they developed flak jacket skins in a bid for world domination?

25 June 2000

A LITTLE HELP FROM MY FRIENDS

Now our new front garden has been planted up, it has met with more enthusiasm among my neighbours. Mrs Mills from the house opposite is now a great fan – in fact, she has taken to propping herself on the picket fence and calling to passers-by to stop and have a look. The comments – from friends and strangers alike – have been encouraging. Even Melvin, the eighty-something Jamaican, who had questioned the wisdom of replacing a solid brick wall with a flimsy wooden fence, had to admit it looks nice. And my husband, whose main concern had been that there should be a place to store my bicycle, seems content with the new arrangement, even though the offending bike is still cluttering up the hall. The only people who seem oblivious to the changes are the council's recycling crew, who missed us on their rounds that week – my plan to make the bins less obtrusive by placing them away from the door is obviously working too well.

I had long ago decided on a purple and grey front garden to offset the paintwork, which is in a fetching shade called "Turkish Plum", not unlike the bloom on black grapes. But when it came to selecting the plants, I called on the help and advice of a garden designer friend, Laura Morland (020 7733 9681), who lives locally. I know I should be perfectly capable of choosing my own plants by now, but it's nice to have someone to bounce ideas about with. My husband's response, when asked his opinion about anything to do with the garden is, "Whatever you do, I'm sure it will be lovely," which is all very well and loyal, but there are times when a girl needs something more. Everyone should have a gardening friend who knows more than them. Just as playing tennis against someone better than you is good for your game, spending time with those who have been gardening for longer or more adventurously than yourself is an easy and most enjoyable way of boosting your horticultural knowledge. So one rainy afternoon in May, Laura and I sat in my kitchen working our way through her well-thumbed nursery catalogues and enthusing about shapes of leaf and shades of grey-green.

Latin names sink in so much more quickly when uttered by a friend intent on converting one to their charms than when encountered in a book. Our conversation went along these lines: Laura: "Have you come across *Penstemon* 'Raven'/ *Pulmonaria longifolia* 'Aucum'/ *Libertia peregrinans*?" Me: "I don't think so, let's look it up in my book." Or, me: "What's that lovely wine-red buttony flower that weaves its way in and out of a border – a bit like a scabious but not one?" Laura: "Do you mean *Knautia macedonica*?" In this way, and at great length, I was acquainted with a whole load of new plants, which I wrote down in the bulging notebook I take to RHS shows. (Tip from one who knows: always add a brief description or sketch as the name alone will mean nothing in a fortnight's time.) She introduced me to *Salvia x superba*, with its electric violet flowers and claret-coloured calyxes; the delicate bells of *Campanula sarastro* 'Kent Belle'; and the gorgeous black-streaked magenta petals of *Malva sylvestris* subsp. *mauritanica*. Her most exciting recommendation was a deep purple clematis to grow up one side of the door – *Clematis macropetala* 'Purple Spider', and she made me a present of *Sedum spathulifolium* ' Purpureum' – a heavenly little succulent with wine-edged grey-green leaves.

In the end, of course, I was too impatient to go for all of these suggestions. When the garden was finally finished, I wanted to fill it straight away, not fiddle about with order forms and phone sales. I already had some unusual French and English lavenders – bought at one of the excellent annual plant sales at the Museum of Garden History near Lambeth Palace – so I headed for the garden centre and made the best of it. The lavenders – in every shade from inky indigo (*Lavandula angustifolia* 'Hidcote')to mauve-tinged pink (*L. stoechas* x *viridis* 'St Brelade') are now interplanted with grey *Stachys byzantina* (lamb's ears), some grey-green or purple-tinged hebes and rosemary, with cardoons and black single hollyhocks for height. As the plants bush out, the idea is that the lavender and rosemary will push their way between the pickets of the fence, releasing their scent as people brush by. This year, while they are still young, I've filled some of the gaps with home-sown white cosmos, dark sweetpeas and black cornflowers. And there's a lovely white osteospermum, whose outer petals are exactly the same shade of mauve as the door. I'll order Laura's clematis, and some of the other rarities to plant in the autumn. That's another joy of gardening friends – you don't have to follow all their advice: it's your garden, so it's ultimately your own decision.

"Garden looks nice," said my husband, as he left for work the next day. And I remembered the words of another gardening friend when she heard we were getting married. "Does Frank like gardening?" she asked. "No, not really," I confessed, feeling that it was a bit of a shame. "That," she said. "Is the recipe for a good garden and a happy marriage." I think she might just be right.

2 July 2000

LONG FACES AT THE ALLOTMENT

This is the time of year when friends who grow their own vegetables start inviting you round for supper so they can show off their home-grown crops. In past summers I, too, would have been smugly reporting in this column the promising first harvests of broad beans and peas, salads and young spinach, and the simple yet delicious meals I have rustled up. Not so this year. We've had nothing but a few portions of broad beans and seven pods of peas. In spite of the recent upturn in the weather, it's been a terrible year for growing vegetables, and everything was extremely slow getting off the ground. Several sowings of peas, beans and courgettes just failed to appear – having rotted, presumably, in the cold wet soil. Even the runner and french beans I sowed in my VW camper van, which becomes an efficient unheated greenhouse for the months of March and April, met the same fate. For the first time in years I had to resort to buying plants from the garden centre – only to have the slugs devour a good half of them. Sometimes I have caught myself wondering why I bother, especially now that the price of organic vegetables is coming down in the shops. By the time you add in the cost of all those unsuccessful seeds and plants, not to mention the compost, manure and sheer back-breaking labour, it becomes clear that I do it for love, not money.

I take comfort in the fact that I am by no means alone. There have been a lot of long faces at the allotment this year. The poor weather has united organic and non-organic growers alike – you can't resort to chemicals against cold and damp. Practically everybody lost their first sowings of peas and beans – you'd see people, hunched over the beds where they'd sown them, searching in vain for signs of life. The only person who got it right was my Indian friend, who now has the neatest and most productive plot on the site – claiming the title from my next-door neighbour, whose baby now takes up much of his time. Mustafa was more patient than the rest of us. Throughout that cold, wet April – and much of May, too – he bided his time. He didn't rush out and sow on the few sunny days we had; nor did he resort to raising plants under glass. Somehow, though, he knew when it was safe to start, and, as a result, his french and runner beans, sown straight into well-prepared trenches, are the only ones in full flower and about to set. His courgettes, too, are fruiting, while my second lot of plants (no need to tell you what happened to the first lot I sowed myself) are still establishing themselves. The other day, I asked him what his secret was.

"Warm soil," he said. "I waited till the soil was warm both day and night. Warm soil daytime, cold soil night time, is no good for seeds." This makes perfect sense, of course – and reminds me of the old farmer's saying that the soil must be warm enough to be able to sit on comfortably with a bare bottom before you plant your seeds.

Luckily, though, there are enough good things happening on my own two plots to prevent me giving up. The pond is full of frogs (clearly a non-slug eating variety – so bang goes that theory) and hovered over by dragonflies which are quite the most beautiful thing I've seen in ages. We've had a stunning display of ornamental alliums, culminating in the massive, quivering heads of A. *giganteum* shooting up among a bed full of cardoons and fuzzy-leaved mulleins. And the living willow bower is a real joy – so bushed out now with leafy growth that it provides pleasant dappled shade. The only trouble is, you can't eat any of those.

My hopes are pinned firmly on the fruit cage, where the first strawberries are ripening, the raspberries are doing well and there are tight clusters of fruit on the red, black and white currants. I shall have to get my friends round for dinner – let's hope they like broad bean risotto and summer pudding.

9 July 2000

CHIPS WITH EVERYTHING?

I've put the finishing touch to our new front garden with some bags of slate chippings. They're like gravel, only a subtle dull grey-mauve colour, and flat, like miniature paddlestones. The colour looks lovely with the grapey grey paintwork and all the purple and silver planting, and when it rains (which it has done rather a lot recently), they turn a darker, glistening grey.

Gravel or chippings are a useful choice for small front gardens, which are often no more than a thin strip of concrete with a wall or fence bordering the pavement. They are cheap – gravel is about £1.60 a sack from builders' yards and my slate chippings were just £5.99 for 25kg (55lb) from B&Q; they are easy to install and, provided you take a few precautions, extremely low maintenance. We laid our chippings in a 2.5–5cm (1–2in) layer on top of existing concrete, so we didn't need to worry about weeds creeping through. This can be one of the major drawbacks with gravel – it looks lovely for a few weeks, but then the chickweed, ground elder and worse find their way up between the stones and the effect is ruined. The best way to deter them is to lay some "landscape fabric" on the ground before emptying your sacks of stones. This black, mesh-like membrane, which lets the water through but not the light, costs around £1.25 per metre from garden centres. Ask for Permealay (call 01285 8600150 for stockists) or Netlon (0114 221 3413). In a larger, wilder style of garden self-sown seedlings can look lovely springing up to blur the edges of gravel paths – check out *Beth Chatto's Gravel Garden* (Frances Lincoln, £25) for inspiration – but town front gardens are usually best kept tidy, and you won't regret the marginal extra expense and effort.

You can lay gravel or slate chippings quite simply on their own, but the colours and textures lend them to some interesting decorative effects. There's a stunning chequerboard of grass and gravel squares in a garden in Kevin McCloud's new book, *The Outdoor Decorator* (Ebury, £25) – and if you don't fancy mowing 25 mini lawns, thymes or sempervivums make an attractive alternative to turf. You'll need to make some sort of retaining edge to prevent the gravel straying and spoiling the pattern – and it's best to recess the gravelled area into the soil so the surfaces are all level. With our own front path, for instance, the gravel is in a narrow sunken channel on either side of the solid York stone path up to the door, and goes on to fill the entire remaining space between pots and raised beds on the right. It might seem an obvious point to mention, but I've walked past many front gardens where no retaining edge has been incorporated, and the gravel is invariably all over the pavement.

One other slightly annoying aspect when using gravel is that the particles are an obvious trap for dead leaves and other debris, which have to be removed by hand. It's not great for beneath deciduous trees, for instance, as one exhibitor at this year's Chelsea Flower Show found out – the clean, modern lines of his show garden, which featured super-trendy transparent *glass* chippings, if you please, were constantly ruined by dead horse-chestnut blossoms descending from above. Seeing him crawling about with a bucket reminded me of one of the most unpleasant chores I've ever had to perform – combing a gravel courtyard for fag-ends after a wedding. Believe me, you want to keep grovelling in the gravel to the absolute minimum.

Although gravel is good to walk on, it's not ideal for areas where bikes, prams or wheelie bins need frequent access – you'll find it heavy going, and the chips will spray everywhere. Go for a solid alternative, such as stone, granite sets or tiles, in such cases. But the scrunch of gravel and chippings underfoot can be useful as a burglar deterrent. It's well-nigh impossible to tread on them silently, as I found out the other night, when I caught someone trying to nick my much-prized wine-red aquilegias. She was clutching a gorgeous bunch of peonies and arum lilies, which she'd obviously gathered from other gardens around our street. We may not have deer or rabbits to contend with in the city, but flower-thieves are something I can do without.

23 July 2000

SOFT FRUIT: HEAVEN ON A PLATE

Bar some excellent broad beans, potatoes and onions, this has not been the finest year for vegetables at the allotment. So it's a real joy to make my way through the slug-infested beds in the first plot to the new fruit cage, which occupies a large part of the second. Compared to the rest of the place, it is a haven of fertility and abundance. Not quite up to my favourite Marvell poem about "luscious clusters of the vine" and "stumbling on melons", perhaps, but definitely getting there. Even from a distance, I can see the glossy red strawberries shining against their thick mulch of straw, and the currants, back-lit by a low sun at the end of the day, glowing like little fairy lights. We have harvested our first gooseberries – sweet wine-red fruits from "Pax" and pale green "Invicta" and are looking forward to the blueberries (still in pots of ericaceous compost, as they need an acid soil). Best of all, I picked two raspberries the other day. The summer-fruiting canes will not do much till next year, but the ten canes of "Autumn Bliss", put in last November, are covered in tiny greenish fruit. A constant supply of fresh raspberries, and organic ones to boot, will be all the compensation I need for the poor show elsewhere this year.

Anyone with an allotment, or even a suitable patch of their garden, should set aside an area for soft fruit next year, if they don't already do so. Compared to coaxing seeds to grow in cold, clay soil and keeping the surviving seedlings free from slugs and other predators, growing fruit is a tea party. You place an order for canes and bushes (and now is a good time to start thinking about this), plant them in the autumn and then simply wait. Well, you have to do a little more than that, but not much. A fruit cage is an absolute must, to prevent the birds stripping your bushes bare, and blackcurrants and raspberries, in particular, benefit from a thick mulch of compost or well-rotted manure to increase the crop and keep down competition from weeds. The best thing is that slugs and snails aren't interested in anything that grows so far from the ground. So you can guarantee that a fair amount of produce will make it to your table – or, at least to your mouth if, like me, you graze while weeding and watering.

We've lost quite a few strawberries to slugs, but the dozen plants are producing enough to make sharing *just* about bearable. Strategically-placed "slug pubs" (sunken plastic cups filled with beer) and a scattering of bran around the plants (which makes the creatures bloated and unable to move) has seen off a good few, and the rest I am learning to live with. Who can blame them, really, when the spoils are so delicious?

Home-grown organic fruit, picked and eaten while still warm from the sun, is heaven on a plate. Despite the recent "organic revolution", it's still relatively difficult to find organic soft fruit in the shops, because it's not durable and damages so easily in transport; what is available is usually confined to the toughest varieties, harvested before they are properly ripe. I spent last Sunday afternoon comparing our various strawberry varieties – purely in the interests of research, you understand. "Royal Sovereign" really does deserve its reputation for flavour – and Waterperry Gardens in Oxford (01844 339226) is one of the few remaining sources of reliable stock. "Elvira" and "Pegasus" are cropping well, and the latter has very large, attractive berries, while "Aromel", which has just started producing delicious sweet fruit, should continue well into autumn. Sun and dry weather cook up the best flavour.

Early autumn is the best time to establish soft fruit for next year. So look at some catalogues – Highfield Nurseries (01452 740266) near Gloucester has tried and tested varieties as well as some new ones each year, including blackcurrants, redcurrants and gooseberries trained as standards. These would look lovely in even the smallest garden, where you could also plant some autumn-fruiting raspberries (which the birds ignore for some reason) in among your roses or flower borders. They'll be a lovely reward when doing the deadheading.

30 July 2000

FLOWERS FOR THE QUEEN MOTHER

Few people outside the East End of London have been to, or even heard of West Ham Park. Yet this 77-acre oasis in the otherwise unprepossessing Borough of Newham is a remarkable place. Not only is it a haven for ancient trees, including an oak planted to commemorate Queen Victoria's Jubilee and the oldest ginkgo in the country, planted in 1673; it is also a powerhouse of plant production, supplying summer bedding to all the little gardens and churchyards within the City of London and plants and flowers to decorate state banquets at Guildhall.

One acre of greenhouses occupies the north-east corner of the park, and in April and May a tarmac area in front of them the size of several tennis courts becomes a colourful patchwork as rows upon rows of bedding plants await their final destination. About 300,000 plants are raised here each year, and between 150 and 180 varieties, which include relative rarities such as *Gaura* 'Siskiyou Pink' and the crab's claw flowers of *Lotus berthelotii*. West Ham Park is one of the very few London parks that have continued to raise their own plant material, let alone supply so many other gardens. In the Victorian heyday of municipal bedding schemes, the modern practice of buying in plants from outside sources was almost unheard of.

"Apart from the obvious financial advantages, the quality and the service are so much better when we grow things ourselves," explains David Jones, superintendent of the Corporation of London's Parks and Gardens, which include Highgate Wood and Queen's Park in Kilburn, as well as West Ham and the gardens within the Square Mile. "We grow the plants in pots not trays, so they are a good healthy size by the time they go out." Mr Jones is a very busy man. Apart from his duties at West Ham, where he began as a technical assistant 30 years ago, he judges at the Chelsea Flower Show and for Britain in Bloom, and breeds dahlias in his own garden in Warwickshire. One of the most enjoyable parts of his job is selecting the flowers for the corporation and civic ceremonies at Guildhall.

In an average year, there might be more than 50 receptions and banquets at Guildhall or the Lord Mayor of London's residence at the Mansion House, ranging from visits from foreign heads of state to the bestowing of the Freedom of the City on the likes of Nelson Mandela and Lady Thatcher. No effort is spared on decking the halls in flowers and foliage – 4.5m (4ft) weeping figs are trundled out of the greenhouses and on to lorries, together with giant palms and banana trees, bird's nest ferns and standard fuchsias in red and bright purple. The construction and installation of the arrangements is conducted like clockwork by a team of 20 over seven or eight days, and watched over by Mr Jones's eagle eye.

There have been several big occasions in the past 12 months, including the banquet in honour of the President of China last October and the presentation of the Honorary Freedom of the City of London to the Queen of Denmark in February. But none has had more care lavished on it than the luncheon held on 27 June in honour of the Queen Mother's hundredth birthday. For 49 table decorations, Mr Jones chose the pink patio rose 'Queen Mother' from the many roses named after her, and a paler pink rose named 'City of London'. After lengthy consultation with RHS colour charts (a bit like paint charts, but giving the names of flowers in each particular shade), these were teamed with pale magenta orchids, pink dianthus and variegated weeping fig. "Getting the colour right is important – people don't always realize what an impact it makes," says Mr Jones. Only once in his career has the colour ever been wrong – and that was because the Lady Mayoress chose to change her dress at the very last moment from mauve to orange. There were no such problems with the Queen Mother. She wore pale blue, and drifted amid the ocean of pink roses like a galleon in full sail.

6 August 2000

SEEDLINGS OR WEEDLINGS?

Walking my dog the other day, I was delighted to see a patch of derelict land between two houses had suddenly sprung into bloom. The entire area – only about a metre square, was a-flutter with the papery mauve petals of the opium poppy, *Papaver somniferum*. They must have self-seeded, blown in from a neighbouring garden or dropped by a passing bird. The patch of ground is in full sun, so each of the many seedlings, crowded though they were, had managed to flower. Surrounded on all sides by bare brick and concrete, it had an enchanting spontaneity. But when I returned home an hour later, it had all gone; razed to the ground by someone's strimmer. A tidy-minded council worker, perhaps? Or an over-zealous gardener from next door, worried lest her own garden be over-run next year by these breathtaking ephemeral flowers?

Self-seeding is a double-edged sword for gardeners. To some, it means a lot of unnecessary weeding to prevent havoc reigning among the borders. To others, it can add a welcome eccentric element to their plans; the pot marigold that pops up in the middle of a border can be responsible for colour combinations you'd never dare engineer, while tall sprays of *Verbena bonariensis*, waving their tiny electric purple flowers on top of spindly square-sectioned stems, are a thrill wherever they choose to shoot up. Such unbidden "extras" need a degree of stage-direction if the real stars aren't to be crowded out, however. And this, in turn, requires the ability to tell self-sown treasures from self-sown weeds when they are still only seedlings. It's one of the reasons why even quite grand gardeners keen to encourage this spontaneous naturalistic look prefer to do the weeding themselves. One false swipe with the hoe or grasp of the hand and that mullein, which might have made a dramatic punctuation mark among the mounds of low-growing perennials, will be gone for good. That "spontaneous, naturalistic look" is harder work than it seems.

Earlier this summer in my back garden, something stopped me grubbing up some young plants whose leaves looked exactly like those of a weed I find frequently at the allotment. I'm glad I stayed my hand – it has turned out to be a beautiful black scabious which I don't remember sowing there at all. I can only think some spare seed got stuck to my clothes while I was sowing in pots elsewhere. Anyway, it couldn't look better, pushing its dark black-red buttons through the acid green foam of *Alchemilla mollis,* the purply stems of *Euphorbia amygdaloides* var. *robbiae* 'Rubra' and the deep-cut leaves and maroon stars of *Geranium phaeum.*

At the Centre for Alternative Technology in Machynlleth, Wales (01654 705950) – which, incidentally, is a great day out for all age-groups, gardeners and non-gardeners alike – there is a rectangular bed, about 3 x 4.5m (10 x 15ft), which is dug over every year to see which plants are brought in to set seed naturally. A little light editing has to occur in order to stop it being taken over by docks, nettles and creeping buttercups, but there are surprises every year, among them teasels, welsh poppies, buckler-leaved sorrel and bronze fennel, Himalayan balsam, foxgloves and yellow and scarlet pimpernel. There's even the occasional interloper from a private garden in the area – one year they found bluebells, a potentilla and the fluffy pink heads of *Eupatorium cannabinum.* I'm reminded of a vacant lot in Manhattan where a similar experiment has taken place, this time in the name of art. Back in the Eighties, an environmental artist was given permission to take over a derelict corner where Houston Street meets La Guardia Place and reclaim it as a "time capsule", to show New Yorkers what the city would have looked like before the white settlers came. Over the years, the oak, hickory, maples and junipers he planted have grown into an impenetrable tangle, held back only by a metal fence entwined with bindweed. But in spite of the care he took to plant only indigenous species, the artist's project looks nothing like the island in the early 17th century. Nature, of course, has taken a hand. Seeds blown in from the neighbouring community garden, dropped from overhead balconies and roof terraces and deposited by birds and other wildlife, have led to nightshade vines, sunflowers, poppies and other brightly-coloured, definitely *non*-indigenous plants taking hold among the so-called "native" planting and spilling out on to the streets. Now, which would you call the "natural" planting there?

13 August 2000

PRUNING LAVENDER

Lavender is such a fashionable plant that it's hard to believe it was once out of favour. Brought to Britain by the Romans, popular in medieval civic gardens and Tudor knot designs, it was widely grown until the First World War for its scent and healing properties as well as for its beauty. At the beginning of the 20th century, however, tastes changed and the lavender fields on the south-facing chalk downs around London were swallowed up by housing developments. Norfolk Lavender (01485 570384) founded in 1932, was, until recently, the only lavender farm left in England.

The revival of interest in lavender began in the Nineties. Suddenly, it seemed, no 'good taste' gardener could live without a lavender hedge or collection of unusual varieties in pots or along a border. The range of lavenders on the market snowballed – particularly the stoechas varieties, with their butterfly-like wings waving above fat magenta or pale pink bracts. Nowadays, the specialist stands at horticultural shows are abuzz with people looking for white lavenders (such as *Lavandula x intermedia* 'Alba'), cut-leaved or fringed lavender (*L. dentata*), dark purple lavenders such as *L. angustifolia* 'Blue Mountain' and silver-leaved lavenders like *L. x intermedia* 'Lullingstone Castle'

Their appeal is not hard to explain: the combination of purple bracts in all shades from white to pale lilac to magenta and rich electric violet floating in a purple haze above mounds of grey-green foliage (again, in many subtle shades) would be irresistible in itself, even without the scent. And, in the Age of Aromatherapy, its heady scent now wafts through the smartest hotels, beauty salons and yoga studios.

Lavenders look good in all kinds of gardens. Can there be a nicer approach to a cottage door than between two lavender hedges spilling on to the path, releasing their scent as you brush past? Lavenders associate well with timeless plants such as peonies, iris and old scented roses. They can be clipped into balls and trained as standards in a formal garden, and they look terrific with modern architecture, too, whether arranged singly in smart zinc planters or set in bold swathes or stripes of subtly gradated colour.

To beginner gardeners lavender seems easy enough to grow. Given a sunny position and well-drained soil it usually establishes fast and flowers for long periods. You can get away with doing very little for a year or two, but then the problems start. There is a lot of confusion about pruning lavender and many people – myself included – lose their first plants by pruning too hard into the woody stems at the centre of untended bushes. But early losses can lead to overcaution, and for the past few years I've been dead-heading the different plants in my garden after they've flowered and taking off about a third of their stems. They have now grown quite large – one hangs over my windowbox like a great leafy beer belly and the two specimens in old dustbins by the front door, planted as small bushes two years ago, now threaten to block the way.

Recently, when buying yet more lavenders from Downderry Nurseries in Hadlow, Kent (01732 810081) I asked for pruning advice. Dr Simon Charlesworth, the director, explained that you can cut down lavender quite dramatically – provided it hasn't been allowed to grow too woody and that you leave at least a few tiny green leaves just below the cut. Timing is important: July for the stoechas varieties and mid-August for the angustifolias. This gives the new growth, which springs back by September, time to establish itself before the winter. It looks like a hacked-about haircut for a few weeks, but soon recovers. Virginia McNaughton's new book *Lavender: The Grower's Guide* (Garden Art Press, £17.50) has reassuring photographs showing a wayward, sprawling bush before pruning; the spiky woody balls with a few leaves showing after it has been sheared; and the well-rounded clump, flush with new leaves and buds, the following spring. Plants of any age can benefit from pruning, and it is the best way to preserve the beauty, health and vigour of young plants. So take heart – and take up the secateurs.

27 August 2000

SMASHING PUMPKINS

Late summer is when squashes and pumpkins begin to come into their own. When close friends are refusing yet *more* offers of runner beans and you've let all your courgettes grow into unwieldy marrows, there are still these splendid autumnal fruits to look forward to.

We planted out our squash seedlings late this year, but they soon got going on the circular mound of earth that was dug out when we made the pond last year. Pumpkins and squashes are traditionally grown on top of compost heaps, and ours certainly benefited from the addition of several inches of well-rotted horse manure and kitchen waste a few months before planting. The mound is now contained by a half-moon of a hurdle fence, which we wove from extra willow wands bought for our living willow bower. Such hurdles are simple to make. Stick a series of upright posts in a line in the ground about 20cm (8in) or so apart – ours were about 50cm (20in) high but you can make the fence whatever height you choose. (The stakes must be dead – you don't want willow roots competing with the hungry squashes.) Then all you do is weave long wippy wands in between, as if you were making a basket – singly and snugly at first, to secure the stakes in the ground, and then in groups of three or five if you want to make more of a textured pattern. Our pumpkin patch now looks most picturesque – with the large leathery leaves spilling over the top of the fence, the odd tendril escaping to race across the path, and a few glossy fruit to be glimpsed in the clearings.

In fact, the only squash patch I know that looks better belongs to some friends with a smallholding down on the south coast. They have surrounded their patch with a wall of hay bales. These cost only about £1 each direct from the farmer, and make a good solid wall which will slowly rot down from inside to perk up the soil for next year, when you may want to add more bales around the outside. My friends' crop certainly looks good on this treatment.

Improve your crop by snapping off the leading shoots once one or two fruits per plant have set. Protect swelling fruit from slugs, snails and damp by placing some sort of mat between them and the surface of the soil – something that lets the air circulate is ideal. Last year, my allotment neighbour Mustafa grew his squash seedlings through an old rusty mattress so the fruits came to lie on the top in the sunshine. And at last year's garden festival in Chaumont-sur-Loire in France I was intrigued to see smaller squashes grown up thick plastic netting, strung at an oblique angle to catch the afternoon sun.

There is no precise time when a squash or pumpkin is ready for harvesting, but they need about 100 days to flower, set fruit and ripen, so most should be ready by the end of September. Clear gaps in the leaves so they can get some sun as they mature, and leave them in the sun for a week or so after cutting so the skins can toughen and dry. They can then be stored for several months in a cool place. There are many things you can do with these delicious, earthy fruit besides making gallons of pumpkin soup. I love to roast great fat slices in the oven, with olive oil, crushed garlic, a sprig of rosemary and lots of black pepper – great with roast pork or poultry. Roasting is also the least strenuous way of producing puree for soups or risotto – leave the rind on and simply scrape away the flesh when it is cooked.

If I've whetted your appetite and your squashes are still far from ready, you could follow the example of Nepalese cooks and use the nutritious young shoots in a curry. Cut 30cm (12in) shoots from the tips of the vines, discard the curly tendrils and tough stalks, and chop up the buds and small leaves. Heat two to three tablespoons of oil with some mustard seeds, fenugreek, a finely-diced red chilli and a few chopped peanuts. Throw in the shoots and cook for five minutes with the lid on, then add some peeled chopped tomatoes (a tin will do) and cook for another three to four minutes. I found this recipe in Christine McFadden and Michael Michaud's *Cool Green Leaves and Red Hot Peppers: Growing and Cooking for Taste* (Frances Lincoln, £25) and it is surprisingly good. It's also a useful way of containing your growing plants if the vines are threatening to take over your garden.

10 September 2000

MADE IN THE SHADE

A combination of small plots and neighbouring buildings mean that urban gardeners are plagued by shade more than others. But I would urge anyone with a troublesome shady corner to pay a visit to Crûg Farm Plants in North Wales. Specializing in shade-tolerant plants, many of which have been hand-gathered by the owners on trips all over the world, it must be one of the most fascinating nurseries in the country. When I headed there last month, I was looking for plants that might thrive in my increasingly shady garden – a few unusual ferns for a black spot of a corner where even the hellebores aren't happy, and some ground cover brave enough to establish beneath my huge acanthus and bamboo.

Crûg (pronounced creeg) means "lookout" in Welsh, and the nursery is on a windy hillside near Carnarvon, with a view over the Menai Strait. Bleddyn and Sue Wynn-Jones were beef farmers here for 20 years before setting up the nursery in 1991, driven by a thirst for the unusual and a conviction that "out there", beneath forest canopies up mountains in the Far East, might be shade-loving plants hardy enough to survive British winters. Every autumn, they head off to Japan, Nepal, Thailand or Taiwan, to return in the new year laden with seed, which is grown on with great care in a series of shaded polytunnels. The mature plants are displayed in a series of show gardens around the farmhouse, which make interesting viewing, particularly if you are lucky enough to have Bleddyn as guide, reminiscing about on which particular island off Korea he found which plant, and reeling off Latin and Japanese nomenclature with head-spinning speed.

The real shade-lovers, such as the curious, cobra-headed arisaemas and more than 25 varieties of polygonatum (solomon's seal), grow in raised beds beneath wooden canopies clad in shade-tolerant hardy climbers. There are beautiful feathery ferns from Vietnam and Taiwan (I succumbed to several), the graceful silvery-leaved *Rubus lineatus,* which makes a stylish substitute for bamboo, and unusual members of the lily family, such as a lovely scented ypsilandra from Tibet, which flowers obligingly from the end of February. It is here that I found my ground-cover – the creeping, silver-mottled *Rubus pectinellus* var. *trilobus*, a member of the bramble family, whose label states it was found "creeping on dark forest floors at 3000m".

But it isn't only shady plants that the Wynn-Joneses target on their travels. "We'll bring back anything we feel is unusual or useful, particularly things that extend the season by flowering at unusual times," explains Bleddyn. And so there are wonderful dark-leafed saxifrages that flower earlier than the usual cultivated forms, stunning colquhounias, whose buddleia-like orange blooms begin in late July, and Himalayan daphnes that flower from October right through winter. There are also many hardy begonias, climbing monkshood and dicentras, and the beautiful *Sambucus racemosa* 'Crûg Lace', whose decorative, deep-cut leaves make it a lime-tolerant substitute for cut-leafed acers. And, for real oddity's sake, how about a sun-loving hosta (*H. yingeri*) found on a sunny cliff on an island off Korea, or a hardy umbrella plant, *Schefflera taiwaniana*, which will grow into a small tree in sheltered gardens? As well as the national collections of coriaria, paris and polygonatum, Crûg Farm has 70 or so unusual hydrangea species (not to be confused with blowsy hybrids) and more than 200 geraniums, including the beautiful bronzy-leaved 'Crûg Strain' and 'Bertie Crûg', (both bred here), and the rampant *G. procurrens*, which is one of the few plants that can compete with bluebells.

Bleddyn is a mine of knowledge and advice – he suggests, for instance, planting aerial-rooted climbers, such as ivies, virginia creepers and climbing hydrangeas, sideways with only the new growth above ground, so they run along the surface of the soil before hitting a wall – "It'll save you three years," he claims, indicating a high wall that a *Parthenocissus trucuspidata* 'Crûg Compact' has completely covered in record time.

Phone for the Crûg Farm catalogue (01248 670232), or check out their excellent website on www.crug-farm.co.uk to find out more. Crûg Farm Plants (Griffith's Crossing, Caenarfon, Gwynned LL55 1TU) has some special opening days with tours and talks – phone for details. There is no mail order service, but the nursery is open from the end of February to 1 October, Thursdays to Sundays and Bank Holidays 10–6pm; guided tours by appointment. If it seems a long way, why not make a trip of it, staying at Portmeirion just down the coast (01766 770228), visiting its creator, Clough Williams-Ellis' own wonderful topiary garden at Plas Brondanw, and taking in the Centre for Alternative Technology at Macchynlleth and the superb gardens at Powys Castle and Bodnant en route?

17 September 2000

GARDEN OPEN DAY

The other Sunday, 150 people passed through my tiny back garden in the space of three hours. Last summer, Penny Snell, who is honorary county organizer (Greater London) of the National Gardens Scheme (NGS), persuaded me to open our garden for charity, and I didn't feel I could say no. In 1999 the NGS raised more than £1.5 million for the charities it supports; and, altruistic reasons aside, I confess I was flattered that Mrs Snell, whose strict standards are quite notorious, should think our garden worth including. For a start, the NGS likes a garden to have 45 minutes of interest – and in a space less than 6 x 6m (20 x 20ft) you are lucky to achieve 45 seconds. But Mrs Snell was keen to have us, and she is a very hard woman to refuse.

On reflection, perhaps the end of August wasn't the best time to fling my borders open to scrutiny, but that is the time Mrs Snell visited last year, and I reckoned if the garden was good enough for her then, it would be good enough at the same time this year. There was some backhanded logic involved too – by settling on the end of summer I'd have none of that "Will they or won't they?" angst about roses and lilies opening or going over that can be such a trial when organizing parties or events in June. By August my garden is seriously – quite startlingly – jungly, with the acanthus in full glory and the glaucous leaves and bronzy plumes of *Macleaya cordata* topping 3m (10ft). The lovely dark sweetpeas would still be hanging on, and the morning glories might be opening. And if no one came, I could use the excuse that everyone was on holiday.

In the event, I needn't have worried. The garden looked lovely, thanks to a bout of timely late-summer sprucing. And there were so many visitors we had to hold them at the front on occasions till things thinned out in the back. Everyone seemed to enjoy themselves and, far from being disappointed at the garden's dimensions, they were genuinely intrigued and inspired to see what had been achieved in such a small space.

There's certainly nothing like opening to the public for spurring one on to get a garden finished. For those who are not "Yellow Book" aficionados, the listings of gardens open through the scheme are published annually in a thick paperback called *Gardens of England and Wales Open for Charity* (£5 from book shops), and the opening dates and details and a short description of all the gardens have to be finalized in autumn the year before. So when I blithely wrote "new purple front garden just begun", I thought I had plenty of time to get it off the ground. In the event, it was February before I found a contractor and the end of May before the work was finished, the purple picket fence painted and the new beds planted up. Round about March, one of the team of local officials called round to deliver a carrier bag full of yellow posters all printed up with the address and opening times for pasting up around the vicinity, cards to send out to likely visitors, and details on ordering free tea to provide on the day through Jacksons of Piccadilly (the NGS is nothing if not organized). I don't think our bell was working, and when I finally got to the door, the poor woman said she'd begun to think she had come to the wrong place. Looking at the stacks of builder's rubbish and bin bags piled up along the wall, I could see why.

The open day also geared me up to getting a proper barrier erected on the galvanized grid bridge outside the french windows which links the kitchen to the deck. For the best part of three years, the only thing that has prevented anyone tumbling to certain injury in the basement area below has been a couple of low troughs of flowers. Not only is this dangerous, it is also illegal, and as we had decided on serving tea and cakes from the french windows, we needed to get it sorted. In the end, I took the opportunity to commission a tall double arch around the windows, a rail and a new narrow but higher trough, all in matching galvanized metal, which Ralph Levy (01273 382474), a talented metalworker based in Brighton, made up and installed in the nick of time. Morning glories and a purple grapevine are already entwining up the arch and the garden finally feels complete.

The day was great fun – many thanks to all the readers who came – and we raised lots of money for the NGS and the Lavender Trust for young women with breast cancer. So it was well worth the effort. Trouble is, I don't think Mrs Snell is going to let me get away with only doing it once....

The National Gardens Scheme is always on the lookout for new gardens to include in their Open Days scheme. If you would like to find out more, contact the NGS, Hatchlands Park, East Clandon, Guildford, Surrey GU4 7RT (01483 211535), who can put you in touch with your local county organizer.

1 October 2000

A LOOK BACK AT THE SEASON

There was a moment, earlier this summer, when I thought that my bullet-like green tomatoes would never ripen and none of my runner beans would survive the slugs. Well, I'm happy to say that time – plus some lovely hot spells in August – has proved me wrong. For weeks now, Clarkey, Simon and I have been taking home as much produce from the allotment as we can carry. The runner beans are the juiciest yet – and because they were so late this year (first picking in mid-August instead of mid-July) we didn't get sick of them as we so often do. The tomatoes, bought as small plug plants from Simpson's Seeds (01985 845004) also got off to a very slow start, but are cropping well in spite of my having neglected to pinch out all of their side shoots. My favourites, apart from the delicious and reliable 'Gardener's Delight', which I grow every year, are 'Golden Cherry', another cherry variety with sweet bright yellow fruit, 'Black Plum', covered in small, garnet-coloured, egg-shaped fruit, and 'Chocodel', which is deep red with brown shoulders and green flesh. We've certainly had some interesting-looking salads, perked up with lots of lovely basil from my mother-in-law's greenhouse.

The potatoes have also been good. As well as 'Pink Fir Apples' and 'Aphrodite', which I have grown for some years now, I was tempted by the 'Cook's Choice' offered by the Organic Gardening Catalogue (01932 253666) – ten to twelve tubers each of 'Red Duke of York', 'Desiree', 'Kestrel', 'Avalanche' and 'Verity', all varieties known for flavour and good cooking properties. Infuriatingly, some of my labels have vanished, but I can report that 'Red Duke of York' is wonderful, with deep red skin and firm yellow flesh; 'Kestrel', which has large white tubers and purple 'eyes', is great for baking, and 'Avalanche' has a good flavour but tends to fall apart so is best kept for mashing. If you have suffered from blight this year, as so many have, the same catalogue offers a "Blight Resistors" selection featuring 'Premiere', 'Cosmos', 'Sante', 'Remarka' and 'Valor'. A booklet outlining the different properties of more than 100 potato varieties is also available for £1.25.

I'm particularly glad to have enjoyed a good harvest this autumn, as I shall be taking a bit of a break from the allotment next year. All the travelling and traffic has begun to get to me, and after five summers there, I was dreaming of a vegetable garden outside my back door, where I could check on my plants daily – even hourly, if I chose – and be there to intercept damage from slugs or aphids or worse before the rot set in. Well, miraculously, we have found it – down on the south coast. So from next month, my husband and I shall be dividing our time between our London house – where I shall continue to write about our tiny back yard and new front garden – and our rented beach house, which has an established vegetable garden, cunningly created in a series of raised beds on the shingle. The owner, who is a talented potter, makes all the terracotta pots and rhubarb forcers for Great Dixter and West Dean, and the garden is liberally sprinkled with his workmanship – wonderful long toms nearly 1m (3ft) high spilling over with bush tomatoes, tiny cane-tops to stop you poking your eyes out, and even custom-made "leek collars" that not only look extremely smart, but mean you can grow a higher yield of leeks in a smaller space, as you don't need to set aside soil for "earthing up" around the stems. I've longed for a proper greenhouse, and this garden has a splendidly rickety one, made from salvaged Crittal window frames, and with its own small heater. There's even a little conservatory off the kitchen, which will enable me to experiment a bit – not to mention an overgrown front garden, which I am free to tame and untangle if I dare.

It's all extremely exciting, and the fulfilment of a long-held dream. But as I sat under our living willow bower watching the sun go down behind the towering cardoons, I felt deeply grateful to this London allotment and all it has given me. I shall not miss the traffic, nor the slugs, nor the committee's 'Weed Police'. But I shall certainly miss this air of leafy quiet on an early autumn evening.

8 October 2000

COUNTRY GARDENER: A NEW SEASIDE GARDEN

Taking over a kitchen garden in autumn is a bit like inheriting the contents of someone else's larder. There are lots of undeserved treats to be used up – in our new seaside garden we have been harvesting pounds of tomatoes, courgettes, french beans and lettuce in whose production I played no part at all. I even found some peas left from a late May sowing, and since this year's yield from my London allotment came to ten pods in total, these were especially welcome. But at the same time, alongside all this unexpected bounty, there is the sense in which the space will not feel truly mine until I have cleared the shelves, as it were, and begun to stock up with my own produce.

I have enjoyed becoming acquainted with my new garden. Watering the raised beds has been a gentle introduction. Since I now have the luxury of a hand-held hose, I find it very relaxing at the end of a hot day to wander through the network of tile and shingle paths, taking time to look carefully at what is growing in the beds as I go. At the allotment, where a committee by-law prohibited the use of any watering device but a can, I was so exhausted by endless treks to the tank that I used to water without thinking and trudge back for more. There's even a simple irrigation system here, with spray-ends on spikes that can be sunk in the soil and attached to various different hoses, but I'm so unaccustomed to such decadence I can hardly bring myself to use it.

Weeding is another good way to get to know a new garden. There is nothing like crouching a few inches from the earth and getting your hands dirty for finding out more about your soil and what is growing in it. Constructed on shingle and filled and re-filled over 18 years with home-produced compost, these beds are chock-a-block with extremely happy plants. The soil is dark, crumbly and free-draining – thanks to a four-bay and two-tub composting system, the intricacies of which I shall be attempting to understand, re-instigate and explain to you over the next few weeks. The speed and efficiency with which garden and kitchen waste is broken down is, I'm assured, thanks to a mixture of equal parts dried nettle and yarrow leaves, a jar of which the owner of this place (my landlord, who lives locally and continues to use his pottery in the garden), kindly left for me in our yard. I had been just about to try it as a herbal tea when he told me what it was.

Some of the beds have crops that will continue over the winter. I have four fine brussels sprout plants, which will be more than able to supply our Christmas lunch. There's plenty of spinach and rainbow chard, a few rows of beetroot and an enormous patch of leeks, which are swelling nicely within custom-made collars. Most exciting of all, there is a square yard of 'Witloof' chicory, which my landlord is going to show me how to grow into blanched 'chicons' under his wonderful terracotta forcers. You have to wait almost until the first frosts, so I shall write about that before long.

I have also inherited some tasty "cut-and-come-again" salads, some of which I had never tried before. Land cress has dark, shiny deeply-cut leaves and a hot peppery flavour almost indistinguishable from watercress. It runs to seed quickly in hot weather, but thrives in damp, even quite dark spots, and makes a neat edging for beds in the winter. Sorrel and the smaller, slightly spongy leaves of 'Buckler's leaf sorrel' stay green all winter in this mild, sheltered garden, as should a fine crop of flat-leaved parsley – these can be protected under cloches in severe weather. I took my landlord's advice and cropped some sections of the salad plants down to the ground when we arrived here in September so they could put out fresh growth in the remaining warm weeks.

I've since sown a strip of rocket, some red mustard greens and lamb's lettuce, all of which, in my experience, overwinter well and are thankfully un-plagued by slugs and snails. And in the greenhouse I've started some coriander and red-hearted lettuce seeds I bought last year in Italy. So my first crops are in. And this lovely new garden is beginning to feel more like my own.

15 October 2000

COUNTRY GARDENER: PRUNING A GRAPE VINE

Pruning has never been my strong point. Friends with whom I shared a house at university remember me hacking down a buddleia with the bread-knife one morning in my nightie, and I have to confess that exasperation and impatience, rather than the welfare of the plant, are still too often my motive when wielding the secateurs. A combination of last-minute poring over books, phone calls to friends or just doing what seems right at the time has served me pretty well – give or take the odd calamity. But now that I have no fewer than *three* grapevines to look after, it is time to take it all a bit more seriously. After all, when and where and how you prune a vine can have a dramatic effect on its fruiting the subsequent season.

The black grapevine in my London garden, bought as an eight inch cutting, cropped well in its first year, covering the back of our house with heavy bunches of dusky dark fruit. This year, it hasn't performed so well, possibly due to the cool summer. Down by the sea I have two indoor vines. One is in the greenhouse at the end of the garden, planted outside but with its main stem trained in at the base of the wall and up around the ceiling, where its foliage provides much-needed shade in summer. The other, in the rickety conservatory just off the kitchen, must be something rather special. Its fruit, which hangs in elegant long bunches from bamboo canes stretched across the corrugated plastic roof, is quite delicious. The ripest grapes turn a glorious chartreuse yellow, and taste sweet but with a dusty, musky after-taste that spreads across the roof of the mouth. From my limited knowledge of wine, I'd guess it must be a Muscat such as 'Royal Muscadine' or the much-prized 'Muscat of Alexandria'. If you're thinking of planting a grapevine – and now is a good time – the latter is said to be one of the best-flavoured varieties for growing inside.

I turned to my bookshelf for advice about pruning. *The Handy Book on Pruning Grafting and Budding* (two shillings in 1924 but picked up for a few pence at a jumble sale) was the only title devoted to the subject, and it did little to instil confidence. "No operation is less speculative in its results than good pruning, or more quickly and certainly productive of good results...." it declared. "On the other hand, unskilled pruning or neglect of pruning causes mischief that cannot be repaired." But gardening books can be contradictory. This one, along with several entries in other, more recent books, says to wait till the leaves have fallen and then prune the main stem by removing two-thirds of the summer's growth, while taking back the laterals, or side shoots, to one bud. Others say to two buds. And some recommend "resting" the branches over the winter by freeing them from their wires and laying them on the ground. This ensures that, when the sap rises in early spring, it runs right to the end of the stems, avoiding the common problem where only the lower growth sprouts. The stems can be tied back as soon as signs of life appear.

I decided to ask my landlord and neighbour about the vines. After all, he makes very good wine (from elderflowers, runner beans and apples as well as grapes) and planted these ones himself. "Ah!" he exclaimed. "I was told by a Spaniard who knew a thing or two about vines that you should never prune your own prize grapevine. You have to ask someone else to do it in your absence. Then, on your return, *in the presence of the vine*, you must berate the pruner for having cut off much too much." Sounds strange, but it seems to have worked here. I'm letting him loose with it next week while I'm in London. The logic (if that's the right word) seems to be that the friend will be more ruthless than you – and that the vine won't "blame" you for the dirty deed.

I, meanwhile, will be attacking the climbers that are taking over our London garden. It's the wrong time for the *Clematis montana*, which is the main culprit and should really be cut back after flowering in spring. But I can take refuge in the advice of Christopher Lloyd: "The best time to prune is... when you remember."

22 October 2000

RECLAIMING THE SKY

I have just reclaimed some sky in our London back garden. This may sound strange, but sky is a limited resource in the city. High walls and tall buildings encroach on all sides, and uninterrupted views are rare and come at a price. This little garden can sometimes seem like a high-sided box, and its open lid to the heavens – already small enough – has been diminishing daily. First there was the new development backing on to our property – the extra courses of bricks that contravened the planning conditions have narrowed our horizons considerably. But the other problem has been of my own making. My climbers have got out of control.

Planting eight or nine vigorous climbers around the periphery may have been a fast way to get a small garden going four years ago. But I've become a victim of my own success. Two years ago, when the jasmine and clematis reached the top of the walls, their tendrils were twirling about with nowhere to go. So I stretched five overhead wires from the rear boundary wall to the back of the house and let them twist their way along, with tiny white fairy lights twinkling in between. It looked lovely. But by the end of this summer the plants had not only reached the house wall but had begun to scramble up it, too, and the older woody growth was weighing down the wires. A *Clematis montana* was making a bid for the roof, clinging to a down-pipe and making it impossible to see through the lavatory window, let alone open it. Despite repeat emergency surgery in early and mid summer, a dense overhang had formed where the walls met the wires, and a leafy crochet of jasmine, honeysuckle, grapevine, clematis and the glossy-leaved evergreen *Holboellia latifolia* was shading out the beds below.

I knew something had to be done, but it was only when our neighbours politely pointed out that they had no light to their back door that I finally got round to the job. As these are the same neighbours with whom we appealed against the increase in the back wall – on the grounds of loss of light – it was embarrassing that I was now the guilty party.

I decided to cut all the climbers right back to the top of the walls and to keep them that way. Pruning at this time means sacrificing the spring blooms on the montana, which flowers on last year's shoots, but the plants would all put on new growth fast enough. Three hours and 11 bin liners full of prunings later, I hardly recognized the place. It felt a bit exposed, and I missed the veil of greenery between us and the neighbouring buildings. But the space felt much larger and airier and I am sure the plants will appreciate it. The best thing was how much more sky I could see. It got me thinking about the role the amount of open sky plays in determining the character of a garden – and urban gardens in particular. Sometimes the sense of enclosure created by surrounding buildings can be comforting; more often than not – even if they do not impinge directly on one's light or privacy – they can cause feelings of claustrophobia. It was this, rather than the hours of direct sunlight lost, that led the local council to rule in our favour over the wall dispute.

I am much more sensitive to the size of the sky since moving part-time to the country. There, just a few hundred yards from the sea, the skies are enormous, the horizons infinite. Even in the garden, which is thankfully hedged round against the harsh coastal winds, I can see the weather coming – the clouds racing across, the woolly tracks of aeroplanes and a layer of light blue spreading from the east. And I can stop and watch the wild geese flying over in arrow formations, preparing for their long journey south. In London, while I was pruning, I heard their familiar call and downed tools to watch them pass. Nearer and nearer they came – and then it struck me: they might not fly over my small square of sky. Somehow, the thought of being able to hear them but not see them was unbearable. I couldn't even tell from which direction they were flying. Then I heard their wing beats and the panic was over. For three thrilling seconds the geese passed right overhead.

29 October 2000

AN INDIAN SUMMER IN LONDON

The pay-off for this year's poor summer is that the flowers, so often burnt out by the heat, seem to have gone on for ever. My London gardens – front and back – are still full of flowers, and the limpid low light of these perfect autumn days illuminates their intense and fragile colours. Best of all have been the morning glories, which are still putting out between 20 and 30 new blooms every day all around our front door. Nothing can compare with their clear electric blue – slightly deeper on a dull day, and suffused with pink in hot sun. The wall is covered with flowers in all stages of growth – the buds, like conical twists of white tissue paper, the blooms themselves in their day-long blaze of glory, and then the crumpled, spent petals, like punctured pink balloons. Passers-by have stopped to stare, and a local artist spent an afternoon sketching them.

Other stars of the front garden are the 'Velvet Queen' sunflowers that come in all shades from palest lemon to deep chocolate brown, with one large flower at the top of the stem and smaller lateral buds for picking. They have looked stunning among scrolling grey cardoon leaves, clouds of white cosmos and spires of the black hollyhock, *Alcea rosea 'Nigra'*. People warned me about rust with hollyhocks, and I have certainly had to pull off a lot of infected, brown-spotted leaves, but I would not have been without these startling flowers, bursting from tight knotted buds into circles of creased black-red silk all up their stems. All the above flowers can be raised from seed next spring – try Thompson & Morgan's new catalogue (01473 688821). Hollyhocks are biennials, but can bloom the same summer if sown early under glass.

The back garden, clearly benefiting from an increase in light after its dramatic pruning, is also still flowering away. There are more morning glories here, hung among the huge red-gold leaves of *Vitis cognetiae* on the south-facing wall, and entwined with orange and ochre nasturtiums up the new metal arch round the french windows. The passion flower is still bravely putting out new blooms, which I stumble on while reaching for late 'Black Plum' and 'Golden Cherry' tomatoes. And all around the top of the walls, the white potato vine, *Solanum jasminoides* 'Album', sends sprays of tiny white flowers down into the garden and in among the last lingering white roses. I've seen white solanums flowering well into December in sheltered spots, and its delicate blossoms, dancing in the breeze, bring a welcome note of lightness into the darkest, dank corners of a late autumn garden. By the basement steps, it has created the most wonderful combination – totally unplanned – with a variegated large-leaved ivy (*Hedera colchica* 'Dentata Variegata') and the purple grape vine *Vitis vinifera* 'Purpurea'. A swag of the three plants intertwined, fit for a Dutch flower painting or harvest festival altar, is now slung between the wall and the new arch. By next autumn it should be twisting all the way round.

Other plants that have put on surprising spurts of growth in this late Indian summer include my lovely *Melianthus major*. Fresh fronds of deep-cut, grey-green leaves are unfolding against a backdrop of dark glossy ivy, looking for all the world as if they were cut out from piles of tissue paper with pinking shears. *Convolvulus cneorum*, another of my favourite silver-grey plants, had a second flowering of bell-shaped white blooms that has only just come to an end. As I always associate these plants with sun-baked balconies in the Mediterranean, it never ceases to amaze me how well it does here. A garden designer I know says it can thrive even in shade – so it's an exception to the rule that silver-leafed plants must always have full sun.

Among this late flowering, though, are timely signs of winter. The honeysuckles are covered in scarlet berries, as luminous as redcurrants in the late sun. The spear-like leaves of *Arum italicum* 'Pictum' are pushing through the ferns and silver lamiums. And there is a palpable chill in the air.

5 November 2000

COUNTRY GARDENER: COOKING UP THE COMPOST

One of the many pleasingly eccentric features of our new house by the sea is that it has two kitchens – well, three, really, if you count the tiny room which contains just a Rayburn, two sawn-off pews to sit on, and shelves full of firewood and books. At the back of the house, looking out onto the lean-to conservatory, is the conventional "winter kitchen", equipped with everything even two townies like us could ever need. But if you walk from here into the Rayburn room and through the back door, you'll come across the "summer kitchen", roofed with clear corrugated plastic and completely open to the yard on one side. It has a fridge freezer, an electric cooker and a big old butler's sink standing on bare bricks. A solid, scrubbed wooden table stands in the middle, loaded with flowers and vegetables from the garden. When we first saw it, it reminded me of places I've known in Crete and the Caribbean, where dogs sleep, children play, chickens scratch about and long lunches are prepared and eaten in the shade of a grapevine. We've had great fun out there so far – even eating outside with the rain hammering down overhead. With potted plants and herbs dotted about, and a *Clematis montana* scrambling around the roof, it lends a new and literal meaning to the term "kitchen garden".

Now that it's time to retreat inside, the outdoor kitchen still has its uses. It's handy for storing pumpkins and squashes, which look good lined up along a long driftwood shelf, and keep well in the cool. The concrete floor makes it a good place for messy but domestic gardening tasks – I've begun to pot up bulbs here, as it feels cosy under cover but is easy to clean up. And the extra space certainly makes recycling a lot more simple – and savoury – than in London. There, the kitchen scraps would often wait up to a week for me to take them to the allotment – longer if, as frequently happened, I'd forget. Down here, the scrap bucket in the outside kitchen can be emptied daily into one of the compost bins in the back.

This garden is a veritable powerhouse of compost making, with four wide bays in various stages of production, and two tall black plastic bins with lids in which kitchen waste is broken down rapidly by a colony of worms. Garden debris goes into the bays – and I had accumulated quite a pile of limp yellow cabbage leaves, spent tomato plants and other remnants of the summer's crops. My landlord kindly supplied me with a hay bale and seven bags of fresh horse manure, so I spent a satisfying morning constructing a proper heap, with layers of garden waste interspersed with hay, manure, wood ash (a useful source of potash) and seaweed from the beach. Seaweed is not only a good compost activator, but also a welcome source of minerals and algins – micro-nutrients, which field tests have demonstrated can increase plant yields and germination rates. I've taken to bringing back a couple of carrier bags full of seaweed if I find some washed up when I'm down on the beach with the dog. It's horribly slimy and hard to manoeuvre but, rather like spinach or steamed greens, it does have that look of something awfully healthy. Infused with a dose of my landlord's special nettle and yarrow brew, the heap should soon be humming away, with more great compost on the way for spring. (Equal parts dried nettle and yarrow leaves, this is his version of Maye E Bruce's famous "Quick Return" compost activator, which I first mentioned in these columns in 1998. Two teaspoons in a pint (568ml) of water is left for three days and then added to the pile by plunging a pole in at 30cm (1ft) intervals and pouring the mixture down. A commercial version of this highly effective "QR" mix can be bought from Organic Gardening for £1.40 a sachet – ring 01932 253666 for their catalogue.)

Composting is a good job for autumn and I can't wait to make some more. It's easy to understand how people get completely obsessed by it, though I doubt I'll ever go as far as a friend in Scotland who saves up the family's hair and toe nail clippings. To me, there is something immensely comforting about the thought of that big old heap slowly cooking away, while we huddle inside against the cold.

12 November 2000

COUNTRY GARDENER: REMEMBERING ROLF

I love planting spring bulbs. For me there are few more rewarding ways to rebuff winter blues. Planting in pots and glass bowls is the most fun – in open ground, harsh weather and shortening days often result in a last-minute rush, a bad back and numb hands. Compared to grubbing out holes in cold wet soil, the ease of setting the bulbs in a nest of warm dry compost or on top of a layer of moist pebbles is such a comfort. And, of course, there is the vision in one's mind's eye of the flowers and fragrance to come. A single white hyacinth on my desk in January, or an amaryllis bursting its buds against a rain-streaked window in the city bring me joys that far outweigh the small effort and expense in making them happen.

This year I started by planting 'Paper White' narcissi (*Narcissus papyraceus*) on pebbles in my glass bowls and blue and white hyacinths in my forcing jars. These are the best types of bulbs for growing without soil, the tracery of fine white roots twisting in the water and around the pebbles only adds to the beauty. Ensure the water line is just *below* the base of the bulbs and add a small piece of charcoal to keep it sweet.

I also planted – in compost – shallow bowls of multiflora hyacinths, which create an effect more akin to bluebells, with several slender stems of smaller flowers to each bulb, and smaller pots of grape hyacinths and different types of crocus. Grape hyacinths (muscari) are more often used outside, but their compact form and clear colours make them ideal for pots inside. They come in many shades, from the pure white of *M. botryoides* 'Album' through pale 'Sky Blue' and mid-blue 'Cantab' to the deep cobalt *M armeniacum* 'Heavenly Blue' (all available from Bloms Bulbs in Bedfordshire (01234 709099). Unlike the usual forced bulbs which exhaust their reserves the first year and seldom perform so well again, muscari and crocus should come up year after year in the same pot, and make great – and long-lasting – Christmas presents. It was a dull rainy day, and the hours sped past as I moved on to the real treats: species tulips and irises purchased at the RHS autumn shows. I can hardly wait to see the pointed purple petals of *Tulipa humilis* 'Persian Pearl' or the maroon-flecked falls of the dwarf iris 'Katharine Hodgkin'.

I had reason for needing this gentle gardening therapy. Rolf, our lovely grey lurcher, has died. He collapsed two weeks ago, after running on the beach he loved so much, and died the next day. The vet thinks he may have ingested a toxic chemical that had been washed up along six miles or so of high tide line that weekend. It is terribly hard getting used to his loss. I trained him from a puppy not to jump in flowerbeds or chew plants, so he was the best of gardening companions, particularly at my London allotment, where he would snuffle about for hours in the morning dew, or make himself a shaded bed in the long grass on a summer afternoon. When I was gardening – or writing, for that matter – I never felt lonely with Rolf around.

We wanted to make some sort of memorial for him – but it was hard to know what to do. Had we a large garden where the dog had enjoyed running about and where we were certain to remain for many years, the first thought would have been to bury him – though digging a secure grave for a large animal is some task, as my husband knows, having buried family pets in the past. Local authorities often have reservations about the practice, and like to be consulted about burying anything larger than a cat in a domestic garden. In the end, we had our dog cremated, and scattered some of the ashes along the beach, some in the park near our home in London and some in a corner of the garden here, where I planted a small silver birch and a sunken pot of the beautiful black and green *Iris tuberosa*. My landlord, the potter, has offered to make a little plaque bearing his name and the dates (1996–2000) of his short but extremely happy life.

That night I dreamed about Rolf, leaping through fields of yellow tulips like a dolphin jumping through waves.

18 November 2000

COUNTRY GARDENER: RABBIT RAGE AND CHICORY TIPS

I have a rabbit in my garden. A few months ago, if someone had said this to me I would have asked what its name was and where they bought its hutch. Now, having become a part-time country gardener, I am getting to grips with one of the most dreaded garden pests. When I think how I have moaned over the years about slugs and snails, I feel quite ashamed. A single rabbit can wreak more destruction than several hundred molluscs in the course of a night, and this one has been getting fat on my winter salad patch. It even ate the rocket; at least slugs and snails have less sophisticated tastes and leave that unscathed.

There is no sure way to keep rabbits out of a garden, but a fence will help. It should be sunk at least 20cm (8in) below ground level, and should stand at least 1.2m (4ft) high. Even better would be to dig a trench around the periphery of the fence and line it with the chicken wire, so the rabbits hit a horizontal barrier of mesh when they dig down. My landlord had already done this, so the rabbit must have snuck in when the gate was open – no doubt emboldened by the demise of our dog. Luckily, at this time of year there is not too much damage it can do. Apart from the winter salads, which I hope will soon sprout again, it has nibbled down all the carrot tops and started on the chicory. But this doesn't matter as the roots remain intact.

Now is the right time for forcing Belgian or 'Witloof' chicory – setting in motion the mysterious process that turns bitter green leaves on top of long parsnip-like roots into delicious crispy white chicons. My landlord is an expert at this, and taught me his time-worn method: lift the roots in mid-to-late autumn, when the top of the tap root should, ideally, be about 4–5cm (1.5–2in) across; cut the leaves down to 2.5cm (1in) with a sharp knife and trim the roots to around 20cm (8in), getting rid of any subsiduary roots. (My landlord very enterprisingly makes chicory coffee from these side roots, drying them out in his Rayburn and pounding them to a powder with a pestle and mortar.)

The roots then need to be packed into a large pot or bucket of compost, with crocks in the bottom for drainage, and soil right up to the base of the crowns. Water well, then invert a similar sized pot over the top and place in a warm dark spot – ours is in the bathroom, with a blanket over the top to shut out all light. The cut-off crowns will soon begin sprouting and should be ready in three to four weeks – it's hard to resist peeping every day. If you sowed a lot of chicory in May or June, you will have enough for an efficient rotation system, with more pots in cooler places ready to be brought inside as earlier ones are eaten. Heat simply speeds up the process. It's said that the method was discovered accidentally by a Belgian farmer who was growing the crop as cattle fodder. When the tops had been eaten, he dug up the roots and flung them into a dark barn. When he returned a few weeks later, he had what would become a culinary classic on his hands.

According to my books, similar but slower results can be obtained by leaving some roots in the soil and covering with a light-tight bucket or forcer. I've done some as an experiment, as the pottery forcers look so pretty, but my landlord is doubtful that it will work. At least the forcers will keep the rabbit off – I've been chasing it all around the garden today to no avail, and fear I may have to enlist a neighbour's dog to see it off.

While on the subject of wildlife, may I take this opportunity to thank the many readers who pointed out that the geese I mentioned in my column a few weeks ago do not fly south for winter. They have already come south, from their Arctic breeding grounds. The birds I fondly imagined were "preparing for their long expedition south" were, in fact, on their daily commute from the ponds to the east of us where they feed to the ponds further west, where they spend the night – a distance of some two and a half miles.

26 November 2000

COUNTRY GARDENER: OH, TO BE A 'REAL GARDENER'

My landlord, the potter, is a down-to-earth, hard-working gardener of the old school who never buys anything new when something handmade or recycled will do. So I was surprised, the other morning, to find him leafing through one of those fashionable mail order gardening catalogues – the sort filled with soft-focus photographs of miniature potted olive trees and women in expensive wellington boots. All was explained when he revealed that the head buyer from the company had seen his terracotta cane tops in a magazine and wanted to stock them in their London shop. "Who on earth buys this stuff?" he asked incredulously, wondering at the obscure accessories and outrageous prices. "They can't be *real* gardeners."

Having long since coveted this company's rubber gardening clogs – not to mention the smart linen tool bag with leather straps – I kept schtoom. After two days of trying to get to grips with my new overgrown front garden, I had already come to the conclusion (not for the first time) that I was not a real gardener, and I needed no further proof.

The garden is lovely – and potentially could be even lovelier. It's about 27 x 9m (90 x 30ft), stretching down from the front of the house to the dirt road, with another 3m (10ft) strip that wraps around the side of the building and abuts the pottery studio, where my landlord comes to work. There are several largish trees, including a bay, a holly, a tamarisk and two enormous leyland cypresses, which block the sea view. There are also some interesting shrubs – I can identify a silver-leafed buddleia, a pyracanthus, a snowberry, lots of sumac – its flame-coloured foliage only just dying down – and a lovely thing with tiny fragrant yellow flowers that I think may be a type of mahonia. These were all planted before my landlord became owner, and have had little attention over the 18 ensuing years as he is rather disapproving of flowers and concentrated on the vegetable garden round the back. So it has become rather jungly, to say the least, with shrubs and trees growing into one another and great swags of old man's beard strung between the branches. The ground – which is mostly shingle, with the odd pocket of soil – is knee-high in self-seeded valerian, St John's wort, dead nettles and brambles. Scattered among it all, like relics from an ancient burial mound, are fragments from the pottery – rhubarb forcers, like huge terracotta bell-jars, upturned bowls, and vases lying on their sides in which birds make their nests.

I have never had to cope with an established but neglected garden – I have had only roof gardens, or our tiny London yard, which I created from bare concrete – and it's hard to know how and where to start. My mind's eye, fuelled by images of Beth Chatto's famous gravel garden, can see mounds of santolina and sedums, and lots of swishing grasses, but I'm loth to clear too much before I know what else may come up. People say it's best not to do too much to an inherited garden in its first year, for just that reason – but we may only be here for a year. For now, I am aiming to clear the worst of the undergrowth and brambles, and make space for a few spring and summer-flowering bulbs around the main path. But I'm making very slow headway – not helped by having to look up every other plant in a book to find out what it is and how to prune it.

That evening, we were invited round to my landlord's house for supper, and one of the other guests was the head gardener from a large and famous garden near here. We had a lovely evening, drinking home-made wine in my landlord's immaculate polytunnel (where neat rows of perky winter salads induced a further crisis of confidence), and dining on roast pumpkin in the cosy kitchen. The following morning, my landlord nearly made my day by announcing that his friend had said that I "must be a real gardener" because I had (I am much ashamed to say) dirt around my fingernails. But then he told me the owner of the rarified gardening catalogue had rung again, wondering if he had any other ideas that could be added to the catalogue. "Oh yes," he had replied, "I've had a very good idea. There's no real money in pottery, so I'm starting a new line of little boxes filled with soil. They fit easily into a handbag, so if you're ever invited out to dinner with a famous gardener, you can just dip your fingers in once or twice and you will immediately be taken for a real gardener." If I'd been able to stop laughing, I might have been offended.

10 December 2000

SIMPSON'S SEEDS

The other day I met one of my gardening heroes. Colin Simpson founded Simpson's Seeds in 1993 from the garden and kitchen table of his house in Surrey. The company's catalogue is now the best source for unusual tomato varieties (95 at the last count), not to mention 100 types of potato, 73 types of peppers and an impressive selection of beans and salad greens. The idea came to Mr Simpson while he was recuperating from a near-fatal accident. Some friends in America sent him a seed catalogue – he'd long grown his own vegetables to feed his family, but was amazed by the variety and prices in this catalogue. He sent for some seeds, and got almost 100 per cent germination, vigorous plants and fruit with super flavour. It struck him that there could be a small profit in selling plants to friends, local shops and allotment societies, and he set about printing up a catalogue. Just the sort of enterprising attitude one would have thought the government of the time would have encouraged. Wrong. Within months he hit a problem with the Ministry of Agriculture. The seeds he was offering were not on the list of approved plants that the EC allowed for sale.

Rather than succumb to this setback, Mr Simpson saw it as a challenge. A veteran foreign correspondent and investigative reporter for *The Sunday Times*, he was not put off by reams of bureaucratic directives, and soon discovered a loophole he could use to his advantage. The only people allowed to buy, sell and grow seed outside these directives were plant trialists. So by turning Simpson's Seeds into the Tomato Growers' Club, and making membership free to anyone who bought seed, he could turn his customers into plant trialists, too. All they had to do was report back on the progress of their plants, a practice the company still encourages.

The Ministry was not amused, and a lengthy legal debate ensued, finally settling in the Ministry's favour. But again, Mr Simpson was undeterred. The EC laws apply to seeds, not plants. Quoting the Court of Human Right's ruling that life begins as soon as germination takes place, he began trading in seeds that showed visible signs of germination. The Ministry had to give in.

Six years later, the mailing list has swollen to 15,000, and plantlets are sent out as far afield as Japan. The business is still run on a personal scale, however, with most of the plants grown in a series of greenhouses and polytunnels in the garden, and requests not to call the helpline after 8pm or during the Derby, Grand National, Cheltenham Gold Cup or test matches. Mr Simpson is now planning to ease up a bit and hand on more of the business to his wife, Jane, and son, Matthew. They hope by next spring to be based in the walled garden on the Longleat Estate in Wiltshire (01985 845004), where for the first time they will be able to welcome visitors.

Matt Simpson kindly gave me a beautiful chilli pepper tree – an orozco plant, native to south-east Mexico. Matt's great passion is for peppers – the large polytunnel in the garden was full of every type of pepper imaginable. There were bell peppers as big as a baby's head, Nepalese 'Friar's Hats', like glossy red Capuchin hoods nodding from slender branches, the fiery 'Jamaican Hot Yellows' used for jerk pork and chicken, and long snaking 'Elephant's Trunk' peppers from India.

Most ornamental and chilli peppers are dealt with as annuals in this country – sown every spring to die down in autumn. But in their natural habitats, many are perennial, and Matt has had some success at overwintering them, by picking off all the fruit in late autumn, cutting the stem back to 7.5cm (3in) and keeping under fleece at a minimum of 10°C (12°F). In early February, increased light and heat and a level teaspoon of dried blood watered in should spurt them back into bushy new growth.

Picking all the pretty purple, red and yellow chillis off my orozco tree will be hard, but I may try drying them on a sheet of baking parchment in the Rayburn (a low oven with the door propped open works as well). They can then be ground into chilli powder using a pestle and mortar – gloves are vital for this task. Then we'll have some of the warmth of Mexico to cheer us through the winter.

24 December 2000
INSIDE OUT GARDENING

People talk a lot about "indoor/outdoor" gardening these days – by which they usually mean thinking of the garden as an outdoor room, whose furnishings can be moved in and out at will or according to the weather. But they seldom include plants in the equation. To me, there is great fun to be had in bringing garden pots in for a spell inside, and introducing cosseted houseplants to the great outdoors. You need to exercise a fair bit of caution, of course. You'll get nowhere by plunging a prize rex begonia outside on a cold night, and sunlovers like lavender won't thank you for being deprived of maximum daylight. No – you have to pick and choose.

I took the opportunity of the autumn downpours to give my dusty indoor plants an al fresco shower, which they greatly enjoyed. And some houseplants – umbrella plants, for instance, and most of the ferns – positively thrive on a summer in the garden before returning under cover. Frost-tender specimens, such as potted pelargoniums and many succulents that spend most of the year in the open, must, of course, be brought in before winter gets underway. I always enjoy the last extravagant blooms of daturas and brugmansias brought into the sitting room in November and December – and the scent is even more heavenly for being confined by four walls and a ceiling. But many other plants, perhaps originally intended for the garden, can bring great pleasure if brought inside, and some may even benefit from the experience.

The most obvious candidates at this time of year, of course, are small evergreens such as hollies and conifers. My little blue spruce has put on a good 20cm (8in) since I bought it at the New Covent Garden Flower Market the other Christmas. It has been kept in its pot at my London allotment all year, and will be re-potted this year after its seasonal spell in the limelight as a Christmas tree. A bay tree clipped as an obelisk looks great in the hall with a spiral of white fairy lights wound around it; a standard mop-head holly bush, provided it is bursting with berries, needs no further adornment. In my experience, none of these plants has been harmed by its sojourn inside – though we do not have our central heating on as much as some people. If your house is very warm it might be sensible to subject your plants to the opposite of "hardening off" ("softening up"?) to introduce them to their new conditions by stages. The one crucial thing to remember is that these plants will need frequent watering while inside – check the surface of the compost daily with your fingers and water when dry to the touch.

Pots of bulbs that may have been intended for outside can generally be brought into flower earlier by bringing them indoors. In these bleak midwinter days, I love to have a house full of bowls of early blooms – miniature iris and daffodils on the dining table; hyacinths perfuming a bathroom; little pots of grape hyacinths on my desk or by a window. I have even been known to dig up clumps of snowdrops in bud and re-pot them as bedside treats for winter guests. As the time for dividing and replanting snowdrops is immediately after flowering anyway, they ought not to suffer too much from the disturbance.

The other thing you can do with outdoor pots is to make sure they can be admired from the house when their moment of glory arrives. In our London garden I have a young fig tree – too big to bring inside now – which has fifty or so tiny *Iris reticulata* planted around its base. Wherever it stands in the garden for the rest of the year, I make sure I lug it over to the french windows when I see the first pale green nibs poking through the soil. Iris are so beautiful in all the slow stages of their unfolding, from tight indigo scrolls to three-point firewheels of breathtaking beauty. Keeping a skateboard (or a small trolley on casters) somewhere in the garden makes moving pots easier. But if you had all your pots on wheels you could scoot them around – and inside and out – all year to your heart's content.

2001

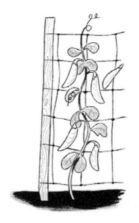

7 January 2001

COUNTRY GARDENER: WINTER TREATS

When we returned after a couple of weeks' holiday, the garden had moved on from the muddy mess of late autumn to the stark beauty of mid-winter. High winds had hoovered up the dead leaves on the paths and stripped the fruit trees and surrounding hedges down to the bare branches. Pruned in October to a height of 2.4 or 2.7m (8 or 9ft), the hedges act like a curtain around the garden, keeping out the worst of the weather and providing a deep green backdrop for the summer crops. Now they look like a lace border around the patchwork of beds, and I can see straight through to the shingle beyond. All our privacy is gone: the outlines and voices of passing hikers and dog-walkers are clearly discernible – and they can see me, too, hard at work for the few hours a week when dry weather and daylight coincide.

There is plenty to do. While I can forgive and even enjoy an untidy autumn garden, the pared-down aesthetic of winter demands a greater degree of order. Nasturtiums and borage, a bright blur around the edges of the beds until only a few weeks ago, have been liquidized by the frost and need to be cleared. The raised beds look bare and business-like without them. The last heads of sunflowers, thistles and fennel, picked bare by the birds, can now be cut down – I usually leave a few to be outlined in frost, but I'm told we don't get much frost, being so close to the sea. There are also wayward, gone-to-seed sprays of chard and chicory that must go on to the compost heap. There will be lots more next year.

I dig up some impressively large carrots – the compost-rich, aerated soil of these raised beds means they grow more successfully here than on the heavy clay of my London allotment. And I pull the last leeks from the clamp – a soil trench that doubles as an outdoor larder, useful for preserving root vegetables once they have stopped growing. The resulting clear space is big enough for a new soft fruit patch. I put in ten raspberry canes ('Autumn Bliss', which, unlike the summer-fruiting varieties, yields a good crop in the first year), lining the trench with garden compost and bone meal, and burying the stalks in 7.5cm (3in) of soil. (It's important not to plant raspberries too deep, as in a wet winter, the roots rot.) Newly planted canes must then be cut down to the ground to allow the roots to establish and throw up new shoots in the spring. I can never resist the gamble of dipping the severed cuttings in rooting powder and sticking them straight in the soil alongside, in the hope of creating a second row for free. In the past I've had about a 50 per cent success rate, which isn't at all bad.

I also have a dozen tiny bushes of the delicious gourmet strawberry 'Mara des Bois' (to order, telephone Ken Muir on 0870 747 9111) overwintering in pots in my greenhouse. This is a cross between a wild and cultivated strawberry, with all the flavour of the former combined with the juiciness and larger size of the latter. The thought of strawberries and cream seems so incongruous in the cold and wet that I find it hard to get excited about these fragile plants with their yellowing winter foliage. But their time will come in spring when they will be ready for planting out.

Also in the greenhouse, I pot up some suckers of garden mint to keep a supply going over winter, and continue to harvest pots of autumn-sown mizuna and coriander. What with the rocket and lamb's lettuce under cloches outside, a fine crop of land cress and parsley, and the last lingering lettuces in the cold frame, we are doing very well for winter salads. Most thrilling of all, the chicory roots I've been forcing under buckets have become fat crispy chicons. They're a rare treat in mid-winter, with boiled eggs, anchovies or crisped-up bacon, land cress, mayonnaise and pepper. Whenever a bucket becomes free, it can be replenished with more roots.

There's one winter crop I've been missing since leaving my London allotment for this year by the sea. I've had a hankering for jerusalem artichokes – there's just no substitute for their unique earthy flavour. Happily, Clarkey and Simon brought us down a bag full last weekend. I have saved a few of the tubers to plant here: they have a habit of taking over, I know, but I simply can't resist them.

14 January 2001

WAR ON SQUIRRELS

It would be nice to have started the new year full of peace and goodwill to all creatures, but I confess I have been feeling murderous towards one type of animal. No sooner have I got rid of the rabbit in our garden in the country – thanks, I'm afraid, to a neighbour's dog – than I am plagued by squirrels back in London. Friends and family have been driven to distraction by grey squirrels over the years – sick of their habit of digging up bulbs and stripping the bark off trees. My youngest sister, who lives in a third-floor flat, has learned to live with an especially acrobatic squirrel who runs along the roof of the neighbour's conservatory, shins up several feet of drainpipe, and then swings precariously, paw by paw, along the underside of the metal grille beneath her window like the man in the Milk Tray adverts. And all because the squirrel loves the crocus bulbs in her window box. And tulip bulbs. And almost any other spring-flowering bulb you spent a freezing cold, finger-numbing afternoon planting. You go to bed dreaming of all those beautiful flowers in embryo under the earth, and awaken to a garden scattered with nibbled remains and badly-buried leftovers. People get desperate. One friend has even threatened to use an air pistol on her local squirrels – and this is in Clapham, not the depths of the country.

I have sympathized with these and many other stories, but it wasn't until we were set upon by squirrels ourselves that I understood how people could be driven to such measures. Maybe we were just lucky, or maybe our dog

used to see them off – but for some reason our garden remained a blissfully squirrel-free zone. Until now. The trouble did begin a couple of weeks after our dog died – I returned home to find tulip bulbs tossed about the flower beds and dug out of pots, and compost all over the deck. Even worse was that they'd vandalized the brilliant "double decker" bird table my father made me for Christmas one year – the "cage" of dowelling rods designed to keep squirrels and larger birds, such as starlings, away from the wire cylinder of nuts on the upper storey had been gnawed clean through, and the nuts, at which a couple of blue tits had been delicately pecking, were all gone. When I came inside, ranting with rage about what I'd like to do to the blasted creatures, my husband said he'd look out his *Elvis Presley Family Cookbook* – apparently, The King's hard-up childhood in Tupelo, Mississippi featured a diet of roast squirrel, squirrel pie and even deep-fried squirrel.

I certainly don't fancy eating a squirrel – nor do I really want to kill them. I just want them to leave my plants and bulbs alone. Squirrels hardly get a look in on the pages of most gardening reference books, so I rang an advisor at HDRA, the organic gardening organization (02476 303517), to see what they could suggest in the way of humane deterrents. I was amazed to find that they could offer no lasting solution. You can cover your bulbs with wire netting and wrap tree bark with protective rings, but beyond that, there's not much more that you can do. Squirrels are legally classed as vermin, so even if you found a way of trapping them you'd have to kill them – you can't cart them off and release them on unsuspecting gardeners elsewhere as some people do with slugs and snails. "Basically, if squirrels like your garden, they like your garden," the advisor said. And that was that.

Do readers have any squirrel-busting tips they could share? In my experience, there's nothing like a bout of pest frustration to generate a healthy postbag. And on the subject of readers' letters, may I take this opportunity to say thank you for all the kind messages – many on cards without an address to reply to – about the death of my dog, which I mentioned several months back. I've always thought gardeners were nice people and these letters proved it. The exciting news to report is that we shall soon be getting a new puppy – and I'm hoping she'll see off the squirrels. Last night my husband suggested we call her Tufty. I hope it was a joke.

21 January 2001

WET WEATHER TACTICS

The heavy rains and thawing snow have played havoc with people's gardens. Making an infrequent visit to my London allotment to return our potted Christmas tree, which is put out to graze there all year after its brief annual spell in the spotlight, I was dismayed to see how wet and compacted the soil was. Many of my friends who garden on heavy clay soil are similarly afflicted: the soil is too wet to work or walk on, and autumn sowings of peas and broad beans have rotted underground.

There are a few simple measures you can take now to help rectify water-logged soil. The most important thing is not to let the soil get even more compacted, so lay planks and boards across the soil and edges of lawns while working. Then, dig in as much organic matter and sharp grit as you can get hold of. Make a thick layer of well-rotted manure and 2–4mm washed horticultural grit (available from builders' merchants) on top of the soil in the worst affected areas and incorporate it with a spade until the soil is crumbly and falls apart. The grit will last in your soil for ever, and will make you better prepared for the next downpour.

The best way to beat the wet, however, is to convert your vegetable patch or allotment to raised beds. My seaside garden, with the beds constructed on top of free-draining shingle, was blissfully unaffected by the deluges, and my November-sown broad beans are now a healthy 20cm (8in) high (the first time I've had such an early overwintered crop). Now is a good time for construction work in the garden, when there are few other tasks nagging at your time. If the wet weather is set to continue, it could be a sensible move.

Raised beds, as many readers will know, are a tried and tested feature of organic gardening. You'll have seen them on allotments, tacked together from old sleepers or scaffolding planks, or in pretty potagers with neat brick borders. Small enough to allow access from paths in between, one of their major advantages over growing directly in the ground is that because you never walk on the beds, the soil structure remains uncompacted and drainage is good. The retaining walls mean the soil can be built up and improved easily every year by spring and autumn additions of garden compost or well-rotted manure, and the soil tends to warm up earlier, too, making earlier sowings possible. As the soil is so rich and well-structured and there's no need for access between the rows, crops can be sown closer together, resulting in higher yields per yard and less space for weeds. The crucial thing is the size: the soil needs to be at least 30cm (12in) and prefer-ably 35cm (14in) deep to allow for a full range of crops to thrive, and the distance to the centre of the bed must never be longer than an arm's length, to allow for easy sowing, weeding and picking from the paths.

My landlord made his raised beds cheaply, pouring concrete into shutter-ing made from wide planks of reclaimed wood, and topped the walls with bricks to make an attractive flat surround. More conventional methods involve lengths of timber nailed or riveted together, salvaged railway sleep-ers, brightly painted breeze blocks or bricks. Woven willow hurdles would look nice, but would need to be lined with cloth or plastic to keep the soil in place, or you could even try hay bales (about £1 each from a farm) – these would slowly rot down from the inside to make next year's compost, and the surrounds would be nice and wide for sitting or placing pots on, perhaps with a wooden cover or cushions on top. The beds only need a base if they are to go on a balcony or roof terrace – ensure you make enough holes for drainage, and fill the bottom few inches with gravel. My landlord laid a layer of old clothes in the bottom of his beds to prevent the soil from leaching into the shingle while still letting out excess water.

For protection, you can build or buy cloches to fit the beds, making early spring and winter crops a possibility. My landlord paid a local ironworker to make some simple arched metal frames and then covered them with chicken wire and clear plastic (like a mini polytunnel; the plastic can be left off if all you want is to protect crops such as brassicas from bird damage). In a small garden, you could even construct your beds to fit multiples of the smart glass lantern-style cloches on sale in garden centres or smart mail order companies such as English Gardenwares (telephone 01243 543804).

28 January 2001

BEAUTIFUL BRASSICAS

There are few prettier sights in the winter vegetable garden than frost on brassica leaves. Those who were sensible enough to sow plenty of cabbages, kale and broccoli last spring and summer will have been enjoying the filigree effect of a frosty white outline around frilly, purple-tinged leaves. Having taken over my new garden by the sea in autumn, too late for sowing over-wintering brassicas, I have only a half dozen brussels sprout plants to admire this year, but very splendid have they looked, and very delicious they have tasted, too. As recommended by many a trendy TV chef, I have also eaten the tops this year, snapped off at the top of the stem, steamed gently and served with butter, or garlic, lemon juice and olive oil. Not only are they delicious – rather like nutty spring greens – removing the leaves in this way can also encourage the smaller sprouts to swell more quickly. With a careful choice of varieties and staggered sowings, it's possible to enjoy brussels sprouts from autumn through till spring, but to me they will always be a mid-winter vegetable. I like to have eight or so plants, which supply enough for Christmas lunch and a few other meals on top. Then it's on to the compost heap with the chopped-up stalks, to make room for something else.

I would like to have more cabbages this year. I've grown red ones successfully in previous years on my London allotment, and hanker after some of the more unusual varieties such as 'Cuor di Bue' and the Savoy-type 'Vertus' (organic seed for both of which is available from The Organic Gardening Catalogue 01932 253666). You can have cabbages in your garden all year round so long as you have enough space and choose the right varieties. 'Greyhound', 'Golden Acre' and 'Spitfire' are among the earliest summer-cropping varieties, and can be started in pots under glass over the next few weeks and planted out in spring. Summer varieties, such as 'Pixie', 'Mini-cote' and 'Stonehead', can be sown in the ground in early spring, while 'Flower of Spring' and 'Spring Hero', sown in late summer and protected against harsh winter weather, should be ready next March when there will be little else to harvest. The early-summer cropping varieties are the only ones that need to be sown under cover; the most reliable crops are sown in a seed bed, thinned to 7.5cm (3in) apart and then planted out in their final positions when they are 7.5cm (3in) or so in height and have two pairs of real leaves. All brassicas attract bird damage, so protect with netting or cloches, especially when small.

Cabbages, like enormous sprouts, are really just buds that swell and swell without opening. To keep the heads large and the leaves tightly packed, they require constant unchecked growth in rich moist conditions. When planting out any brassicas, work a handful of sieved garden compost and calcified seaweed into the planting hole. Cabbages do well with scented herbs such as sage, rosemary, chamomile, peppermint and dill planted nearby, as the smell of the herbs confuses pests – principal among which are cabbage white caterpillars and the cabbage root fly. Club root, the other main disease to which cabbages and other brassicas are prone, is almost incurable, but can be fought with some success by liming the soil. If you do well with your cabbages and get some large ones, you don't have to cut and use an entire head at once. Bob Flowerdew on *Gardeners' Question Time* recommended cutting a segment from the plant when it is still in the ground and covering the cut surfaces with foil. And when it's finally off with the whole head, a crop of smaller cabbages will cluster round the stem if you leave the stump and cut a cross in the top of it.

I'll also sow some Tuscan kale or cavolo nero (from Simpson's Seeds 01985 845004) – both for its strong peppery flavour when shredded in a bacon risotto, and for the look of its crinkly dark leaves. And I'll make sure to have a good crop of purple sprouting broccoli for next winter. I miss it terribly the years that I don't have it, and can never seem to plant enough. Early purple, late purple and white sprouting varieties can be cropped in succession from early spring, while a new variety called 'Rudolph' (The Organic Gardening Catalogue) is claimed to crop as early as October in warm areas the same year it is sown. In the meantime, I'm enjoying the few plants that are interspersed with the shrubs and perennials in my London front garden. (Don't ask why; it's a long story.) I've still to spy any purple sprouts, but the foliage looks lovely behind our mauve picket fence.

4 February 2001

LOVELIEST OF TREES

When in London at this time of year, I take great pleasure in all the winter flowering cherry trees (*Prunus* x *subhirtella* 'Autumnalis'). The one I see most is in our tiny back garden, where its tiny, pink-tinged white flowers stand out against a backdrop of glossy green ivy. Like many of the ornamental cherries, this variety came originally from Japan, and the delicate blossoms, borne on bare black branches, have all the lightness and grace of a Japanese pen-and-ink sketch. The flowers first appear in October, when the leaves are beginning to fall, and continue to open, with an extra burst after each hard frost, until March or April the following year. This long season makes it particularly valuable in gardens when there is little else in bloom – a few clumps of snowdrops or aconites or even bright blue scillas around its base can only accentuate the tree's beauty. By the time it comes fully into leaf and merges into the background, the later spring bulbs and other fresh foliage will be coming into their own.

There is a front garden in Hampstead with a row of small *Prunus* x *subhirtella* 'Autumnalis' along its roadside frontage, and over Christmas and new year tiny white fairy lights are woven in among the branches. The effect, though simple enough to achieve, is charming. There's another row of the trees by the cafe in the park where I walk our new puppy, Wilma, and on a sunny winter's morning, the sight of the blossom against a clear blue sky while I drink a cup of coffee can make me believe it's spring already. *Prunus* x *subhirtella*, also known as the rosebud cherry, is a good choice for small gardens, as it grows fairly slowly, averaging a height of 3m (10ft) at ten years, 4–5m (15ft) at 20, and only 6m (20ft) when fully mature. It is hardy, and likes a dry-ish soil in sun or part shade. The pink-flowered *P.x subhirtella* 'Autumnalis rosea' is also a possibility, though I prefer the contrast between the pink buds and white flowers that 'Autumnalis' provides. *P.* 'Pendula rosea' is less of a tree than a flowery hummock, with a profusion of single pinky-white blooms in April. It is best planted on top of a rock garden or on a tiny island in a pool, or as a bonsai-like curiosity in a sparse Zen-style garden, if you like that type of thing.

Now is a good time for planting trees, provided the soil is workable, so it's worth considering other good choices for small gardens, or smaller areas within large ones. Silver birches (*Betula pendula)* look good against all styles and periods of architecture, yet their graphic black and white bark and graceful tracery of branches complement modernist architecture especially well, and provide the perfect foil for all those straight lines. Even an ugly Sixties office block, glimpsed through a haze of soft new leaves in spring, is touched by the tree's charm. Silver birches grow quickly, reaching 7.6m (25ft) at ten years, and up to 30m (100ft) when fully grown, but their open habit and small leaves mean they cast only light shade. Cutting the trunk right down to the ground when the tree is young should result in several smaller stems springing up – what is known as a multistemmed specimen. This can look extremely attractive amid grass and spring bulbs in a wild woodland garden, or even among moss or gravel in an urban back yard. The architect Richard Rogers specified multistemmed birches around many of his earlier buildings, including the London house he built for his mother in the Sixties. When the trees got too big he simply chopped them down and planted younger ones in their place. However you grow a silver birch, it is worth removing any twiggy shoots from around the base of the main trunks to promote cleaner and whiter bark, which is enhanced by exposure to winds. The cut-leaf birch, *Betula pendula* 'Laciniata', has very pretty deep-cut leaves and smooth, extremely white bark, but needs full sun whereas other varieties can cope with part shade.

Another of my favourite trees for a small garden is *Cercis siliquastrum,* also known as the Judas tree. It needs some protection, and is perfect in the summer warmth of a courtyard or south-facing corner. Its moment of glory is short-lived compared with the winter-flowering cherry, but if you plant one you will never want to be away from home in April again. Tiny violet and magenta pea-like flowers are borne not just on new shoots, but burst from the bark all along the bare branches before the bronzy heart-shaped young leaves appear. From a distance, the whole tree seems to have been outlined in purple. As it is only 10.5m (35ft) high at maturity it won't overpower a small space. It comes from the Mediterranean, where avenues of Judas trees lining the streets of Sicily last spring are a sight I won't forget.

PET-FRIENDLY GARDENING

Some years ago, I used to stay with a friend in the outskirts of Naples, whose mother, Adriana, loved gardening. Whenever I left for home, it would be with jars of basil leaves preserved under oil, or of her own delicious tomato sauce for pasta, wrapped up in jerseys in my luggage – all the smells and flavours of a Neapolitan summer to eke out in spoonfuls over the cold English winter. Adriana also loved flowers. If you woke early, you'd see her out in the garden in a floor-length tartan dressing gown and pull-on woolly hat (this was her garb, no matter what the weather, till at least 11 o'clock), pottering about the circular flowerbeds that punctuated the lawn and picking bunches of bright, voluptuous blooms to bring inside. All was a picture of peace.... unless one of the three family dogs had transgressed. Then a string of best southern-Italian expletives, invariably involving the Madonna, several saints and the parts of the dogs' anatomy Adriana would like to boil, grill or fry in punishment, would fill the air, followed by a long, low wailing as she inspected the damage wrought by Carboncella rolling in a dahlia bed, or Scruffy (pronounce it with a wide Italian accent) playing tug-o'-war with the roses.

Knowing my interest in gardening, she would ask my advice on how to keep dogs off the beds – but in those days I didn't have a dog and can't have been much help. The last time I visited – and sadly, Adriana has died since – I was marched into the garden as soon as I'd arrived. The dog problem had been solved for good and all was well in her world. "Ecco!" she said, standing hands on hips and nodding proudly at the flowerbeds. I looked, but I could hardly see them. Yards of brightly coloured plastic-covered wire fencing, wound round and round the beds with the blind zeal of one who has finally found The Answer, had all but obscured the flowers from view. Well, at least she was happy.

I was thinking about Adriana the other day as our new lurcher puppy, Wilma, leapt through my vegetable beds for the eighteenth time. It is possible to train dogs not to hop on flowerbeds, but it certainly takes patience. I was hoping to have succeeded in time for sowing and transplanting, but that's now only a few weeks away. Several of my broad bean seedlings came heroically through weeks of frost only to be felled by lolloping puppy paws, and she's dug up some garlic bulbs. I can see myself resorting to some sort of temporary fencing – a foot or two of chicken wire, or even some miniature hurdles – if I'm to avoid any further damage. The important thing is to get the message through to the dog while she's still small and light on her feet.

In ornamental flowerbeds, damage from dogs and cats can be lessened by dense planting. Bare earth is their greatest temptation: to a dog it's an invitation to dig, to a cat it's a litter tray. A fair percentage of evergreens and permanent ground cover should put off all but the most determined, and will also prevent pets from using your beds as a short cut. Include a few pricklies, such as hollies or berberis, to be sure, or choose plants that are resistant to the sort of damage pets can cause. The much-vaunted "new perennial" style of planting, using lots of ornamental grasses, is not only fashionable, it will also put up with dogs and cats prowling among it – cats will stalk through it like a jungle, while dogs will find a shady corner to lie in all summer.

It may seem far-fetched to plan your garden around your pets, but a new book, *The Pet Friendly Garden* by Richard Barrett (Pan, £12.99) shows you how to do just that. As well as advice on pet-friendly plants, ornamental scratching posts and "dog loos", it even includes DIY "plunge pools" for dogs and trickle fountains for cats, which will, of course, double up as attractive garden features for human enjoyment. In his foreword, John Noakes (who else?) says, "pets and gardens go together like fish and chips", but then goes on to say that "it is better to remember past times fondly and keep the garden as though Shep were still here with me." Someone give that man a puppy – isn't it time he moved on?

24 February 2001

COUNTRY GARDENER: A HEAD START FOR SEEDLINGS

Seed sowing time will soon be here, and for the first time in my life I have a proper greenhouse in which to raise early crops. For too long, every spare windowsill in our house – and even the interior of my old VW camper van – has been crammed with pots and seed trays at this time of year, the seedlings always slightly leggy due to not having *quite* enough light. This year at our new house by the sea I shall be able to do things properly. I've cleared out the greenhouse in preparation – the pots of spring bulbs are either flowering away inside the house or waiting in the wings of our outside summer kitchen to take centre stage when their time comes. And my prized 'Mara des Bois' strawberries will be ready to plant outside soon, along with the October-sown sweetpeas and cornflowers, pinched out at a few inches high to encourage bushier growth. This leaves a lot of room to fill with seed trays. When we arrived here last September, one side of the greenhouse was covered with 20 large pots of cordon tomatoes; this entire raised bed, filled with the free-draining shingle on which our house is built, is available for use, along with the wooden work surface on the other side. It will be so exciting to see the place alive with young plants.

I've now learned the hard way not to trust seed to the open ground too soon. If it's as cold and wet as it has been here, the seed won't germinate, and even if it does, the tiny, silky seedlings soon fall prey to slugs or birds. Giving your plants a head start under glass not only means they'll be ready

for harvesting or flowering earlier; they should also be large enough and tough enough to withstand a few nibbles when transplanted to the open ground. The traditional method of raising seedlings under cover involves sowing them in shallow seed trays of compost, and then "pricking out" the seedlings into larger pots of a few plantlets, or into individual units, when they have formed a set of "true" leaves. This can be fiddly work, and it's hard not to damage, inadvertently, the delicate root systems of the plantlets, thus setting back their growth. These days many people, particularly commercial growers, get around the problem by sowing directly into "cell trays" – sheets of plastic ready-moulded into individual "plugs", in which you can either sow a single seed, or a few, which you later thin out to leave the strongest seedling. The advantages of this method are that the plants can grow on undisturbed until it is time to plant them out in the open ground (after a few days "hardening off" (acclimatizing to the change in temperature) outside or in a cold frame). The major disadvantage is that the system is hopelessly unecological – the plastic used to manufacture cell trays is so brittle that most people are obliged to buy them new every year.

In an effort to do my bit for the planet, I'm going to have a bash at making my own recycled, biodegradable planting plugs this year. I've been sent a rather nifty set of templates for something called the "Potta System" by Grassroots Gardening, which helps you create a whole seed tray full of planting tubes made from old newspapers, at break-neck speed. You can vary the width and depth of the tubes according to the needs of the plants you're sowing, and then carefully fill them with potting compost – the theory is that a thick and healthy root system develops quickly, and will not be disturbed on planting out because the whole thing – paper, plant, soil and all – goes into the ground. And as the newspaper absorbs water, the seedlings should need less watering than those raised in plastic trays. (A kit costs £19; ring Grassroots Gardening on 01189 712085 for mail order.) Other DIY options include the "Potmaker" from RK Alliston – a wooden mould which, the catalogue boasts, is made from wood from a cedar planted by Gertrude Jekyll (£17, ring 020 7751 0077). One does wonder, though, whether the people prepared to spend out on such gadgets will have the patience and inclination for the Blue-Peteresque pursuit of making dozens and dozens of tubes from newspaper and filling them with soil. I can only do it for an hour at a time before all the stories on the newsprint make my head spin and I have to come inside and play with the puppy.

4 March 2001

COUNTRY GARDENER: A SALAD GURU SPEAKS

I have begun to sow this year's salad crops, inspired by a visit to Frances Smith, a "salad guru" who lives nearby. Until her semi-retirement last year, Frances used to supply top chefs all over London with succulent and picturesque salad leaves, raised in polytunnels behind her home above Romney Marsh, Kent. Rosy-cheeked, outspoken, and possessed of a whirlwind energy that belies her years, Frances recently handed over the running of the business to two former employees, but her advice and experience are invaluable – there can be few people who know as much about growing salads on this scale.

Even this early in the season, her eight polytunnels are bristling with neat rows of lettuces, spinach, curly kales and other, more unusual crops. "This is claytonia – or miner's lettuce," says Frances, pulling off a diamond-shaped, slightly spongy leaf for me to try. "It's everybody's favourite," she says, as I indicate its tastiness, "But it's seldom grown commercially as it's fiddly to pick". She moves on to a mustard-like leaf with a peppery flavour. "'Fordhook Fancy'," she declares. "I've been saving seed since one of my chefs brought it back from America – you can't buy it over here." 'Par-Cel' confuses me – it looks like curly parsley but tastes just like celery – but I recognize rocket and the raggedy green leaves of mizuna, both growing under cloches in my own garden.

Almost all the salads are harvested as "cut-and-come-again" crops, with outside leaves picked off repeatedly from the young plants when they are 5–10cm (2–4in) long. "That's how the chefs like them," says Frances. "They want young springy leaves that will make a nice heap on the plate. Curly leaves are especially popular. And nice bright colours." Both desires are met by curly kales and ornamental cabbages, which come in all shades of cream, green and purple and keep going through the winter. More colour is provided by bright red chicories and mustards and the mixed packs of red, pink, white and golden-stemmed chard sold as 'Bright Lights', which Frances lets go to seed so she can save the strongest colours.

Seed is sown in a tiny greenhouse in moulded plastic "cell trays", and the seedlings are planted out in the polytunnels through holes dibbed in a wet newspaper mulch. "It may not look very pretty but it keeps the weeds out and the moisture in," says Frances. When I tried out this method at my London allotment, I was soon beset by slugs, for whom conditions beneath the newspaper were ideal for snoozing by day after a hard night's snacking on my seedlings. Frances admits to a sprinkling of slug pellets beneath and above the paper. "It's the only way, when you're gardening on this scale," she says. "In a small garden you can pick the things off by hand – or you can flame the ground with a blowtorch."

Though not totally organic, Frances prides herself on using the barest minimum of chemicals. Blood fish and bone mix and local poultry manure are her only soil conditioners, while natural predators help keep down aphids and other pests. "I let things like borage self-seed in the tunnels as they bring the beneficial insects in," she explains. Outside, teasels and foxgloves act as "sacrificial victims" to attract aphids and, consequentially, their predators. Swarms of hover flies, along with lacewings, ladybirds and lots of blue tits means she seldom sees an aphid. Sprays are only used as a last resort or to combat sudden infestations.

Overwintering salads are sown no later than August – except for claytonia, which benefits from the shorter days in September. Popular winter lettuces include 'Passion Brune', which Frances bought on a trip to France, red and green 'Parella', 'Rouge d'Hiver' and 'Winter Density'. When supplies are inevitably lower in the winter months, the chefs have to content themselves with a sprinkling of leaves to perk up bags of market-bought lettuce, but for them there is no substitute for Frances' salads. In the past they have, she says, fallen over themselves to remain in favour and safeguard their supplies.

Frances's own favourite leaves, which she will continue to grow for her own kitchen table, include 'Frillice', a frilly iceberg-type lettuce which she treats as a loose-leaf, picking leaves as they are ready, and the traditional corn salad or 'Mache' – best served, she says, in a nice heap beside a slab of foie gras. "Never mix mache and lettuce in the same salad – you need one or the other as a background taste but not both," she says. "Likewise, mustard and rocket cancel one another out if used together." In the world of speciality salads, it would seem it is possible to have too much of a good thing.

Almost all the above salad seeds can be obtained from Suffolk Herbs (01376 572456 for catalogue).

11 March 2001

OPERATION SQUIRREL

In January, driven to distraction by grey squirrels ransacking my bird table and digging up spring bulbs, I appealed to readers for advice. Pests of any description are guaranteed to generate a lively postbag, and I was prepared for hate mail from the Grey Squirrel Protection League. I needn't have worried. Among the stacks of letters there was only one that stood up for squirrels. The rest of you, it seems, are even more fed up with them than I was and have been driven to surprising lengths of ingenuity, cruelty and even deception in search of the ultimate deterrent.

The kindest cures involve either a physical barrier, or substances with a strong smell or taste which the squirrels do not like. Mr P Tillotson from Oldbury in the West Midlands spreads a thick layer of half-inch gravel on top of pots and beds where bulbs are buried. "If you select the right blend or colour it looks good into the bargain," he says. "And cats and foxes don't like it either." Lydia Skinner advises via email to lay chopped gorse or holly leaves on top of the soil, while Mrs DA Wright of Benfleet in Essex is among the many who stretch wire or netting over pots or lay large stones as a mulch around the roots of plants to keep the squirrels away. "Vivian and Ray" email that they sprinkle a few drops of Oil of Olbas (a cold cure available from chemists) on tea bags placed in strategic positions around the garden – the strong eucalyptus smell apparently deters squirrels, but defences must be replenished weekly or after heavy rain. I was interested to hear of a product called 'Squirrel Away' (from CJ Wild Bird Foods at £2.99 (01743 709545/0800 731 2820 for stockists), a harmless peppery-tasting powder that can be sprinkled over bird food and bulbs. This helpful suggestion comes from Mrs Brenda Ross of Abingdon in Oxfordshire, who also adds that chasing squirrels while making a loud noise (she recommends an old screwdriver on a tin saucepan lid) soon sees them off. "Repeat each spring," she advises. "Best to explain to your neighbours first or you get some funny looks." Possibly the most curious idea came on email from Lee Skinner, who advises spreading human hair (begged from the barbers or beauty salon floor) on the surface of the soil. "It is supposed to deter moles," he muses. "And I wonder if it might work with squirrels. Try to use dark hair as it will be less visible."

Then things start to get nasty. By far the majority of the letters were from those who have resorted to traps, and most withheld their name and address for fear of repercussions from animal lovers. Some buy mink traps from farm suppliers, while others obtain rat traps under false pretences from their environmental health office. Of the proprietary traps available, those by Agriframes seem the most popular – its "Humane Squirrel Catcher" costs £34.99 (01983 209209 mail order). But now comes the crunch. Once you have trapped a grey squirrel you cannot, by law, release it into the wild again because grey squirrels are not indigenous – the only option is to kill it. Most people who wrote to me drown squirrels by tying a string to the full trap and lowering it into a water butt. "It was hard to do it the first time," writes one Anon, "But after all the trouble they have given us, my heart has hardened." Others are less squeamish. "If awards are to be handed out for squirrel culling, I believe my husband should receive one, for in a period of about ten years he has rid this area of about 1,500 squirrels," claims another Anon. "This he has achieved with a basic trap made from chicken-wire on a frame, a strong polythene bag and a heavy right foot." (The RSPCA endorses neither method, and instead recommends contacting a reputable pest control firm before setting any traps.)

After that, I was relieved to find Ann Rawlings' letter from Worthing, West Sussex. Having cracked the bird problem by suspending a feeder on a long wire from a branch (squirrels don't like to travel downwards and can't bite through thick wire, she says), Mr and Mrs Rawlings gave their squirrels their own nut pot in the hope that they would not dig so much. "This has worked quite well," she says, "And we have a close-up view through the kitchen window of their comings and goings. Some have become quite tame and will take nuts from the hand. Given the choice of bulbs v squirrels, I would not part with my grey gang. They are graceful, quick, adventurous, resourceful and funny, and unlike bulbs they are around all the year." Perhaps I can learn to live with mine, too.

18 March 2001

COUNTRY GARDENER: A NEW FRONT GARDEN

Having slumbered unchanged all winter, our new front garden at the seaside is springing into life. Violets and lemon yellow gorse were in bloom by the end of February, and most of the trees and shrubs are in bud. I spent a few sunny mornings wandering among my overgrown new domain, cutting back the old, spent stems of fennel, valerian and wild marjoram to let the rosettes of bright new leaves take over. I'm glad I left so much standing when we came to live here last autumn. It was partly out of laziness, and feeling overwhelmed by all the work that needs to be done. After all, the last garden I tackled was bare concrete – daunting, maybe, but a blank slate. It would fit five or six times into this new plot, which is crammed to bursting with trees and shrubs in severe need of pruning and many other plants with which I am not entirely familiar, all growing out of an unpromising mixture of soil and shingle. But now I'm glad I did so little last year. Apart from having fed the birds all winter, the spindly seedheads, now as dry and brittle as touchpaper, offer me further clues, along with the new leaves, to the iden-tities of my new charges. There's a large clump of red hot pokers (Kniphofia) to one side of the gate, lots of Japanese anemones, and what look to be many different types of buddleia. Lambs' ears (*Stachys byzantina*) and lavender line the path to the front door, and I was pleased to see the frilly pale-green leaves of aquilegias pushing up among them.

Leaving old growth on the plants as long as possible has also enabled me to keep track of how large and high the existing plants grow, which has been useful when putting in new bulbs and plants. The area near the path, where

I have concentrated most of my efforts, is now beginning to come together, with greenish-white nibs of alliums and pendulous nectaroscordums pushing through the soil, and drifts of white and spotted foxgloves under the trees beyond. Nearer the path, I've put some lower-growing plants given to me by knowledgeable gardening friends who know which plants will flourish in this sort of garden. There's lovely *Libertia peregrinans* with its fan of grass-like leaves – olive green with a rusty orange central vein, and in front of it a group of the wild buplureum, *B. falcatum*, which will have a haze of acid yellow flowers in a month or two's time. Spreading on to the path are tufts of *Dianthus carthusianorum*, a member of the pink family that has large purply blooms, and a plant with red-tinged pointy leaves, which has been careless enough to lose its label.

I'm ashamed to say that I can't name most of the trees and larger shrubs, but as buds and blooms unfold I am confident they will declare themselves. The two enormous leyland cypresses that cast dense shade and obscure the view to the sea need no introduction – I'm not yet sure what to do about those. And the scarlet stems of dogwood are unmistakable, creating a splendid contrast with the ochre lichen that covers the candelabra branches of stag's horn sumac. There are bay trees and a couple of hollies, all growing into one another like nobody's business, a sprawling pyracanthus and that favourite among seaside gardeners, the tamarisk. I can also make out a hawthorn, some sort of laurel and a pair of young larches. Many of the larger trees or bushes have roses or honeysuckle scrambling up into the branches, which should look charming, come the summer.

There are, however, two initially unfamiliar plants which may, I fear, prove invasive. One is the creeping St John's wort (*Hypericum calycinum*), whose scruffy bronzy leaves cover much of the ground to the right of the main path. The other, to the left, is a rather pretty thing with starry, pink-tinged white flowers and leaves, which shoot up through the earth like spearheads but open into bright green hearts. Neighbours tell me that it's known locally as 'butterbur', and that nothing, but nothing, will grow anywhere near it. My reference books defeated me till I tried Richard Mabey's superb *Flora Britannica* (Sinclair Stevenson, £30). There I found it as winter heliotrope (*Petasites fragrans*), praised for its vanilla-scented early flowers, but described as "extremely invasive, spreading rampantly by means of underground stems, and its naturalized colonies on roadsides tend to exclude all other species." Hmm. Definitely one to watch.

25 March 2001

COUNTRY GARDENER: SEA KALE FOR SUPPER

One of the advantages of having a potter for a landlord is that I get to use his beautiful pots. He is one of the old school which believes that the traditional shapes, tried and tested over centuries, are hard to improve on. He lends his own signature to a range of Gopsall Pottery designs by leaving sculptural ridges with his fingers during throwing and thumb-marks on the handles, and by naming them after various local characters. A wide squat planter with a wiggly edge is known as 'Betty Wiggly' after the friend who works at the local filling station, for instance, while 'Mabel', with a rim crimped like a Cornish pasty, commemorates a long-departed sprightly ex-Wren named Mabel Mussett.

The garden was full of these terracotta wares when we arrived last September. 'Long toms' more than 0.6m (2ft) high had tumbling tomatoes spilling over the sides, the raised beds had small pots of chives and other herbs ranged along the edges, and every bamboo cane was crowned with a tiny, bell-like cane-top. Even in midwinter, this liberal sprinkling of terracotta kept the garden looking well-furnished. Most splendid of all is a range of forcers – for blanching early crops of rhubarb, sea kale, chicory and endive. Those for rhubarb are more than 0.6m (2ft) high, with lids like minarets and handles for lifting, while the other vegetables have bell-like cloches in decreasing sizes. As well as being useful, these wonderful shapes inhabit the garden rather like sculpture. Slightly misshapen or cracked 'seconds' are scattered through the overgrown front garden, where they have become homes to hibernating creatures and nesting birds. But now it is time for those in the vegetable garden to be pressed into use.

Rhubarb and sea kale can be forced and harvested now, although existing rhubarb plants can be forced from January onwards. Cover the crowns with a forcer or plastic bin, shored round with compost or straw to keep in heat and speed up the process. Nothing can beat the pink stems of 'Champagne Early', sliced and baked slowly, to keep their shape intact. I bought a couple of new crowns from the local farm shop, which I have planted in a sunny open spot with plenty of well-rotted manure mixed into the soil. The new plants must be left to establish for at least a year, and forcing for early crops can be done only once every two years, so it is good to have several plants on the go.

Sea kale is something completely new to me. I have admired the plants, with their thick cabbage-like leaves and clouds of white flowers, on the beach down here and at Dungeness, but have never eaten it. Apparently, sea kale is the new rocket among trendy London restaurants, so it would be fun to try growing my own. The tradition, since sea kale became a delicacy in the 18th-century, was for local people to shore up the shingle around the emerging shoots in late winter to deprive them of light, and return two months later to harvest the blanched, celery-like stems and crinkly purplish leaves. It is, of course, not done to uproot plants that are growing in the wild, so I tried our local garden centre for some 'thongs' – the pencil-thin side-shoots that are removed in the autumn and grown on in bundles over winter. These are not due to arrive till the end of March, but you can still get a crop the first year if you feed with seaweed-based fertilizer and cover with a forcer surrounded by compost or straw.

Impatient to sample its apparently sublime flavour, I sent off for some mail order sea kale to Sandy Pattullo of Angus in Scotland (01307 840303; £6 for 225g/8oz). The pallid bundles arrived the next day, and we ate them that evening with melted butter and a squeeze of lemon, just like asparagus. With the texture of braised celery, a delicate earthy aftertaste and a pleasant hint of the sea, they were absolutely delicious. I can't wait to establish a crop of my own.

Rhubarb, sea kale, chicory and endive forcers from Gopsall Pottery are available from the shops at Great Dixter, Northiam, E Sussex (01797 253107) and West Dean Gardens, Chichester, W Sussex (01243 818279) – strictly no mail order.

4 April 2001

THE PERILS OF OVER-PLANTING

Our redesigned front garden – slate chippings and deep raised beds behind a purple picket fence – may have been a hit last summer, but it has been looking distinctly sorry for itself for the past few months. Once the splendid 'Velvet Queen' sunflowers and scramble of sweetpeas and other annuals died down, there was simply not enough structure in the beds to carry it through the winter. My original vision was of soft mounds of different types of lavender that would grow into one another and bush out between the fence posts on to the street. Given how well my lavenders in the window boxes and old dustbins by the door had performed, this didn't seem a bad plan. I love the colour and scent of the flowers, and the subtle greys and greens of the foliage look good all year round. However, I was done for by my own impatience. I bought lots of lovely lavenders at one of the Rare Plant Fairs that are held in various places across the country each summer. But in spite of having spent the sort of money that makes me blush when doing my accounts, the little plants looked rather sparse and forlorn when I planted them out in the big new bed. I'd been able to buy the more common varieties as larger bushes – but some of the rarer French lavenders, with their waving 'butterfly wings' petals in palest pinks and mauves, were available only as tiny twiggy things a few inches across.

Had I just left them to establish, I'm sure the plants would have been fine as lavender grows quickly when it is happy – indeed, the problem is to keep the bushes compact by means of regular light pruning so they don't go woody in the middle. But I couldn't wait. It wasn't just the usual thirst for instant gratification; I did have the excuse of the garden being open to the public through the National Gardens Scheme in August. So between the lavender bushes I popped in lots of annuals that I'd raised from seed – white cosmos, bronze fennel, 'Velvet Queen' sunflowers in dark shades from crimson to brown, and the heavenly black hollyhock, *Alcea rosea* 'Nigra'. The trouble was, that in the deep, freshly manured new soil, the seedlings took off like triffids. In no time at all, the hollyhocks were putting out enormous rosettes of leaves and the sunflowers and cosmos – the latter, usually a graceful, feathery plant, in my experience – had stems several feet tall and almost an inch across. In spite of my efforts to free some space around them, my poor lavenders were swamped. When you add the damp summer into the equation, together with all that rampant foliage, they didn't really stand a chance. If there is one thing lavenders like, it's sunshine, and they certainly didn't see much of that. By the time the firework show of the annuals was over, a lot of them were dead.

I am left with a couple of hebes, a rosemary and lots of furry grey lambs' ears (*Stachys byzantina*), along with the few surviving lavenders and some self-seeded fennel and hollyhocks. Now we are in the country so much, the garden could usefully be more low-maintenance, so I think I'll forget about replacing the fussy lavenders and go for some easy-going but attractive shrubs. Senecios, with their silver-rimmed leaves in soft felty grey, would look nice against the purple fence, and I've been given a small *Garrya elliptica* by a friend. This will eventually grow into a tree, but is just right for the garden now, where its ghostly grey catkins can be admired at head height. I could do with a few cranesbill geraniums and some purple sage. There are still gaps between the plants, but thank goodness I had the foresight last autumn to fill patches of the bed with bulbs. Black and white tulips ('Spring Green' and 'Black Swan' – a subtler colour than the more widely-grown 'Queen of Night', with a luminous white base to the petals) will be flowering soon in large informal groups, as well as the odd 'Prinses Irene' (flaming orange, with a purple sheen on the outside of the petals) just to stop it all becoming *too* tasteful. I was suddenly tempted to sow some peacock blue cerinthes in between, but for once I held back. I have finally learned my lesson – the hard way.

8 April 2001

COUNTRY GARDENER: IN PRAISE OF PEAS

Ask a group of gardeners which home-grown vegetable they couldn't do without and a good many will say peas. Picked, shelled and cooked straight

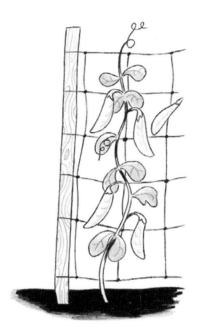

away, for just a few minutes, they have a freshness of flavour and firmness of texture that is a world away from the watery mush you were once served at school. People are often put off by all the shelling, but I find that guests often like to help out, and it is a very sociable job for a small group, chatting in the last of the evening sun with colanders on laps for the peas and a box on the ground for all the spent shells.

Greediness aside, pea plants also look good. The flowers – smaller, usually white versions of the sweetpea – are pretty and the leaves an attractive grey-green. Once the pods start to form, that bright 'peapod' green looks dramatic with the sun shining through it and the embryonic peas clearly visible as dark shadows within. Peas are not difficult to grow, provided you don't try to start them off too early. After many years of pathetic results with autumn and early spring sowings of hardy varieties such as 'Pilot', I have given up with the rounded seed types – which are not supposed to be as tasty, anyway – and gone over to sowing only the wrinkled seed, or marrowfat types, which are sown later. I have started a few rows already, but am going to wait till the end of April, when the soil has had a chance to warm up some more, for my main sowing. Pea seeds rot quickly in cold, wet ground; the most frequent reason for a poor show. You can go on sowing till mid-June, but later plants will be less productive, and prone to mildew.

Pea sticks made from the bushy top growth of hazel, hornbeam and birch are an attractive feature in a vegetable garden. You can train peas up netting or chicken wire, but the traditional twiggy stakes, stuck into the ground in a double line, perhaps meeting in the middle as a rough rustic arch, look much nicer. Check the seed packet for the height of the variety you are growing before cutting your sticks. Alternatively, a teepee frame will bring a welcome vertical element into the garden, and you can make another for sweetpeas. The crucial thing is to stake peas early. Leave it too late and the brittle stems will snap as you try to lift and train them, and slugs and other pests will attack any foliage or seed-pods that are touching the ground. Peas like a well-manured soil – preferably prepared the previous autumn, but if not, a good digging over now, incorporating some well-rotted garden compost or concentrated chicken manure into the soil, should do the trick. If your soil is good, the seeds can be sown a couple of inches apart – grown this close together, they will help support each other as they grow.

When I first grew peas, I was so deliriously happy to have my own home-grown supply of this delicious vegetable that I didn't much care which varieties I grew. But after a few years, curiosity set in, particularly after hearing experienced gardeners wax lyrical over their favourites. One of the most vociferous pea-fanciers I've met is Laurie Woods, a volunteer gardener at the beautiful Gilbert White House and Museum in Selborne, Hampshire, which I visited recently. He very kindly gave me a bundle of brown envelopes containing some of the peas he is growing in the vegetable garden there – a re-creation of the sort of kitchen garden that the 18th-century clergyman and naturalist Gilbert White wrote about in his *Garden Kalendar*.

If all goes well, my new vegetable garden will be filled with delicious peas come midsummer, including two rare Dutch heritage varieties, 'Langedyks Pale Flowering' pea, which has ivory white flowers and grows to 0.7m (2.5ft), and 'Early Veen's Marrowfat', slightly taller with two-tone flowers in pink and lilac. There's also the 'Carlin' pea, usually grown for drying and believed to have been brought to England in 1577 after a shipwreck on the East Coast – and the 'Asparagus' pea, whose attractive, four-seeded pods are eaten whole when young (less than an inch long). Mr Woods also included the 'Lincoln' pea, first grown in this country in 1884 – his favourite of all the more commonly grown varieties and one of the best for flavour – which has white flowers and long, well-filled pods.

'Lincoln' is available from The Organic Gardening Catalogue (01932 253666) and the asparagus pea from Thompson & Morgan (01473 688821). The 'Carlin' pea, together with other unusual peas and old-fashioned varieties, is part of the HDRA's Heritage Seed Library – ring 02476 303517 for details of how to join.

22 April 2001

COUNTRY GARDENER: AN ABUNDANCE OF BASIL

On the first day of spring – which, true to form, turned out to be one of the coldest of the year so far – I sowed several trays of basil seed. As snow whirled around the greenhouse windows, it felt almost like an act of defiance in the face of the weather. After all, what can be more summer-like than the smell of fresh basil in the sunshine? As I fiddled with the seed packets with frozen fingers, I tried to imagine us in a few months' time, eating tomato salads and grilling fresh fish on the barbecue under the chestnut tree. There are some wall-mounted pots in that area of the garden and it would be good to have some basil growing there, just where you need it for cooking.

Sowing basil at this time was not the foolhardy gesture it might seem. A native of the sun-baked Mediterranean, basil is a very tender herb, and you'd wait forever for your first crop if you sowed it outside when all danger of frost has passed. The first sowings of the year should be made under glass and in the warm – basil likes a steady temperature of 18–21°C (64–70°F) to germinate. Taken inside the house and set on a wooden shelf above the Rayburn, mine was oblivious to whatever the weather was throwing at us, and showed a rash of tiny round green leaves after only a few days. They were unmistakeably basil leaves. Unlike many other seedlings – tomatoes, or beans, for instance, whose first 'seed' leaves bear no resemblance at all to the finished article – basil looks like basil from the very beginning. And what's more, it smells like basil, too.

In the past, I've sown only two types of basil – the usual kitchen basil (*Ocimum basilicum*) and the purple-leafed variety, 'Purple Delight'. Inspired by the American cooking and gardening guru, Martha Stewart, who grows no fewer than fifteen types of basil in her immaculate Connecticut garden, I succumbed this year to Thompson & Morgan's collection of six different basils in one packet, sold under the silly name of 'The Spice Boys' (01473 688821). As well as the familiar Greek and purple varieties, there is also 'lettuce leaf' basil, which has leaves like a frilly lettuce; 'lemon' basil, which has a strong citron scent and is ideal with fish, chicken and peas; 'cinnamon' basil, with a marked cinnamon-clove flavour and pretty purple flower spikes, and 'Ararat', a rare heirloom variety with dark mottled green foliage and a sweet spicy aroma. Had I chosen to compete with Martha, the Terre de Semences catalogue (01227 731815) is a good source of other unusual basils. There, you can choose from a further 18 varieties, including 'Peruvian' basil, whose flavour is said to be a mixture of mint, oregano and camphor; 'Thai' basil, which tastes of aniseed and clove; and the curious-sounding 'Mammoth', with leaves the size of a human hand. Suffolk Herbs (01376 572456) has 17 varieties, including lime basil, dark red basil, and a miniature fine-leafed Greek basil.

The point of this mass sowing is to have enough basil to be able to cut it in large handfuls to make pesto sauce and sprinkle all over salads all summer long. I always feel bad about massacring those poor little plants you buy in supermarkets, and there is no point in sowing your own basil if you don't sow lots. You can always give it away if you become swamped by it – a few strong plants in an attractive pot can be a good present. Make successive sowings from now on under glass, and prick out the seedlings into pots or large planters that you can have on the kitchen windowsill or outside the back door. Transplant outside no earlier than the beginning of June, after hardening off (acclimatizing in a cold frame) for ten days or so. Basil hates cold soil and will droop and fail if conditions are not right. Once the soil has warmed up, you can try a later sowing outside – Greek basil is a good one to try as it does not flower until the middle of autumn, when the other varieties will have already run to seed. Now half an inch or so high, and giving off the most delicious range of aromas, my trays of basil are a wonderful promise of the summer to come.

SCENTED PELARGONIUMS

At the very top of our London house, beneath a skylight leading to the flat roof, are four large shelves devoted to plants. My friend Clarkey installed them shortly after we moved here as I was keen to make the most of the light from another large Velux window we had cut into the sloping side roof of the house. The shelves range in length from 0.6–1.2m (2–4ft) long, and are staggered across the wall in the manner of flying ducks so that the last is directly beneath the skylight. In a stylish feat of construction, Clarkey designed the shelves so they have no visible means of support – they appear to float straight out of the wall, and are painted the same colour.

Packed with plants and bathed in light that throws leafy shadows across the walls, these shelves are one of my favourite features in our house. Any sun-loving houseplant does well here, and it is a good place to raise seedlings or bring potted spring bulbs into early bloom. But after we'd had the stairwell repainted recently, my motley collection of plants looked decidedly dusty and scruffy. Some tired zonal pelargoniums, brought in to overwinter several years ago and never moved outside again, were ripe for retirement, and an enormous aloe vera, bought as a seedling from the Lambeth Country Show, had outgrown its pot and keeled over. There were pots of amaryllis bulbs that had flowered in the distant past and then produced nothing but strappy green leaves. A few pots were empty save for a dead central stick – no doubt the victims of over- or under-watering. It was definitely time for a change.

Rather than the colourful jumble of plants I'd had before, I decided to go for a more restrained approach – one particular type of plant per shelf. As there are not an awful lot of houseplants I like – I can't stand rubber plants, cheese plants, cactuses or anything that looks like a miniature tropical shrub – that isn't hard to do. I am dedicating one shelf to scented-leaf pelargoniums, one to different aloes, one to attractive succulents, such as aeoniums and echeveria, and the last to something I hope will take my fancy in the course of this research.

I began with the scented pelargoniums. This is a wonderfully varied family of plants with leaves that can smell of peppermint, roses, lemon, camphor, apple, cloves, aniseed and even coconut. The leaf shapes and textures range from the velvety soft bright green of *Pelargonium tomentosum* to the crinkled heart-shapes of *P. odoratissimum*, ('apple geranium') and the deep-cut spidery foliage of some of the rose-scented cultivars. Most enjoy lots of light and average warmth, and must not be over-watered – just the conditions they will encounter on my shelves. At the RHS Westminster Shows in March and April I came across Pearl Sulman, a specialist whose theatrical displays of pelargoniums have won many awards, I bought 'Lillian Pottinger', a delicate camphor/pine-scented plant with tiny white flowers and small lime green leaves; 'Joy Lucille', a peppermint-scented one with larger deep-cut leaves and white flowers, and a beautiful grey form of the old favourite 'Lady Plymouth' with variegated grey and cream leaves and small pale pink leaves. (Pearl Sulman, 54 Kingsway, Midenhall, Bury St Edmunds, Suffolk IP28 7HR (01638 712297, mail order.) Fibrex Nurseries of Warwickshire (01789 720788) tempted me with the peppermint-scented *P. tomentosum* and its gorgeous sister 'Chocolate Peppermint', which has a dark brown blotch in the centre of the leaf. I also succumbed to the stunningly beautiful *P.* 'Splendide', not strictly scented, but with attractive long grey serrated leaves and two-tone flowers, the top petals of which are red and the bottom palest pink. *P. ovale* x *Tricolor* 'Diana Hull' is similar, but with magenta and pink flowers. These last two are so striking they are in danger of knocking my erstwhile favourite pelargonium, *P. sidoides* (small round, felty grey leaves and tiny deepest magenta flowers) off its pedestal. They are apparently tricky to keep, but the secret is to pot on every other year into fresh John Innes no. 2 compost and to feed weekly when in flower with liquid tomato feed. They give me such a thrill now when I pass them all on the stairs. I shall certainly do my best.

13 May 2001

COUNTRY GARDENER: SPRING IN MY STEP

"Do you go down to the garden with a torch when you arrive at night?" a friend asked me, soon after we'd begun renting this second home by the sea. He'd bought a weekend cottage in Norfolk several years ago and suspected that I, like him, would be bursting with excitement to see what the garden had been up to during my absence. For the first few months at least I was able to inform him I could contain myself till morning – though he didn't see me rushing out at dawn in my nightie. But I cracked during the flurry of sunny days in April, when spring seemed as if it might *finally* be arriving. Last night I didn't even bother to unpack our bags from the car; I grabbed the big torch from the boot and headed straight for the garden. There was a bright, unclouded half moon, and once my eyes had become accustomed to its light, I found I didn't need the extra beams from the torch.

At this time of year so much can happen in just two or three days. On warm afternoons I swear I can see buds swelling before my eyes. I hate the idea of missing a moment, and often wish I could pull on the reins to make it all last a little longer. This time, we'd been away in London for longer than usual, and I was anxious, as well as curious, about my young plants. I needn't have worried. The tiny lettuce seedlings I'd planted out last week had turned into healthy little plants, and the mizuna that went out two weeks ago was ready for picking. The newly sown rocket was a rash of green in one raised bed, with a reddish haze of giant red mustard leaves in a strip beside it. And over in the large cold frame, a sowing of 'mixed salad leaves' (sold as 'Saladisi') was beginning to come through.

The next morning's early sunshine revealed other changes. The row of little fruit trees that frame the entrance to the garden had burst into blossom, the pear pure white and the cherry slightly pink-tinged, while the back hedge was covered in crimson ribes flowers and buzzing with bees. In my little cutting garden, three lines of tulips were almost ready to open, with pointy nectaroscordum buds and posies of bright blue forget-me-nots between the rows. The first batch of autumn-sown sweetpeas, planted out against a "see-through wall" of bamboo canes and sheep fencing, were just coming into bud. My landlord, a keen vegetable gardener, who disapproves of flowers as "frivolous things with one-track minds", will think it scandalous. Better draw his attention to the broad beans, which are about to set their first pods, and to the many different varieties of pea which are pushing their pretty young leaves through the soil.

Inside the greenhouse things were even more exciting. Fortnight-old sowings of dill, coriander, leeks and more sweetpeas were all promising, while the seedlings I'd potted on from newspaper plugs into larger pots had grown out of all recognition. The tomatoes were now proper little plants, with several sets of leaves all with that unmistakable tomato shape and smell. And the globe artichokes – purple 'Roman' ones from seed bought in Italy last year – had developed deep serrations in their scrolling silvery leaves. I spent a good hour watering, weeding and wandering about before I realized it was almost ten o'clock and I was still in my nightie and wellies.

People ask if it is hard having two gardens to look after, but I find it's just double the pleasure. Neither garden is too large, so I don't feel overstretched, and because they are very different from one another, I'm never bored. I live in a permanent state of excitement and anticipation as I move between the two places. The London back yard, whose tiny size had become a frustration when it was my only garden, has now come into its own as it needs only minimal care. And the thought of what I might find on my return makes leaving the countryside less of a wrench. This week I found that two of my favourite plants were in flower for the first time: *Euphorbia mellifera*, with its tawny clusters of honey-scented blooms, and the gorgeous, purply-brown bells of the chocolate vine, *Akebia quinata*. What a wonderful treat.

20 May 2001

THE WINDOW-BOX ALLOTMENT

I've always said that no garden is too small to grow a few vegetables, but the other day I met a woman who puts to shame the smallest plot's sole runner bean teepee and tubs of tomatoes. Penelope Bennett is a true urban gardener, and an inspiration to anyone with the tiniest of roof terraces or balconies – or even just a sunny window ledge. A writer in her early sixties, she lives in a first floor flat on a busy road in Chelsea with two cats and several hundred plants. Her west-facing terrace – which was an unpromising patch of asphalt before she decked it over and made the window overlooking it into a french door – measures just 3m (16ft) wide by 1.5m (8ft) deep. But it is home to several fruit trees, including a comice pear, a Victoria plum and a cherry, troughs of year-round 'Perpetual' spinach and herbs and, in summer, all manner of containers spilling over with dwarf beans, tomatoes, "cut-and-come-again" lettuce and oriental salad greens, potatoes, baby beetroot, carrots and parsnips, and even aubergines and cucumbers. An old plastic water tank beside a small pond with a trickling fountain overflows with strawberries and lavender, and she has somehow also found room for a wormery and several other compost-making devices. Scented climbers scramble up the back wall, and in summer the perfume of regale lilies, planted in tubs, wafts in through the windows. It is one of the most productive gardens – regardless of its remarkable size – that I have seen.

All summer long, Ms Bennett hardly has to visit the shops for salads, fruit and vegetables. Yet she insists that self-sufficiency is not her motive – she does it for the sheer joy of sowing, raising and reaping her own produce. "My produce is gathered not in trug-loads but in snippings, clippings and handfuls," she says. "Yes, it is delicious, but all the happy hours spent germinating the seeds, watching and looking after them and then finally picking and eating the finished product, make it even more so." She raises her plants with the protective passion of a mother rearing her young. In spring, her bedroom becomes a "seedling kindergarten", with removable shelves that fit across the window on

permanent brackets to house young plants of basil, lettuce, tomatoes and aubergines till it is warm enough to establish them outside. She likens the "hardening off" process, in which plants raised under cover are gradually acclimatized to the great outdoors, to "putting a baby out in its pram for the first time", and once rushed home from a party because she had forgotten to take her melon seedlings in for the night.

Ms Bennett has recently published a book, *Window-box Allotment* (Ebury, £9.99) which is packed full of entertaining and idiosyncratic advice about growing your own food on such a small scale. As well as probably the best step-by-step seed sowing guide ever (she knows from experience that the books take a degree of knowledge for granted and don't tell beginners what they really need to know), there are tips on growing your own potatoes in 8in pots (just enough for a single large portion), raising unusual crops such as oyster mushrooms, wheatgrass for juicing and saffron crocuses, making a pond in a plastic container, establishing a wormery and sprouting seeds for salads in jars on a windowsill. There are seasonal guides to what to sow, and simple monthly recipes using home-grown produce – her "Chinese sweet-sour radish salad" is delicious.

The book is suffused with Ms Bennett's humour and joie-de-vivre. She manages to make a day-by-day journal of a runner bean seed germinating as gripping as a passage from *Bridget Jones's Diary*, and her series of 'Wormery Disasters" had me in fits. Somehow, she converts you to her cause and you end up thinking that, when it comes to gardens, small is the *only* size to have. "Window-box gardening is quite different from garden gardening," she writes. "Because such gardening is intimate, you are more a part of it and can observe more of what is going on... the cucumber slowly fattening and lengthening, the alpine strawberry flower mysteriously turning into fruit. Although it is small, the enjoyment, interest and enrichment it produces are great." As I leave, she is still warming to her theme. "Oh I'd *hate* to have a big garden!" she cries. "You don't need much to look at, if you really know how to look."

27 May 2001

COUNTRY GARDENER: A FRONT GARDEN FULL OF FLOWERS

Last October I cleared and re-planted the area around the path in my new seaside front garden, and it is now looking rather pretty. In the pale pinks and lemons of faded summer dresses, aquilegias are pushing up among a carpet of silvery lamb's ears (*Stachys byzantina*) and the violets along the path's edge have given way to little lamiums. Further back, the white and spotted foxgloves I put in are doing well – I'm particularly interested in the progress of 'Pam's Choice', a variety that can top 3m (10ft). And amid clouds of crimson valerian – a classic seaside plant – my groups of different alliums are coming into bloom. The largest, *Allium giganteum*, are dotted around at the back; they can reach 1.8m (6ft) tall, with a flower-head 15cm (6in) across, and their rosettes of strappy grey-green leaves need space. In front of them are *A. hollandicum* 'Purple Sensation' (similar to *A. giganteum* but only half as tall), *A. cristophii* with its spheres of star-shaped lilac flowers and *A. karataviense*, a white-flowering variety which I love most for its broad grey-green leaves, tinged with purple.

My favourite, though no longer known by the old names of *Allium bulgaricum* and *A. siculum*, are the nectaroscordums. The spear-like leaves appear early, leading me to search in vain for signs of flowers, but just when I think the bulbs are coming up blind, long thin buds are released from sheaths within the leaves themselves – 5cm (2in) long and pointed like fairytale minarets. Slowly, the buds swell, to open in May in cascades of small bell-shaped flowers – sometimes I have to remove the papery casing which gets caught in the flower-head. Suspended above stems that can reach 1m (3ft) or more, these are some of the most elegant flowers around – they sway gently in the breeze and look wonderful floating above mounds of lower-growing plants. If you can bear to pick them – and if you have enough (they self-seed rapidly if allowed) – they also make wonderful cut flowers in a tall glass vase. In his splendidly opinionated *Garden Flowers* (Cassell, £30), Christopher Lloyd sneers at nectaroscordums slightly, complaining that, "they do not want to stand up and be counted, but will help to earn you a reputation for good taste." But Beth Chatto delights in them, planting the two subtly different forms in drifts in her famous Gravel Garden at Elmstead Market in Essex. "In *Nectaroscordum siculum* subsp. *bulgaricum,*" she writes, "the basis is alabaster cream, heavily overlaid with plum, producing from a distance a curiously beautiful brownish-pink shade. *N. bulgaricum* has much less plum, its petals striped alternately in plum, cream and green creating a paler effect." I couldn't better her descriptions.

The other area where I've made progress is by the front fence. Both for privacy and to provide some colour along the boundary, which is overlooked by hikers and dog walkers at weekends, I've planted lots of sweetpeas, sun-flowers, globe artichokes and hollyhocks, all raised from seed in the greenhouse. Taps, a local character who sometimes helps me with heavy gardening, dug a long trench the length of the paling fence, and I planted the seedlings out quite close together. I hope they'll make a good display. My landlord, with his disapproval of purely ornamental plants, is of course doubtful about my devoting my efforts to flowers at the expense of the much more worthy vegetables. "I see you've been doing some weeding," he said to me the other morning, as I walked past the pottery with an armful of fresh-cut tulips.

And I must get down to some serious weeding if I'm ever to make anything of the rest of the front garden. I'll need to thin some of the self-sown trees and sumac bushes, and attack the dense tangle of couch grass, St John's wort and brambles which make up my ground cover. The main problem, however, are the two huge leyland cypresses, which block out two of our windows and obscure the main view from the first floor balcony to the sea. I've been pondering what to do with them – more about which, later.

3 June 2001

COUNTRY GARDENER: RUNNER BEANS RULE OK

Am I the only person in Britain who still likes runner beans? My husband certainly does not care for them – and I have noticed over the years that they are less enthusiastically received by friends than other surplus garden produce. Trendy gardening and cookery writers scorn old-fashioned runners in favour of french beans, which come in desirable colours such as purple and yellow as well as boring old green. But I shall continue to grow both types. French beans are undeniably tasty (and look neater on the plate, should you care about such things) but a mound of bright emerald green runner beans, sliced up small and lightly cooked to preserve that watery crunch is, for me, a real treat. The crucial thing is to pick them while they are still young and tender. Unless you are entering a horticultural show, there is no point in waiting till the pods are 25cm (10in) or more long. Harvest at 10–15cm (4–6in), when any tendency toward stringiness will be avoided and the flavour will be at its freshest and best. The other day I saw a pack of runner beans on sale in a well-known supermarket: they looked like the neglected crop you find on return from two weeks' holiday – dark dull green, at least a foot long, and bulging where the seeds had swelled within the pods. And yet they still bore the proud label: "Picked young for tenderness and flavour". If this is what we're being offered, it's no wonder runner beans are out of favour.

Taste apart, my other main reason for growing runner beans is that I like the look of them. I find it hard to imagine a vegetable garden without its staked rows or teepees of scarlet-flowering beans. Even the most makeshift contraptions cobbled together from old canes and timber off-cuts look jolly on allotments, but with only a little more effort and expense you can have something really smart. Hazel poles look lovely lashed together with stout string, or how about a woven willow wigwam? You can make your own using whippy young willow wands (English Hurdle (01823 698418) sell a kit for £14.10 for a 2m [7ft] support) or buy ready-made ones for £12–15 from garden centres or mail order. This year I've made a simple circle of 12 bamboo canes lashed together at the top and crowned with one of my landlord's hand-thrown terracotta cloches. In an inevitable compromise I've sown half the circle with runner beans (three to a station, to be thinned out to two later on) and half with climbing french beans. The spare four corners of the square bed are devoted to annual herbs such as borage, dill and coriander.

Many of the french beans grown today are dwarf varieties. They are easy to grow and require no staking, but they are not as decorative and are more of a chore to pick. In terms of yield per square foot of ground, you get a better deal from the more old-fashioned climbers – I chose 'Blue Lake' (from the Organic Gardening Catalogue 01932 253666), which has purple pods – though disappointingly, these revert to green when cooked. Other tasty and decorative varieties of climbing bean include 'Burro d'ingenoli' (from Simpsons Seeds 01985 845004) with flat, stringless yellow pods and 'Mantra', an early cropping variety with sweet-flavoured stringless pods (from Thompson & Morgan 01473 688821). Or contact Future Foods (01398 361347), who can always be relied on to come up with something really unusual, for 'Morada' – a French bean with "a gorgeous pinkish dusty colour", according to the fascinating catalogue, or – apparently excellent for flavour – the runner bean 'Rateski V', from the former Yugoslavia.

French and runner bean seeds sulk and rot if they linger in chilly soil. In a fit of optimism inspired by two solid days of sunshine, I sowed my beans outside a few weeks ago. A week of cold and wet naturally followed, but the beans have started to surface and a few are beginning to twine up their canes. I was chancing it a little, but the soil in my small raised beds tends to warm up and dry out earlier than the open ground. You can raise these beans in pots or plugs under cover to gain a head start, but the young plants will have to be hardened off in cold frames before planting out, to avoid a check in growth. Far simpler to sow seed now, straight into the ground – but be sure to protect from slugs. A second sowing can be made in late June or July to keep supplies coming till October – provided you're confident that you, and everyone else, won't be sick of them by then....

10 June 2001

COUNTRY GARDENER: TO FELL OR NOT TO FELL?

I was pondering the other week about the two large leyland cypress trees in our new front garden by the sea. As summer sets in, we are increasingly frustrated by their gloomy presence – although they are on the north side of the house, one of the trees is fewer than 1.8m (6ft) from a study window and they almost completely obscure our view of the sea. My landlord, who remembers them as smallish bushes when he moved here 18 years ago, is quite happy for us to cut them down. This seems a radical move, especially since I hate the idea of felling a tree. But a leyland cypress is not just any old tree. Widely used and abused as fast-growing specimen and hedging plants, they have become the scourge of sensitive gardeners everywhere. My friend Alice had neighbours she'd never met knocking on her door to congratulate her when she got rid of one that dominated her front garden in north London. Left to its own devices a leyland cypress can top 15m (50ft) in just

20 years – the reason ours have only managed a paltry 12m (40ft) is that the soil in our front garden is almost pure shingle. I've only ever seen one leyland cypress that looked good in its setting: it was at Westonbirt Arboretum in Gloucestershire. A majestic 33m (110ft) tree with a great forked trunk that had been planted seventy years ago, it looked splendid in a woodland glade, towering above the surrounding maples and larches. Translated to a small suburban – or sunny seaside – garden, however, the tree's silhouette looks bulky and out of place.

I have been considering our options. Rather than chop down both trees straight away, I've decided to start by pruning out the lower branches on one of them. Raising the canopy in this way will let in more light and air, and help us to imagine what the space would be like if the entire tree should go. The effect can be dramatic. I've seen it done to good effect in a garden designed by James Fraser in south London, where he pruned the branches to leave a bare telegraph-pole trunk with just a small cloud-like canopy at the top. The result looked surprisingly good – not like a leyland cypress at all but, according to Mr Fraser, remarkably similar to the tea tree (*Melaleuca alternifolia*) of his native New Zealand. He recommends working in careful stages (well after the bird-nesting season is over, of course) to allow you to assess the ultimate shape of the tree and ensure that any upper branches which may have been resting on lower growth will have adequate support.

If we do end up felling the other tree, I'm reluctant to remove the remaining stump. This can be a difficult and time-consuming operation, involving disturbing the earth for many yards around the tree and/or dissolving the wood with noxious chemicals – and there are other, more creative ways of dealing with tree stumps. I've seen them carved into wonderful sculptures: a totem pole, where all the children in the family carved and painted their own fantasy face – and a figure doing a handstand among the bluebells. Or what about using the stump as the support for a table? I'm tempted to do this with ours, as that part of the garden gets good morning sun and would be a nice place to drink a cup of coffee, while admiring the sea view. You'd need to treat the stump with something to avoid it rotting and attracting honey fungus – a proprietary solution of ammonium sulphamate is what most books recommend, but this would destroy a lot else beside the fungus. Armillatox, another potent preparation, is said to be effective against honey fungus but, according to the Tree Advice Trust, whose excellent Tree Helpline (09065 161147) offers expert advice on tree care, planting, felling, etc, there would still be a chance that the fungus might attack, and spread up to 9m (27ft) around the trunk. If your garden contains prized plants within that area, the Trust recommends removing the trunk.

Large trees should really be tackled by a tree surgeon (telephone the Arboricultural Association on 01794 368717 for a list of approved contractors) and you should check with your local authority that the tree in question is not subject to a Tree Preservation Order or conservation area regulations. In a conservation area, even the most lowly self-seeded sycamore may be protected if its trunk measures more than 7.5cm (3in) in diameter at 1.5m (5ft) above ground level, and penalties of up to £20,000 can be incurred. Even if you have permission, cutting down a mature tree can cost several hundred pounds, depending on its size, where you live, access to the site, etc. But one of our neighbours has just offered to fell our tree for free. He's a blacksmith with long hair and pagan leanings, who has made it his personal crusade to rid the world of upstart conifers and re-instate our native oaks and other species. This kind and unexpected offer has made my mind up for me. Well, it seems rather rude to refuse.

17 June 2001

COUNTRY GARDENER: AN UNTIMELY HOLIDAY

It is hard to leave a garden when it's in full summer sail. A wedding in Chicago at the end of May meant we had to leave the country at one of the best and busiest times for gardeners. As we were travelling so far, we decided to make a holiday of it, with a week in California and a few days in New York at the end. All great fun, but I couldn't help fretting about our garden by the sea. I haven't been away at this time of year since I began gar-dening in earnest seven years ago. Like many keen gardeners, I prefer to wait until winter to head for the sun, when the garden has relinquished its hold on my time and energies. To my mind, there is simply too much going on at home in May and June. Who would *choose* to miss the tulips, the cow parsley, the alliums and first roses? And who would run the risk of all their newly sown seeds and young plants dying of under-watering or neglect?

My landlord has very kindly offered to keep an eye on things while we are away. He is by far the best person for the job – not only does he come by to use the pottery in the garden every morning, he is also the person who made the garden in the first place, so he knows all its ways: that the different sizes of raised beds dry out at different rates; that a window at the far end of the greenhouse needs opening on warm days; that the little pots of seedlings on tables will need extra attention. In return, he gets to pick all my exotic let-tuces to put in the bags of mixed salad leaves (usually grown in his own polytunnel half a mile away) that he sells to the local shop. It seems a fair deal, and I'm very grateful. Now my only remaining worry is that the garden won't live up to his exacting standards.

My landlord is a very tidy person. His pottery workshop is always immac-ulate, with every tool in its place and the thrown pots in serried ranks waiting to be fired. He has even managed to make a polytunnel – not the most picturesque of structures – look beautiful. I don't know the secret of how he transforms his claggy clay soil into the finest crumbly tilth for sowing, but I intend to learn. And I think he must use a peg and line to measure out his rows of seedlings – either that or he relies on a very good eye. The place is a picture of neat productivity, with plants graded in height from the broad beans at the back, which are pushing the 2.4m (8ft) ceiling, through the french beans and tomatoes to the patchwork of different lettuces by the door. There is never a weed to be seen. The polytunnel has become my landlord's leafy outdoor sitting room – there is an armchair in it, and a desk – and I can picture him at the end of the day, patrolling the tiled paths with a glass of his elderflower wine in his hand, eyes peeled for any weeds that dare to show their faces.

My own style of gardening is slightly more relaxed – it has to be, what with all the whizzing up and down the motorway to our house and garden in London. I try to keep on top of the weeds, but unless they are about to seed, they are not my main priority – there always seems to be something else to do. I was determined, however, to leave the garden in a state that would impress my landlord. I had been so encouraged by his words of praise for the greenhouse after I'd washed it from top to bottom that I have kept it uncharacteristically tidy ever since – partly as I know it's his habit to pop in while we're away to see what's going on. So in the build-up to our departure, I spent several long sunny days outside, weeding each of the raised beds in turn, and getting all my remaining salad and vegetable seedlings into the ground. It was happy and pleasant work, with the sun on my back and one of the robins that have nested in an old teapot in the hedge never far from my side. A garden composed of raised beds is like a book with short chapters – it's easy to feel you're making progress.

I planted out four courgette plants – with a few nasturtiums and poached-egg-plants (*Limnanthes douglasii*), to attract beneficial insects – in between. I sowed a square of dwarf french beans, and filled the gaps among my climbing beans with young plants from the farm shop. (Many of the seeds I sowed a few weeks back did not germinate, in spite of the warm weather, and I fear I may have set them too deep – there is a huge variation between the temperature of the first couple of inches of soil and that further down, and bean seeds rot if they remain too cold and damp.) I sowed more salad leaves and radishes, and planted out artichokes, sweetcorn, strawberries, sunflowers and more sweet-peas. In the greenhouse, I sowed more basil and morning glories, and transferred all the tomato plants to their large terracotta pots along the wall. By the time I had finished, the garden was bristling with well-groomed good health. As for me, I needed my holiday.

1 July 2001

CALIFORNIA DREAMING

"California is a Garden of Eden, a paradise to live in or see," goes the old Woody Guthrie song and, after a week exploring the coast between Los

Angeles and San Francisco, I have to agree. For several centuries, America's south-west coast has attracted migrants from all over the world, lured by its year-round sunshine, dramatic mountain scenery, the promise of gold or, more latterly, fame and fortune in the film industry. Many of the incomers have made gardens and it is fascinating to see the ways in which settlers from so many different cultures have responded to the area.

The cities we visited were far greener than I'd expected – especially Los Angeles, which I'd imagined to be a high-rise hell-hole chock-a-block with hideous celebrity mansions. True, parts of the city are undeniably tacky, but they are redeemed by the colourful exotic plants that seem to spring up everywhere. The beaches are fringed not only by palm trees but by spongy bright green grass, and day lilies and agapanthus are planted in swathes by the roadside. Boulevards and avenues are lined with lilac-flowered jacaranda trees, and the central reservations overflow with bronze phormiums and blazing Californian poppies (*Eschscholzia californica*). High in the canyons, clumps of fuzzy mauve *Pennisetum* grasses frame fabulous views of the distant hazy city far below.

With no risk of frost, tender succulents, pelargoniums and daturas can be planted in the ground and left to grow to impressive jungly sizes. I was surprised to see so many roses, but was assured that they love the west-coast weather – they bloom well in the sunshine and escape the blackspot and mildew that beset them in England. The perpetual sunshine isn't only enjoyed by the plants. Many Californians take the notion of the outdoor room to its ultimate conclusion and live outside all year long.

All of the Californian gardens I visited contained ideas for outside living that could be adapted for use in this country. Many have elements in their design that are stylistic leftovers from the Spanish missions (large fortress-type churches) that were dotted up and down the coast under colonial rule. Courtyards are popular, with high walls to provide shelter from sun and wind as well as the wild frontier. Some gardens incorporate a simple loggia, under which a table and chairs might be set; others are designed around the space beneath a large tree canopy. Most include water in a central pool or fountain to cool and humidify the air.

One of the most attractive gardens I saw was in Santa Monica and belongs to Nancy Goslee Power, a landscape designer. Inspired by visits to South America and Morocco, she has used unexpected colour on the plaster walls of her 11 x 11m (35 x 35ft) garden, including an ochre yellow copied from a building in Brazil and a piercing cobalt blue, while a thick strip around the overlooking windows is picked out in olive green. Seating, shelving and a simple fireplace have been built into the walls, with low ledges for candles and other ornaments. The centrepiece of the garden is a raised pool, divided into two. One half is thick with waterlilies, while the other, cool and still by day, doubles up as a Jacuzzi at night. Permanent plantings include palms and bamboos, while decorative pots – containing chartreuse nicotiana, delphiniums the same blue as the wall and pink stargazer lilies – are replanted and moved around at will.

Another LA garden had a round stone-edged pool in the shade of a Chinese elm, and an exuberant formal potager, where strings of coloured glass beads were strung among the flowers and vegetables to ward off birds and create kaleidoscopic light effects. But by far the most eccentric was the fantasy landscape high up in Beverly Hills created by the late theatre and set designer Tony Duquette and his wife, Elizabeth. Here, a small and unpromising site in a steep dark valley has been transformed into a surreal Shangri-La, complete with hanging walkways, pinnacled temples and candlelit dining pavilions. The effect, though suitably opulent and ornate from a distance, is pleasingly makeshift close-to. Sculptures turn out to be made from salvage and scrap: what appear to be gilded pillars turn out to be posts clad in sari fabric and yachting varnish. Hanging pots of spider plants and trailing succulents are strung throughout like leafy chandeliers. The place seems the perfect expression of the larger-than-life ambition and kooky eccentricity that characterizes this part of California.

8 July 2001

COUNTRY GARDENER: THE ROVER'S RETURN

Two weeks is a long time in gardening at this time of the year. And the fortnight we were in America turned out to be gloriously hot back home, with no rain at all. The seaside vegetable garden, still at an embryonic stage when I left at the end of a dull May, was like a jungle on our return. After a few false starts, spring had finally sprung in my absence, and the place felt like a different country. It was if I'd arrived at a party when the best part of the evening was already over. But that's the price you pay if you go away in spring.

Spring is a process. It's about daily changes rather than an end result. Over a period of hours, days, weeks, you *watch* the buds unfold, the flowers open, the seeds germinate and put out their first leaves. The thrill is in the watching and witnessing. The end result, if you need one, is summer. When I left, this whole process was just beginning, and weeks of cold and grey weather meant it was taking its time. But the sudden heat was like a loosening of the reins. The neat, weeded plot I'd left behind me, with all the new seedlings planted out in rows, was almost unrecognizable.

The first impression, as I opened the door into the garden, was of deep green leafiness. When I'd left, the small cherry trees that flank the entrance were still hanging on to their blossom; now they were in full leaf, with one or two small fruits among the branches. Behind them, all the climbing beans showed signs of flower buds. Broad beans and peas had fine pods swelling, and spindly salad seedlings had filled out into plump butterhead lettuces and crêpey Cos. Inside the greenhouse – suddenly shady due to the plate-sized leaves of the grapevine rampaging the length of its roof – the foot-high tomato plants I'd set out in pots had turned into triffids, some nudging the ceiling and already in flower. And the pots of morning glory seedlings, just showing their first set of leaves two weeks ago, now made mad scribbly tangles, the tiny tendrils snaking in every direction. The best surprise was the sweetpeas I'd raised from seed and planted out in April. Just showing their first buds when I left, they were ablaze with mauve, white, pink, purple and indigo blooms, which I picked straight away and arranged in fragrant bunches around the house.

All credit for the garden surviving in the heat must go to my landlord and his artist friend, who obviously had to do a lot more than "the occasional watering" I'd envisaged, while still having to tend their own two acre plot. If they hadn't tied in the tomatoes to their canes and begun pinching out the side shoots, the plants would have bowed over, and put all their energy into excess leaves instead of flowers. And the plants in the conservatory must have demanded frequent attention. I felt rather sheepish as I handed over the small presents I'd brought them from America.

Still, it was fantastic to be back and I set straight to work. Rather than use the sprinklers, I took a hand hose and went to each of the raised beds in turn, slowly reacquainting myself and taking full note of all the changes as the water poured into the parched soil. Of course, there were bound to be casualties. The rocket, red mustard, sorrel and mizuna had all bolted in the heat and were waving flag-like flowers 0.9–1.2m (3–4ft) high. The parsley bed, sown by my landlord but my pride and joy since our arrival, was also threatening to flower. A bed of perpetual spinach had gone to seed, and so had the splendid 'Jacob's Coat' chard, its improbably pink, yellow and scarlet stems swollen to the size of my wrist. I consoled myself with the thought that since they were survivors from my landlord's crop of last summer, they've had a good innings. In the hope they might sprout anew after watering, I cut back the parsley, sorrel and spinach, but pulled up the rocket, mustard, mizuna and chard.

It seemed the most awful waste. To cut my losses, I saved the spinach and salad leaves for my landlord's sheep and arranged the budding parsley stalks – not unlike cow parsley – in a big vase on the table in the yard. The woody chard stalks and tattered leaves went on the compost heap. I went inside to make some sorrel soup. And then it rained for three whole hours.

15 July 2001

COUNTRY GARDENER: FIRST OF THE SUMMER WINE

I returned from London recently to find our outside kitchen (an enclosed yard with butler's sink, cooker, fridge and covered eating area) in a flurry of activity. Three huge grey plastic water butts had been installed at the foot of the stairs, along with a Heath Robinson contraption made from a copper cylinder with hose attachments. Crates of lemons and sacks of sugar were propped against the wall, and a small blackboard was marked up as a chart with chalked calculations. A 1m (3ft) high duvet of freshly picked elderflowers was piled on the kitchen table and the air was thick with their sweet musty scent. My landlord's annual elderflower wine production had begun.

Each year he makes more than 370 litres/100 gallons of the stuff – a wonderfully heady brew that smells of hedgerows in summer and is stronger than you think. As all his equipment is still here, we'd agreed that he should make the wine in our yard, and I'd promised to help pick the flowers – the reward was to be a share of the end product. Towards the end of May, a daily inspection of the local elder bushes commenced. You didn't want to pick too early, my landlord explained, when there were still too many unopened buds. But you didn't want to leave it till the blooms had begun to turn brown. The weather had to be right, too – ideally a sunny dry morning after a couple of dull days. The middle of next week, he reckoned; then the weekend; then the week after that. As it turned out, I was away in Wales when the most auspicious day dawned. By the time I turned up, my landlord and his friend had been picking for four hours, starting at 8am, and were embarking on the time-consuming task of trimming the stalks off the flower heads. I pulled up a chair to join in, and we gradually worked our way through the fluffy white mountain, tossing the snipped blossoms into one box and the discarded stalks into another.

Then the alchemy began. Into each of the grey butts went 7kg (16.5lb) of flowers, 27kg (60lb) of brewing sugar and the juice of a hundred lemons, along with 85 litres/22.5 gallons of water, heated to boiling point in the copper cylinder by a roaring gas burner. My landlord kept check of the amounts on his blackboard while his friend and I snipped on. By the end of the afternoon the butts were full of the pungent mixture, the flower heads floating on the surface like dumplings in a stew.

Bright and early the next morning, my landlord arrived to test the temperature and add further ingredients to each bin. In went 140g (5oz) tannin, 60g (2¼oz) of Pectalase (a clearing agent), seven packets of yeast, 100g (3½oz) of yeast nutrient, and a 5 litre/9 pint tin of white wine concentrate. Contrary to what I'd believed, the flowers don't ferment, they only add flavour; you need fruit sugars to make wine.

Fermentation was soon underway, filling the yard with the unmistakeable smell of elderflowers and alcohol. My landlord appears daily to inspect and stir, before rushing back to his smallholding to finish his planting out and sowing. The air locks on the lids have begun to bubble – the butts feel like a distinct life force that is inhabiting the yard. After ten days, when the most fervent action should be over, my landlord will strain the wine off the 'must' or solids, and transfer the liquid to 26 litre/7 gallon fermenters. Then it'll be a matter of watching and listening and the occasional tasting until the wine is ready – this usually takes five to six weeks at between 20–30 °C (68–86°F). The wine is then 'racked' – separated from its sediment – and sterilization tablets added – before syphoning off into demi-johns for drinking as required. Any initial cloudiness should soon clear, but there are many folk remedies for this problem, including fuller's earth and isinglass (from the bladder of a fish). My landlord swears by a fluid made from rotten bananas. He starts drinking the wine straight away, and very good it is too.

The secret of his success, he says, is that every year he makes the same mistake. Because he makes the wine in 150 litre/40 gallon drums, he calculates the ingredients for three times 150 litres/40 gallons of wine. But when the ingredients are all in place there's room for only 95 litres/25 gallons or so of water. The end result is a much stronger than intended – but who's complaining? There's an undeniably heady magic in the process – all the quivering promise of a sunny June morning distilled into bottles to drink through the year ahead.

The above recipe for elderflower wine is adapted from CJ Berry's *First Steps in Winemaking* (Argus Books/Amateur Winemaker).

5 August 2001

COUNTRY GARDENER: KNOWING YOUR ONIONS

I'm not normally one for trying unusual vegetables simply for the sake of it, but this year I have been enjoying quite a few new discoveries. Some are crops inherited from my landlord – the Witloof chicory, for instance. I enjoyed forcing the roots under buckets over the winter for the crunchy blanched chicons, and am now entranced by the clear blue flowers on the couple of plants I left behind. My landlord also introduced me to land cress, a good alternative to watercress which, as the name suggests, does not need to grow in water. Though it runs to seed fast in summer, it is useful for providing a bit of bite for winter salads when there is little else in the garden to pull. Sow in a shady spot in September and you'll be picking through to spring. (The Organic Gardening Catalogue 01932 253666 has seeds for both the above.) Red orach (*Atriplex hortensis* var *rubra*), a colourful relative of spinach, which can top1.8m (6ft) tall, is another welcome addition to our salad bowl. Its bright magenta leaves are as good as flowers for enlivening a green salad, and they look wonderful in the garden, too, with the late afternoon sun shining through them. The plants self-seed readily, so unless you want it all over your garden, it's best to pull the plants in late summer. (Red orach seed is available from Terre des Semences, 01227 731815).

There were also bunching onions in the garden when I arrived – they resemble a spring onion but grow in clumps like shallots. Pull a clump to slice and eat in salads, put one of the onions back in the ground, and a new clump will form in a matter of weeks. Seed for bunching onions is available from Suffolk Herbs (01376 572456), and can be sown under cover till September for an early spring crop. They also offer 'Purplette', a decorative purple-skinned variety, 'Red bunching crimson forest', which has bright red stems, and 'Ishikura', a bulbless Japanese variety useful in Eastern cooking, whose long white stems can be lengthened by earthing up.

It's easy to confuse the bunching onion with the Welsh or leaf onion; indeed, in some books and catalogues their names are interchangeable. As I understand it, the leaf onion is more like a large member of the chive family – a perennial which produces clumps of hollow leaves up to 0.6m (2ft) tall and attractive white flowers. It's an excellent evergreen substitute for chives and spring onions in soups and salads, and seed is available in both red and white varieties from Suffolk Herbs. Strangest of all my new onion discoveries has to be the tree onion. This unlikely vegetable matures much as a normal onion until it flowers, when a cluster of tiny bulbs starts forming *on top* of the stem. Eventually the stem arcs down so the bulbs can take root. I haven't yet tried eating it, as I'm so enjoying the plant, which is guaranteed to attract attention in the garden. Seed is hard to come by, but Future Foods (01398 361347), a great source for unusual vegetables, have it in their autumn catalogue.

I can't say I've been as enamoured of the other new vegetable I tried this year. The asparagus pea may sound appetizing and appealing, but I have found it a waste of space. Even if I'm around to pick the crinkly winged pods before they reach an inch long, their taste, to me, is neither like asparagus nor peas, and not worth bothering with again. Leave the pods to grow a fraction of an inch larger and they become so fibrous to be inedible. Thank goodness for a great crop of 'Lincoln', 'Langedyks Pale Flowering' and 'Carlin' peas from seed given to me on a visit to Gilbert White's house in Selborne earlier this year.

New vegetables I'd like to try next year include scorzonera, a root vegetable similar to salsify but with black roots (a bolt-resistant variety from Suffolk Herbs) and 'Red Russian' kale, which can be sown now to over-winter (from Future Foods). I was also most taken by a friend's 'Salad Blue' potatoes – as much for the taste as much as the startling purply-blue flesh. It's an old variety newly available in plantlet form (order by February) from The Organic Gardening Catalogue.

12 August 2001

TOWN AND COUNTRY

What makes a plant right – or wrong – for a particular place? I normally subscribe to Beth Chatto's philosophy that you should choose plants that would grow naturally in your soil type and garden environment, but what about when style is at stake? I was pondering this issue as I replanted three of the 0.6m (2ft) high 'long tom' pots in my vegetable garden in the country. Till recently, they'd been filled with an elegant mix of regale lilies and *Cerinthe major* 'Purpurascens' – two of my favourite plants. Somehow, though the peacock-blue bracts and violet flowers of the cerinthes are the perfect complement for the fragrant lilies, the combination never looked right here. It would have been wonderful at home in my London garden, where that style and colour scheme prevails. Here among the courgettes and cornflowers it looked awkward and overdone – like a London guest arriving in full evening dress for a barn dance. When the flowers had faded I replaced the dead flowers with 'Tumbler' tomatoes and different types of thyme.

My black and greenish-white tulips had a similarly jarring effect earlier in the year. Our landlord was extremely rude about them – to him it was sacrilege that someone should waste good vegetable-growing space on flowers, and he made no secret of the fact he found them hideous. I was too stubborn to admit it at the time, but he did have a point. The tulips' glossy, sophisticated profiles *did* look out of place – both in my little cutting patch and, what's more, inside the house. These rooms have never looked more beautiful than when I decked them out in enormous bunches of cow parsley, gathered in armfuls from the hedgerows, for my birthday party in June. Fashionably coloured tulips, which look so chic in a jug on the table in London or in pots on the deck outside, just can't hack it in the country with the Rayburn and "old lady" armchairs.

I'm not saying there are "town plants" and "country plants", as it's all a matter of style and taste. But this vegetable garden certainly looks best with wilder, less manicured flowers, such as nasturtiums, borage, purple loosestrife and limnanthes – which are all, incidentally, either edible or useful in companion planting. The sweetpeas look fantastic – even the trendy dark purples like 'Midnight', 'Maudie' and 'Matucana' – but then they look good in London, too. And so do the hollyhocks, which one might almost consider the quintessential country cottage flower. My urban front garden is full of stunning spires of *Alcea rosea* 'Nigra', its blooms like shiny black silk rosettes. Is it the exotic colour that stops them looking countrified?

As it happens I need not concern myself with such questions for much longer. Our year's tenancy here will soon be up, and we shall be moving out in the autumn. The landlord has kindly allowed us an extra month, so we can see the cycle of the garden through, but it will be hard to leave this lovely place. It's odd how quickly nostalgia can kick in – the journey down here is already bathed in a sad sort of longing. My husband and I are dealing with the prospect of leaving in very different ways. We're a bit like two people reacting to the news that a love affair which has been going on for quite some time has got to end. My husband, sensible soul that he is, is taking the "don't get involved" line and is already distancing himself emotionally from the place. I, on the other hand, being a foolish romantic, have deemed that if I only have a couple of months left to be in love, I am going to be truly, madly and deeply in love for as long as I can. I am spending as much time as I can down here, swimming in the sea every morning, taking the dog on long walks and visiting local gardens and nurseries.

Yesterday I made a trip to the excellent Madrona Nursery in Bethersden, Kent – a favourite haunt of the late Derek Jarman for plants for his Dungeness garden and still worthy of his accolade, "the most charming nursery in England", even after a terrible arson attack (01233 820100 for mail order catalogue.) I succumbed to a clump of echinacea, its bold daisy flowers just opening in shades of pink and greenish cream. I bought them for our London garden but ended up planting them here, in the vegetable garden, where they look lovely amid clouds of bronze fennel. Well, it *is* a traditional healing plant, used to make herbal cold cures – and I've got to leave something for the garden to remember me by, haven't I? That and a hundred self-seeded cerinthes, of course....

NEIGHBOURLY GARDENS

Like walking a puppy or wearing a silly hat, planting flowers on the street is a sure-fire way to help the basic British urge for friendliness overcome our famous reserve. I've just been out watering our London front garden, and was touched by the number of people who stopped to say how much they enjoy it. Mothers hold their young children up to see the sunflowers, and one man even told me he makes a long detour on his trip to the tube just so he can walk past. It is always good to know your garden is giving pleasure, but it seems even more apt this year, when our prolonged absences at our house by the sea mean we're hardly ever here to enjoy it ourselves. Thriving on neglect, the plot has been flowering away for months and shows no sign of stopping – a mad mass of tall purple flowers amid silver and bronze foliage.

Since I created the raised brick bed and purple picket fence last spring, the permanent planting has begun to bush out nicely. I'm particularly pleased with the silvery lambs' ears (*Stachys byzantina*), which have spread obligingly over a third of the bed, their woolly spires of mauve flowers rising from a velvety-soft mat of leaves. Their colour is echoed by the dwarf *Senecio compactus*, whose white-edged grey leaves have a felty white underside. Like many colour-sensitive gardeners, I initially pruned off the yellow daisy-like flowers, worried lest they clash with my mauves and dark purples. But they responded to that treatment by putting out a new flush, bolder and brighter than before, so I have relented and let them have their heads. After all, a splash of bright colour can actually enhance the other, more subtle hues. Among the latter are a large hebe with purplish young shoots and spires of mauve flowers (I think it might be 'Purple Queen' but it has long since lost its label) and some lovely dark-leaved heucheras (*H. micrantha* 'Palace Purple' and *H. chlorantha* 'Chocolate Ruffles'), which are adding to the ground cover.

Within this pemanent structure, the idea was to play with striking flowering plants and annuals to provide some height and interest. I've certainly got height – a cardoon I planted as a young slip from one of my old allotment plants now towers at 3.6m (12ft), its thistle-like blooms in electric violet attracting attention from passers-by. Next to it, seven or so dark 'Velvet Queen' sunflowers, their petals and centres a deep chocolate brown, have been opening in succession from mid July, and dark maroon and lilac sweetpeas look good scrambling up a folding hazel pyramid on the other side of the gate – I'm glad I wasn't deterred by my husband's fears that the frame might be vandalized. Star of the show, though, are all my black hollyhocks (*Alcea rosea* 'Nigra'). Raised from seed in spring 2000, they flowered into autumn last year, and have now come back as many more smaller plants, which are preferable to the five or six giants whose enormous leaves shaded out other plants. There must be at least twenty of them in the 4.8m (16ft) bed, and I love to watch as their tight balls of buds burst open. Hollyhocks are prone to rust, so I've had to remove some of the lower leaves, but their nakedness is hidden by a haze of bronze fennel. I'm hoping that the *Verbena bonariensis* in a large tub nearby will self seed into the bed to work its magic next year. I love the way its tiny violet flowers, held on 1.8m (6ft) square-sectioned stems, create a translucent purple haze in the breeze.

I'm in London a couple of days a week at the most, so I seldom have time to do more than water the front garden. It takes well over half an hour to lug a watering can back and forth from the tap outside the back door, but I'm always in the garden for longer, chatting to my neighbours, many of whom I met because of this little garden, and now count as friends. Back gardens are our attempts at urban privacy, but front gardens are more extrovert, made for giving to the street. If you have a front garden that could do with brightening up, just try it and see. You could start at the garden centres, which are still selling plants in full bloom – you might even get them cheap as the decks are cleared for autumn. Crocosmias look wonderful now, from the blazing scarlet 'Lucifer' through orange to pale lemon, and come back year after year. Or try the pineapple lily, *Eucomis bicolor*, whose maroon-edged greenish flowers cluster to form a sort of elongated pineapple below a topknot of spiky leaves. It doesn't matter what you plant in your front garden – but I'd say, the bigger and brighter the better. The important thing is to plant something. You won't be the only one who enjoys it.

26 August 2001

KEEPING A FEW HENS IN YOUR GARDEN

Having grown up on a farm where I had my very own bantams to look after, I have longed to keep chickens again. Apart from the appeal of a constant supply of freshly laid organic eggs, I enjoy the gently bustling presence of hens in a garden (and the manure comes in handy, too). I was reminded afresh of the mutual benefits of chicken-keeping when I visited Francine Raymond at her house in rural Suffolk. A real chicken aficionado, Francine has built up a small business that revolves around chicken-keeping on a domestic scale, and her pretty garden is a show-case for how it can best be done.

If you want hens just for the pleasure of them, and for eggs for your family, she suggests you start with two or three, keep them in a hen house and allow them as much access to the garden as possible. For Francine, having the birds with her in the garden is almost as important as the eggs they supply. "I actually garden with my hens," she says, in her little book *Keeping a Few Hens in Your Garden* (£5.35). "They follow me round, darting between my feet for insects as I turn the soil with my trowel – they are excellent pest controllers and first-class weed seed devourers. Of course, I'm less keen on the craters left by their dust baths and damaged plants, but over the years I've developed strategies to minimize the problems and make the most of the benefits."

In late spring, Francine confines the hens to their large run, to protect new growth in her vegetable and flower garden, and tips all waste plant material and lawn mowings in for them to scratch through for food. They are let out once more in July, by which time the garden is less prone to damage. Vulnerable plants are protected with pretty wire or wicker cloches, and in the vegetable garden, low permanent cages or cloches cover new sowings and salad beds. Mulching with mushroom compost also seems to deter the hens from doing damage.

In autumn and winter, the chickens come into their own, foraging for pests and finishing off the old crops, and the manure they leave on the beds breaks down in time for spring. Chicken manure is rich in nitrogen and phosphates, but too strong to use neat. It can be layered into the compost pile as an activator, or combined with sulphate or muriate of potash to make a balanced plant food. In the autumn the droppings can be mixed with dead leaves to make a good soil conditioner (spread fallen leaves on muddy patches in the run, or use them as bedding, after which they will compost down quickly).

Chickens, of course, are decorative additions to the garden in themselves – especially the pure breeds such as Orpingtons, Rhode Island Reds and Brahmas, with their fine feathery trousers. Hen houses and runs can also be made into attractive features – Francine's looks more like a summerhouse with painted doors and window shutters. You could build one in the style of your garden.

I'm not sure how chickens would take a beach hut on the shingle down here by the sea. But on reflection, I don't think our peripatetic lifestyle – a few days in London, the rest of the week here – is geared to keeping hens. You need to be there every day to let them out of their coop in the morning and see them in safe and sound at the end of the day. Earlier this summer, when my landlord forgot about his chickens for one single night, a fox got in and reduced his brood of eight to four. But I've heard of an intriguing invention which could help me one day. The garden designer Arne Maynard divides his time between a flat in London and his garden in the Lincolnshire Fens, but still manages to keep chickens, thanks to a clever light-sensitive coop. As dawn breaks, the door opens automatically to let the chickens out into their run, which contains enough food and water for several days. At dusk, the cockerel leads the hens back inside in plenty of time for the door to close – again automatically – when it gets dark. A fail-safe device on a timer doubles up in case the first system fails. This ingenious idea is the brainchild of Maynard's partner, who I think ought to patent it. There must be other frustrated chicken-lovers besides me out there who could put it to good use.

The Kitchen Garden, Church Lane, Troston, Bury St Edmunds, Suffolk, www.kitchen-garden-hens.co.uk. Open Fridays and Saturdays 10am–6pm, May to October, teas, plants and chicken accessories on sale. Please phone 01359 268322 before visiting, and send an sae for mail order catalogue.

3 September 2001

COUNTRY GARDENER: TOO MUCH OF A GOOD THING

Normally I'm only too eager to get out into the garden on arriving at our house by the sea from London. But for the last month or so I've almost been dreading what I might find. Not *more* runner beans! The fridge is already bristling with last week's offerings. How can several more pounds have been conjured up in my absence? How can those courgettes, the size of my little finger when I last saw them, have become ten-inch torpedos in just a few days? And *what* am I going to do with all those ripe tomatoes? Of course, I'm not really complaining – but at this time of year, crops can seem relentlessly prolific. Compared to the last few summers, this has been a good year for growing – and the produce from this little garden has more than lived up to expectations. It's just hard to know what to do with it all.

Of course, you can give it away – and I hardly go anywhere these days without a bag of courgettes and a bunch of sweetpeas tucked under my arm. You can slice it up and freeze it – but I have never been a fan of watery out-of-season veg. Much better, I think, to cook up the excess as chutneys, soups and pasta sauces, which can be bottled up or frozen and used when needed. The best recipes are invariably the simplest. With courgettes, I simply chop them into quarter-inch cubes – you can use a food processor for this, but it doesn't take long if you slice them long-ways first – and fry them, with a crushed clove of garlic per two courgettes, for two or three minutes in a little olive oil. Add enough water *just* to cover and simmer till the courgettes are soft enough to mash with an old-fashioned potato masher. This is one of my favourite pasta sauces, topped with lots of parmesan cheese. I learned it when I was an au pair in Italy many years ago – it may sound boringly simple, but trust me, it's delicious.

Runner beans are more problematic. My husband does not care for them at the best of times, and quite rightly refuses to eat any that are more than five inches long. But I never could bear to throw good food away, so the big bulging monsters hiding in the foliage get sliced up small and turned into chutney. 900kg (2lb) of runner beans, 450kg (1lb) of green tomatoes, six onions, six apples, 4 tablespoons of minced raisins, 2 tablespoons of stem ginger, 2 table-spoons of honey, 1.1 litres/2 pints of cider vinegar, salt and pepper, all boiled up together, makes six good-sized jars. This year I have another use for runner beans, thanks to Mrs Ager of Hertfordshire, who kindly sent me this Hungar-

ian recipe for runner bean soup. Fry a small chopped onion in 28g (1oz) of butter till soft. Add 28g (1oz) of plain flour and cook, stirring constantly, for three minutes. Stir in the liquor from boiling a joint of hock or gammon, together with 225–450g (0.5–1lb) cooked sliced runner beans, bring to boiling point and season with pepper and lemon juice. To serve, add a swirl of double cream and a little chopped dill or mint. At last – a runner bean recipe my husband likes – and it freezes well, too.

There are some great tomato recipes in *The Tomato Book* published by Simpson's Seeds, from whom I order seeds and young tomato plants every year. The first half of the book is devoted to useful growing tips, while the second is packed with recipes from friends, customers and admirers – the chutneys and salsas are particularly tasty. This little book is excellent value at £5 including post and packing, from Simpsons Seeds, The Walled Garden Nursery, Horningsham, Warminster, Wilts BA12 7NQ (01985 845 004). Actually, if my tomato plants in the greenhouse had cropped even half as well as those outside, I'd have chutney and salsa coming out of my ears. But, for all my excitement at having a greenhouse for the first time, the indoor plants have failed to set many fruit. I wonder if the grape vine trained across the ceiling has made it too dark and uninviting for pollinating insects? When I rang Simpsons to ask their opinion, Mr Simpson thought insufficient ventilation might be the culprit. He also suggested putting a bowl of honey mixed with hot water near the plants to attract more insects. My landlord, however, lays the blame squarely on my having planted so many flowers in the garden. Why, he says, should bees bother to go inside the greenhouse, when I've given them what they wanted right outside the door?

16 September 2001

SWEETPEA SECRETS

This has been a good year for sweetpeas in our garden by the sea. I picked my first bunch in early June, from plants sown in the greenhouse last October, and am still picking a couple of bunches a week from a mid-February sowing. Their fabulous scent and colours – white, pink, crimson and maroon, and every shade of mauve from the palest lilac to blackberry ripple to indigo – have been a delight all summer long. The stems are getting much shorter now, so the vases are becoming smaller and smaller, but they still look pretty in the bath-room or on bedside tables. Earlier in the year I had beautiful long stems of ten inches or more topped by lovely large blooms – the sort of flowers I'd only ever seen in florist's shops or flower shows. I put it down to the good drainage here, and the addition of a couple of sacks of well-rotted manure about a month before I planted the seedlings out in April.

There's a lot of mystique surrounding the cultivation of sweetpeas. Fanat-ics used to dig beds to "the depth of your bottom waistcoat button" as old gardening lore had it, but for anyone over five feet tall this would have been a most laborious task. A certain amount of mumbo-jumbo decreed what, apart from manure, was added to the soil, and I've heard of many strange ingredients including soot (which is said to make the colours more intense) and the corpse of a cat or sheep. Books still recommend double-digging (turning over the soil to two spits deep, while transferring the soil from the bottom layer to the top), and adding well-rotted manure and a slow-release fertilizer to the lower spit. As regards the longest stems and largest flowers, there is still a surprising amount of secrecy among growers. My landlord, whose aversion to flowers does not preclude a bed of sweetpeas and corn-flowers for selling on a roadside stand, made the mistake of asking a fellow flower-seller how he managed to get his stems so long. "Do you think I'd tell *you?*" was the short answer.

At a lunch at this year's Chelsea Flower Show, I sat next to a man who trials sweetpeas for the RHS at Wisley. During most of my main course and the whole of pudding he regaled me in great detail with the secrets of his sweetpea success. So here, for my landlord and any readers getting ready to order their seeds for sowing from next month, are the distilled fruits of his wisdom. Serious sweetpea growers swear by the cordon method, which is akin to that used for training tomatoes. A double row running north to south is best, in order to expose the plants evenly to sunlight. At each end of the row, place a stout 1.8m (6ft) post with an 46cm (18in) cross piece tacked to the top, and stretch two parallel wires along the row between the cross pieces. A line of 2.1m (7ft) canes should be spaced at 23cm (9in) intervals at a slight incline along each side and secured to the wire with clips or ties. Raise the young plants in individual pots under cover from October to February, pinch out the growing tips at 10cm (4in) high, and harden off in a cold frame before planting out, one seedling per cane. After a couple of weeks, when the plants are well-established, pinch out all but the strongest shoot on each plant (this may not necessarily be the longest) and train this up the cane, tying loosely to the cane at each leaf node. Side shoots and tendrils should be removed as the plant grows. When flower stems form, the keenest growers remove any with fewer than four buds.

Then comes the peculiar bit. When the plants reach the top of the canes, they should be carefully untied, one at a time, and laid flat along the ground. The growing tip should then be attached to a new cane further down the row – or even doubled back to one in the opposite row – so it reaches about 1ft up a cane. It will continue to grow up to the top of its new cane, producing large flowers on good long stems. This process, which is known as layering, can be repeated again and again until the total growth tops 6–7m (20–24ft). Laying the plants down gives them a new lease of life, as the sap no longer has to be pumped seven feet high to produce blooms. The inferior flowers on short stems that usually abound at the end of season are thus avoided, and prime blooms on super-long stems ensured all summer long.

30 September 2001

SMALL BULBS IN SMALL POTS

For once, I got my bulb order off in good time this year, instead of leaving it till the last minute. Next spring is now sitting in our London hallway – two large boxes filled with brown paper bags containing tulips, alliums, hyacinths, narcissi and a few other little extras for good measure. The crucial thing now is to get around to planting them. I opened the bags straight away, to give the bulbs some air and prevent mould setting in, but the best place for them by far is under the soil. Bulbs start to degenerate pretty quickly unless they are kept in optimum conditions, which ideally means an electric fan and a constant temperature of about 17°C (63°F) (9°C/48°F for prepared bulbs for early flowering indoors). Wet weather is my excuse for delaying planting in open ground, but the bulbs destined for smaller pots can be done inside right now.

I had some success last year with small bulbs in small pots – the sort of flowers that tend to get lost in an open border, and benefit from being brought up to eye level. Species tulips did unexpectedly well, and I have ordered more for this year. These delicate pointed flowers, just three or four inches off the ground, bloom wild on the hillsides of Turkey and Greece, and are as far removed from their big, bold, cultivated cousins as is a dog rose from a hybrid tea. Some, like *Tulipa turkestanica* and *T. tarda* are multi-flowered, with several dainty heads nodding on each stem. Others come in stunning colour combinations, such as *T. humilis* 'Persian Pearl', with its silver-backed purple petals and golden throat, or 'Little Beauty', whose petals move from lilac to rose to deepest blue, with moss green at the centre. (All available from Bloms Bulbs 01234 709099.) Some of these bulbs may seem expensive, at £5 or £6 for ten, but they provide much more lasting pleasure than a bunch of flowers at the same price, Plant them five or ten to a pot, at twice the depth of the bulb, feed once or twice when the flower buds start to show; they should come up year after year. Though they can be naturalized in the garden. I like them on a desk or dining table, where I can watch the little flowers open and close with the light. Remember they'll last longer in a coolish room.

Grape hyacinths are good to have in the house in March, when there's little to pick inside, and growing them in pots helps keep their colonizing tendencies under control. Last year I grew *Muscari azureum* and *M.armeniacum* 'Heavenly Blue' in little pots of ten as Christmas presents. The crucial thing to remember, as with most indoor bulbs, is to keep them outside until the flower buds are showing. Bring them in to the warm too soon and you'll have lots of long leaves but little in the way of blooms.

Dwarf iris are wonderful in pots, where their stunning flowers can be appreciated at every stage of their unfurling. One of my favourites is 'Katharine Hodgkin', whose palest grey-blue petals have a rich yellow tongue flecked with deepest maroon. I also love the melancholic green and black *Iris tuberosa* and the gorgeous soft blue and violet *Iris reticulata* 'Springtime'.

I always do lots of 'Paper White' narcissi in glass bowls of pebbles or gravel, and hyacinths in glass forcing jars. These are my salvation in the depths of winter, as their scent fills the house with the promise of spring. Don't make the mistake of planting them all at once – I do a new batch every two or three weeks from October to January, keeping the unused bulbs cool, dark and aerated in an old plastic milk crate in the cellar. This year, in addition to my usual 'White Pearl' hyacinths, I shall be trying 'Blue Star', a stunning variety I saw for the first time while sitting on the panel to judge the 'Best of the Best' spring bulbs for the International Flower Bulb Centre (www.bulb.com for details). To force them into bloom in August, the bulbs being shown had been specially frozen and cultivated in Holland, and it was slightly off-putting to be seeing and smelling a hyacinth at the "wrong" time of year. Even so, its beautiful delphinium blue petals, fading to sky blue near the stalks, and unbelievably heady scent, prompted three out of six judges to put it in first place. In the end, however, *Allium hollandicum* 'Purple Sensation' won on points for its dependability and versatility in the garden. About the only word said against alliums was that they didn't perform in pots, but I begged to differ. I've grown many different alliums successfully in large metal pots outside, including the stately *A. giganteum*, whose blooms can be 15 or 18cm (6 or 7in) wide on top of 1.2m (4ft) stalks. Because of their size, I've never considered alliums for inside, but why not? I'm planting one of the smaller varieties, *A. triquetrum*, which has greenish white flowers on 25cm (10in) triangular stems.

7 October 2001

REVENGE OF THE CACTI

When I was a child, my mother had a "plants' graveyard" outside the kitchen door. The back steps were a repository for plants that were deemed to have had their day: sickly cyclamen, tatty post-Christmas poinsettias, weeping figs with leaf-drop. Even the odd perfectly healthy specimen would

find itself in plant purgatory, awaiting death by frost, its only crime being that my mother didn't like it. I used to think my love of gardening stemmed from an early desire to rescue these poor exiles, but I've been perturbed to discover the same heartless streak in myself.

While tidying up our country garden the other day, I came across a very sorry sight: a terracotta trough containing my husband's dead cactus garden. In happier days, this jaunty little tableau of cacti set in sand sat on top of the television in my husband's bachelor pad, a tin cowboy on wheels trundling through its simulated desert landscape. My long-seated dislike of cacti was, for a time, conquered by its charm. But when we moved in together, the cactus garden came too, and I found myself unwilling to accommodate it on the few sunny windowsills in our new house. The fact that the then-fashionable eastern art of feng shui regarded spiky plants in the home as an invitation to disaster in health, love and finances only fanned the flames. So the cactus garden languished in my husband's basement den, where daylight seldom penetrates the TV haze.

When we de-camped to the south coast a year ago, my husband decided to bring his poor plants for a seaside cure. I think he was hoping I would give them the loving care they needed, trimming off the dead bits and replenishing the soil. But I'm afraid I just left them where they were, and hardly even watered them. Well, cacti are desert plants, aren't they? Eleven months on, I'm now faced with a sight that would make the Cactus Society clamour to put us behind bars. The once-perky *pachycereus* is all suckered in and dried out, while the aptly-named 'Old Man Cactus' (*Cephalocereus senilis*), is slumped over the side of the trough as if he's sunk too much tequila. The only plant showing any signs of life at all is the *opuntia,* nick-named 'Mickey Mouse' after its ear-like protuberances.

I'm certainly not proud of this, but nor am I prepared to take sole responsibility when my husband eyes the trough reproachfully. Most gardeners with any opinions at all have a category of plants that they dislike and simply won't tolerate in their gardens. For some it's carnations, for others variegated foliage, or anything orange. Perversely, perhaps, I adore almost all other succulent plants. I love crassulas, with their fleshy glaucous leaves, and the geometric rosettes of aeoniums and echeverias. I have pots crammed with sempervivums in every shade from acid green to ruby red. And a cherished aloe vera sits on shelves beneath a skylight at the top of the house – I snap off the odd leaf to rub the gel on cuts and bites, and the plant has just sprouted five new offspring.

The other day in a large garden centre, I succumbed to a few more succulents for my skylight shelves: a beautiful silver jade plant (*Crassula arborescens*), its silvery-blue leaves edged with pink; a sugar almond plum (*Pachyphytum oviferum*), which looks exactly as it sounds, a couple of new echeverias and the lovely string of hearts vine, (*Ceropegia woodii*), which trails like a rosary of variegated green and silver hearts. Just for good measure, I threw in a *Crassula ovata* – the money plant beloved of feng shui practitioners. Well, it can't do any harm.... None of these plants is hardy in this climate, of course – they need to be kept on a sunny shelf or in a conservatory in winter. They do like a spell outside in summer, however, and look good grouped on stairs or around entrances, as done by Christopher Lloyd with such flair at Great Dixter.

Feeling bad about spending all this money on myself, I then picked out five or six new cacti for my husband, planning to amass my new succulents on one shelf, and let the cacti and their cowboy reclaim their place in the sun on another. But the cacti had the last laugh. On emptying their trough on the compost heap I felt a painful pricking on my stomach and arms. When I lifted my clothes my entire torso was covered in raised red wheals, which have lasted the best part of two weeks. Revenge of the Cacti? Not for nothing are opuntias known as prickly pears.

14 October 2001

SAVE OUR ORCHARDS

This year, as I've sped through the Kent and Sussex countryside to our rented house by the sea, I've been heartened to notice some recently planted orchards. There are few things as lovely as an old apple orchard; the gnarled old trees with their crabby branches bent this way and that create an atmosphere somewhere between the enveloping quiet of woodland and the ordered abundance of gardens. But many of our lovely old orchards have been grubbed up and destroyed – of the 62,200 hectares of British orchards in 1970, fewer than 22,000 remain today, with Devon and Wiltshire among the counties that have lost more than 90 per cent of their fruit trees. The sight of apple trees just coming into their first proper harvest is therefore a good cause for cheer. Some old orchards have been rescued – bought up by the local authority or by Trusts set up by residents and turned over to community use. And a few new ones are being planted, buoyed up by the small but growing demand for old-fashioned English apples at food fairs and farmers' markets. Perhaps, as too often seems the case, it takes the threat of near-obliteration to make us realize what we have and inspire us to save it.

Regeneration of orchards is by no means confined to the countryside, however. As much, if not more activity is taking place in towns, with the planting of new orchards in parks and schools, under-used allotments and patches of derelict ground. Blondin Community Orchard in Ealing, West London, was created in 1997 on land that was formerly a fruit nursery in the 18th and early 19th century. Named after the Frenchman Charles Blondin, who famously walked a tightrope across the Niagara Falls in 1859 before retiring to Ealing, the new orchard is home to 46 trees planted and cared for by a Friends Group in conjunction with the council. In Brockwell Park in Brixton, south London, where I walk my dog, an old council dump has been transformed into an organic community orchard. It is now in the process of becoming a "Forest Garden", the fruit trees under-planted with currant bushes, perennial vegetables, culinary herbs and edible ground cover. And in Tyneside, Walbottle Community Orchard, planted four years ago, has been integrated into local play schemes and has a programme of visits from primary schools. Inspired by such places, many urban schools are now turning part or all of their tar-mac playgrounds over to orchards.

Many of these new urban orchards will be celebrating Apple Day, an event launched by the arts and environment charity Common Ground in 1990 to celebrate apples and draw attention to some of the varieties we are in danger of losing. (*The Common Ground Book of Orchards*, £18.99, is something of a bible to those interested in preserving orchards. Contact Common Ground, 21 High Street, Shaftesbury, Dorset SP7 8QU, for details.) There is now a nationwide network of Apple Day events in or around the last two weeks of October, with displays of different apple varieties, tastings, cookery demonstrations, games and children's activities. Ring your local council to find out what's on in your area, or check the information on www.commonground.org.uk.

Some of the most spectacular Apple Day celebrations are held every year at Brogdale Horticultural Trust near Faversham in Kent. Home to the National Fruit Collections, Brogdale has the largest collection of fruit trees and plants in the world, including 2,300 different varieties of apple, 550 of pears, 350 of plum, 220 of cherry and 320 varieties of bush fruits, as well as smaller collections of nuts and vines. The enormous orchard is like a living reference library of apple varieties, from modern strains such as 'Katy' (a modern Worcester Pearmain and James Grieve cross) to the ancient 'Decio' variety introduced by the Romans. Guided walking tours around the orchards take place between mid-March and the end of November, and the nursery is one of the best sources of unusual fruit varieties. Brogdale's Apple

Day Celebrations continue from today until 21st October. More than 500 apple varieties, many available to taste and to buy, are on show, and there will be workshops, cookery demonstrations, an apple identification service, and a grand "Apple Jamboree" next weekend. (Brogdale is signposted off the A2 south of Faversham, ring 01795 535286 for details.)

Now is not only the time for celebrating apples, of course, it is also a good time to think about planting them. Even if you're short on space, some excellent varieties are now available on dwarf rootstock for small gardens and containers. It's best to buy from a specialist fruit nursery, where advice on pollination partners will be available. (Few apples are self-pollinating and require the presence of companion trees that flower at the same time, in order to fruit.) Highfield Nurseries in Whitminster, Gloucestershire, is an excellent source of fruit trees and bushes, and will also be holding Apple Day celebrations next weekend (ring 01452 740266 for details and mail order).

28 October 2001

COUNTRY GARDENER: FAREWELL TO THE SEASIDE

The house is full of sunflowers – large smiling suns with speckled brown centres, tawny brown stars with orange velvet petals, and the deep maroon flowers of 'Claret', the darkest variety – arranged in front of doorways and windows, where the low autumn sun shines through the petals, illuminating the different colours. Though I usually have misgivings about picking sunflowers, as they leave such a gap in the garden, this was part of my end of year tidy-up. I have spent the week getting ready to leave our seaside house and head back to London for the winter. Cutting down the sunflowers not only helped me clear the garden; it made the house look bright and cheerful, even if its contents were fast disappearing into packing cases.

It feels sad to be leaving, as we have had such a wonderful year here. But the place will travel with me – not only in my heart, but also in my cooking and gardening back in London. Cuttings and seedlings of plants I have discovered and enjoyed here have been potted up and taken back home – a large pan of land cress (dry land's alternative to watercress), a pretty variegated apple mint, and mats of the pungent creeping Corsican mint. Two large pots of sea kale will make the journey inland, to see if they can survive so far from the sea – well, it's an excuse to buy a splendid terracotta sea-kale forcer from my landlord, the potter. And I've saved seed from my favourite plants and flowers: the lovely purple orach, whose burgundy leaves have enlivened the sweetcorn patch and our salads alike, papery poppies in every shade from crimson to white, love-in-a-mist, red valerian and the delicate purple spires of toadflax.

Between clearing and tidying, I found time to pick and process some of the produce from the garden. The inevitable glut of runner beans became a spicy chutney; tomatoes and garlic were chopped into jars of salsa; black-berries and apples were stewed into a base for a winter's worth of pies and crumbles. While out harvesting, I was struck by the incredible beauty of this time of year. The low slanting sun seems to intensify colour: the scarlet of hawthorn and rose hips, the shiny black of elderberries and brambles, the tawny ochre yellow of leaves on the turn. In the garden, a flame-coloured nasturtium has climbed way up into an elder tree, and the last morning glories are scrambling among the leaves of a sycamore. They look like blue and orange bunting thrown up in a defiant challenge to the frosts: come and get us, if you dare.

As I tidied out the greenhouse, my mind filled with images from this past year: the magic of discovering the place, and arriving for our first weekend; the view from the greenhouse in winter, with shelves of seedlings and pots of spring bulbs lined up against a backdrop of deep snow outside; the first crops of spring creating new patterns in the patchwork of raised beds; chats with my landlord in the pottery; the death of our dog and the arrival of the new puppy; the garden filled with friends and flowers for my birthday on midsummer weekend. It was as if, along with the vegetables, flowers and seed, I was harvesting my own store of memories.

Some people do not like autumn. They find it depressing – an unwelcome herald of the winter to come. True, there is sadness in the sap ebbing away and the dry lifeless rustle of the leaves. But there is a valedictory splendour in the season that I always find uplifting. And in the country, much more than in town, I am aware of the enormous natural bounty of autumn – not only in the garden but in the orchards, fields and hedgerows, too. There are cobnuts on sale in the farm shop, and striped squash and pumpkins piled up around roadside stalls. From my study window, I can see people out picking sloes and blackberries among the woody scrub that borders the shingle fields beyond our garden. There is a peculiar balletic grace to their move-ments as they teeter, on tiptoe, to stretch for the best and biggest fruit, just out of reach. Are we really so very different from the squirrels, gathering up the fruits of a long hot summer to sustain us through the winter? As we pack the car to leave, I know that what I take with me – both physically and emotionally – will keep me going in the months ahead. New life, too, will come from what we leave behind. My last act before I lock the gate will be to throw the wilting sunflowers on the compost heap.

18 November 2001

21ST-CENTURY SELF-SUFFICIENCY

My teenage kicks weren't those of your average south London schoolgirl. While my classmates were listening to the Bay City Rollers and learning to snog boys, I was ploughing my way through John Seymour's "Complete Book of Self-Sufficiency" and dreaming of a smallholding with goats, lambs and chickens. More than twenty years on, the fascination with growing my own food and earning an independent living has remained – and, indeed, has never seemed more relevant than in today's GMO-, recession- and war-ridden times. Yet the image of self-sufficiency is still stuck in the 1970s – either jolly old Tom and Barbara soldiering on with *The Good Life* in Surbiton, or earnest hippies tending scraggy goats and knitting their own yoghurt in the back of beyond.

When a beautiful hand-bound book entitled *My Kind of Self-Sufficiency* arrived on my doorstep a couple of years ago, I was intrigued and delighted to discover a worthy and totally 21st-century alternative. The book's author and self-publisher Phil Rooksby not only has four earrings, two nose rings and a snappy line in hats; he and his wife Maureen also eat lots of chocolate, drink strong coffee and have a good sense of humour to boot. "Very early on, I knew that although we wanted to grow our own organic food, it didn't have to mean being marooned by a mortgage up a hillside in Wales, coping with the rain and pulling the heads off chickens," he writes in his introduction.

The Rooksbys came to self-sufficiency through necessity. Fifteen years ago they bought Midsummer Cottage, a two-up, two-down terraced house in North Yorkshire with a third of an acre of garden – enough to grow a few herbs and vegetables, but not to do it seriously. When the orchard next door came up for sale they bought it, more with a view to scotching future development than growing their own produce. Then Phil lost his job – which he had never liked anyway. "We'd doubled our mortgage and halved our income, all within a fortnight," he remembers. "It began to dawn on us that rather than getting turned down for yet another dead-end office job, it made more sense for me to stay at home." He taught himself carpentry, plumbing, chicken- and bee-keeping, not to mention the finer points of organic fruit and vegetable growing. A decade down the line, the couple was financially far better off, even on a single income. And Phil's self-esteem, buffeted by years of being a square peg in a round hole at work, had recovered to such an extent that he was keen to spread the word. *My Kind of Self-Sufficiency* was written on a friend's old Amstrad, printed on re-cycled paper and hand-bound – all 2,000 copies – with screen-printed calico and raffia.

Having read and enjoyed the book, I went up to meet the Rooksbys in the summer of 1999. I spent a fun and inspiring day in their company, and was extremely impressed by what Phil had achieved in the garden. In contrast to many "grow-your-own" plots, this was an immaculately tidy and stylishly designed garden, with a neat patchwork of raised beds and criss-crossing gravel paths, edged with upturned wine bottles sunk in the soil – "They look lovely in the moonlight after a rainfall with water glinting in their dented bottoms," says Phil. There was a polytunnel with tomatoes, aubergines and even honeydew melons among the brimming marigolds and nasturtiums; a winding covered walk made from living willow woven into patterns overhead; an intriguing irrigation system and no fewer than five ponds. Nearer the house, the original vegetable patch had become an abstract take on a formal garden, where Maureen was growing herbs and cut flowers in amorphous box-edged beds. It was hard to believe that only a few years beforehand the place had been bristling with brambles and every persistent weed in the book.

Phil tackled it little by little, with no overall plan, quick to point out that the physical labour keeps him fit in a far more enjoyable and productive way than running on a treadmill to nowhere in the gym. His growing methods are unorthodox – a self-devised mixture of traditional organic and Biodynamic techniques, which he learned either from books or visits to a local Steiner community farm. But the proof is in the healthy and prolific produce. The couple never shops for fruit and veg – any excess is bottled or frozen, and they finish last year's tomatoes just as the new crop ripens. "We may not have fresh strawberries in winter, but we enjoy looking forward to things like the first sweetcorn," enthuses Phil. "We live with the seasons, which means in winter we go to bed early and sit inside making clothes and Christmas decorations to sell."

Last year, the couple took their dream of self-sufficiency one step further. Maureen left her job, they sold the cottage and drove a customized camper van to Portugal, where they hope to buy a house. Two new books bring their story up to date (see below), and they have plans to experiment with wind and solar power and composting loos. They could never go back to the way things were. "It's that caveman thing," laughs Phil. "If you can provide your own food, fire and shelter, working for someone else seems like slavery. I used to feel guilty about not having a job. Now I know it's the only way to be."

My Kind of Life by Phil Rooksby (£9.75) has useful and entertaining advice on everything from first-time seed-sowing to keeping chickens, bottling fruit and installing a woodburning stove. *The Cook Book* (£5.50), illustrated by Maureen, has simple and delicious recipes for using your home-grown produce. Both would make excellent Christmas presents, and prices include p&p. Email philandmaureen@hotmail.com for details.

CURE-ALL COMFREY

One of the plants that did well during my year's absence from the allotment is Russian comfrey. This is hardly a surprise, as comfrey is something of a horticultural thug and you'd be pressed to get rid of it once it's established. But nor should you want to – in the organic gardener's top ten useful plants, comfrey can have few contenders for prime position. It's the leaves that you want – with their high concentration of potassium to help form healthy vegetables and fruit – but you need them in pretty large quantities to be useful. In fewer than three years, the two tiny root cuttings I begged from a neighbour have colonized one corner of our plot, and somehow managed to run amok in the shade of the oak tree, too. At last, enough comfrey to put to good use.

"Comfrey tea" is perhaps its best-known use in the garden. To make it, loosely fill a large bin or bucket with comfrey leaves and then top up with water. Leave for three or four weeks, during which time it will start to smell quite revolting and you'll be relieved it's the plants that will be drinking it, not you. Dilute the dark brown brew before use – roughly one part solution to 12 parts water as a general rule, but weaker for seedlings and stronger for hungry courgettes and tomatoes later in the season. Don't waste the dregs – the remains can be thrown on the compost heap, where they aid decomposition. The leaves grow back so fast that they'll be ready for a second cutting by the time the bucket's empty.

I learned some more unusual uses for comfrey when I visited Phil and Maureen Rooksby, whose innovative organic garden in North Yorkshire I mentioned last week. A self-taught gardener who has since moved to Portugal, Phil uses an unorthodox mixture of traditional organic and Biodynamic techniques to produce some of the happiest, healthiest fruit and vegetables I've ever seen. He uses chopped comfrey leaves straight from the plant to line potato or runner bean trenches, or to pack around the root ball when transplanting tomato seedlings into the soil. Unchopped leaves can also be used as a mulch around large-stemmed plants such as sweetcorn or taller brassicas like broccoli and brussels sprouts. The rough hairy leaves and stems, placed as a barrier around vulnerable plants, may also act as a deterrent for slugs and snails. The couple even use comfrey on themselves – Phil swears by a poultice of steamed comfrey leaves and flower shoots to heal a gamut of garden injuries, while Maureen says the sticky fragrant sap makes a great natural hair gel.

Comfrey has been used in herbal medicine for hundreds of years. Indeed, its Latin name, *Symphytum,* which derives from the Greek word for "to unite", refers to comfrey's almost magical ability to knit together broken skin and tissue. It's usually the native common comfrey, *Symphytum officinale,* that is used for healing purposes. Russian comfrey (*Symphytum* x *uplandicum*) is the best type for organic gardeners, as it has a much higher potassium content. It is distinguished by its attractive dark bluey-purple flowers (common comfrey has cream or sometimes mauve flowers). *S.* x *uplandicum* 'Bocking 14' is the real caviar of comfreys, with more than double the potassium content of other varieties, and is well worth getting hold of. The Organic Gardening Catalogue (01932 253666 for mail order) often has a good stock of 'Bocking 14' – you can order now, but plants are usually sent out in the spring – and it also offers a booklet, "Comfrey for Gardeners", price 75p. The Beth Chatto Gardens in Elmstead Market, Colchester, Essex (01206 822007) are also a good source of comfrey plants, particularly the more decorative varieties. If you are after something that will look good in the border as well as being useful, try *S.* 'Hidcote Blue' as an attractive weed-proof ground cover between shrubs, or *S. ibericum*, which has burnt-orange buds opening to creamy-yellow flowers and thrives in shade – the catalogue lists eight varieties.

Beg a bit of Russian comfrey from someone who has some now – an offset, or small plantlet formed at the base of the parent plant, is ideal, but even a rough chunk of root should take readily. Be careful where you put it, though. Common comfrey self-seeds like mad, while the smallest section of *S.* x *uplandicum* root can form a new plant. Right next to the compost bin is a good place to plant it. Not only will it be handy for chopping down and adding to the bin to accelerate decomposition – and I shall be doing this now, before the leaves die down for the winter – it also looks good into the bargain, creating an attractive floral screen around the bin all summer long.

2 December 2001

'WEEDLESS GARDENING'

A combination of rain, sloth and ambivalence about being back in London meant I'd delayed our annual autumn digging session at the allotment. But it turned out to be just as well. While I should have been wielding a spade, I was reading a new book that has converted me to the "No-Dig" school of gardening. "Introducing a system of gardening from the top down that protects the soil, eliminates heavy work, and reduces water needs," boasts the cover of *Weedless Gardening* by Lee Reich (Workman, £6.99). The book makes a most convincing claim for giving up digging like a bad habit, and instead relying on an annual covering of mulch, both to keep down weeds and to increase the soil's nutritional, structural and moisture content.

"Nature abhors bare soil, and so should you," declares Reich, an American organic gardener who writes for *The New York Times*. Bare earth, he explains, is vulnerable to erosion by wind and water, compaction beneath pounding feet and rain, and dehydration by the sun, not to mention colonization by weeds. Nature, whether in a prairie meadow or a forest, avoids these problems by building up layers of dead leaves, stems and roots around the plants, and we can emulate nature by spreading an annual layer of anything from bark or wood chippings, seaweed, straw or well-rotted compost on top of the soil's surface.

The advantages of mulching are many. Not only has Reich done away with the back-breaking work of annual digging and double-digging, he has also cut the weeding in his large garden down to just five minutes a week. "An unintended effect of turning over or stirring soil is, essentially, to sow weeds," he says, reminding us that exposure to air and light through digging is exactly what dormant weed seeds need to sprout. Mulchers also become masters of their soil in a way that those of us plagued by alternate rains and droughts in recent years would find seductive. A blanket of mulch protects the soil from the extremes of weather, providing a soft permeable landing for raindrops, so water can sink in slowly rather than puddle or run off, and preventing the soil from drying out in a heatwave. No need to delay spring planting or sowing due to wet or cold soil – seeds can be sown direct, or seedlings nestled into the warmer ground beneath. Nor do you have to wait for the burst of biological activity brought on in the soil by digging in large amounts of organic matter to die down. (Conventional methods advise delaying planting for at least two weeks after digging in compost or manure.)

Rather than being mixed into the soil all at once by digging, the organic matter in mulch rots down slowly at the interface with the soil, or is dragged down piecemeal by earthworms. This not only releases nutrients gradually and in tune with the plants' needs; it has the added benefit of improving drainage. In un-dug soil, the network of miniature tunnels formed by worms and roots, freezing and thawing is left undisturbed, and there is no danger of forming a "plough pan" – the compacted subterranean layer that can form after repeated digging and ploughing to the same depth of soil.

The principle of mulching is by no means new – it has been adopted throughout history, from the ancient Aztecs, who scooped up mud and vegetation from waterways to create their famous "floating" gardens, to the American, Ruth Stout, who mulched her vegetable garden with huge quantities of hay with astounding success in the 1950s. What Lee Reich has done is to incorporate ideas from across the centuries and continents into a fully integrated system, in which the principle of mulching is backed up by minimal soil disturbance (no digging), avoiding soil compaction via a system of raised or sunken beds with paths in between, and drip irrigation, which supplies the optimum amount of water effectively and economically. For first-time gardening in a previously uncultivated area he recommends sprinkling fertilizer over the area to be cleared, stamping on existing weeds or vegetation followed by close-mowing, and then covering with four layers of newspaper to prevent re-growth before spreading 2.5–7.5cm (1–3in) of mulch.

Bark and wood chips, grass clippings, dead leaves, pine needles, seaweed, crushed shells, straw and sawdust can all be used as mulch, according to their availability in your area and suitability for your plants and style of garden. *Weedless Gardening* analyzes the various properties of each kind in a two-page, "Mulch Guide", but for vegetables, and most kinds of intensive flower gardening, nothing can beat home-made garden compost or well-rotted farmyard manure for its combination of balanced nutrients and stucture-improving humus.

With the zeal of the convert, I ordered a ton of two-year-old rotted-down horse manure from an advert in the back of a local magazine. It arrived in a splendid, crumbly, chocolate-brown heap (bagged was double the price). Mulching must be done when the ground is moist, but not too cold and certainly not frozen. We spent one of those gorgeous Indian summer Sundays spreading it on the beds at the allotment, leaving me enough to do the beds back home. Lugging the compost about was hard work, but nothing compared to digging. And it is most satisfying to survey my freshly tended beds, all tidy and tucked up under an earthy brown eiderdown for winter.

9 December 2001

INSTANT INDOOR TOPIARY

This time of year finds me prowling around the garden on the hunt for interesting potted plants to bring inside. With the last of the cut flowers at the allotment gone, and most of the flowering bulbs still to come, the house

needs cheering in the run-up to Christmas. There's no solace at the florist's – white chrysanthemums are funereal; reds and tawny oranges seem too autumnal now, and I refuse on principle to buy daffodils before new year. So it's up to the garden to come up with something decorative to banish the winter blues.

I've already brought the tender plants in, to save them succumbing to frost. A white datura is now sitting in my study window, along with an unruly rose-scented pelargonium, which is taking so well to the indoor life it is threatening to take over the room with its leaves as well as its heavenly scent. But other plants are awarded a spell inside simply because they look nice. That grey-leafed French lavender in a green-glazed pot, for instance, would be lovely by a bedside. And wouldn't that hellebore, just coming into bud, get more admiration on the kitchen table than among a huddle of other pots out on the deck? This is where good-looking containers come into their own – tatty plastic or mouldy terracotta can be slipped inside a cachepot for the plants' indoor sojourn. I don't tend to keep them inside for long. Nor are they subjected to extreme changes in temperature, as I don't believe in over-doing the central heating. If you have the central heating on a lot, it might be an idea to stagger your plants' progress, placing them in a cool unheated room before bringing them into the warm. And make sure their water supply is constant.

What I'm really on the lookout for is plants that can double up as impromptu Christmas decorations. My little bay tree, clipped as a pyramid in a tall cobalt-blue pot, will be transformed once again into a smart miniature Christmas tree for the hall by the simple addition of a swirl of tiny white fairy lights. And it struck me that a trailing ivy, quietly growing around a spiral of wire in a pot in a corner for years, could benefit from the same treatment. I lugged it on to the table on the deck to give it a haircut worthy of its new calling. And as I trimmed the surplus growth to show off its shape, I began to get excited about the possibilities of some instant indoor topiary of my own.

Ivy looks particularly good growing up openwork metal frames. All you need to do is sink the frame, which usually comes with long prongs and a 'U'-shaped base to anchor it, into your chosen pot, fill with compost and plant some attractive ivy varieties around the base, tying in shoots at regular intervals with soft string or ties. The small-leaf varieties look prettiest, with perhaps a variegated one thrown in to add a bit of light and texture. A range of wire shapes, including pyramids, spheres, cones and even animals is available by mail order from Rayment Wirework in Thanet, Kent (01843 821628), and The Romantic Garden Nursery in Swannington, Norfolk (01603 261488), who also sell ready-grown examples if you are too impatient to wait.

Ivy can be planted at any time of year, but winter is best, because the long growing season that follows gives the plants a chance to establish. It's tempting to choose large plants with long stems to get the shape well covered at the outset – and for Christmas, you could do worse than dig up or buy a plant or two with long trailing stems and tie them in. However, you'll achieve a more even and lasting effect by using young plants and keeping the growth trimmed to encourage the development of dense young shoots. Ivy is slow to start, but once it gets going, should cover even quite a large frame within two years. Luckily, these openwork wire shapes are attractive in themselves, even when the foliage is only part-way up – let a few fairy lights do the rest. For more instant cover try winter-flowering jasmine (*Jasminium polyanthum*), which smells as good as it looks. Or for a conservatory, how about the glory lily (*Gloriosa rothschildiana*) with its glamorous, shocking pink spidery flowers?

There's no need to spend a lot of money on frames. Warming to the Blue Peter potential of my theme, I fashioned a six-pointed star on a long stem from wire coat hangers and have planted it with a jasmine, trimming off all the lower growth to create a bare-stemmed standard and training the leaves and flowers around the star itself. Just the smallest string of fairy lights, perhaps, and it will look like a magic wand. When it outgrows the frame in a couple of years, it can be planted back out in the garden. And I think I've just sorted out a few Christmas presents into the bargain.

16 December 2001

A GOOD TIME FOR GARLIC

One of the few vegetables that can be planted now is garlic. Indeed, tradition has it that garlic is set in the soil on the shortest day of the year and harvested on the longest. I try to get mine in the ground a good few weeks earlier, as a longer growing period produces bigger, juicier bulbs. Timing may well be dictated by the workability of your soil – planting will be out of the question if the ground's too hard and cold, and if there is any risk of waterlogging it is better to wait till spring. Garlic is an archetypal Mediterranean vegetable and hates prolonged wet – that said, it is also remarkably tough, and will not only tolerate but even relish a certain amount of cold. One to two months at below 10°C (50°F) is said to ensure a good head of cloves – comforting to know when tufts of young foliage are poking through the snow.

It's almost impossible to have too much garlic if, like me, you enjoy cooking with it. We had a good crop this summer, which I braided into a plait, but we'll be down to the last bulb soon. Garlic stores well, so I'm planting more this year and experimenting with different types. Though it's possible to stick any old cloves from the supermarket in the ground and get a crop, you'll get best results from garlic that has been raised specifically for cultivation. My elephant garlic (from Mr Fothergill's Seeds 01638 552512) has to be seen to be believed – each clove measures up to 3.8cm (1.5in) across and weighs up to 85g (3oz) so goodness knows what the bulbs will look like. It is supposed to have a mild and sweet flavour, and the bulbs can be roasted whole and spread, like a paste, on toast or meat. "Purple Wight" has an attractive violet skin and is best eaten "green", as soon as it is harvested, while "Giant Wight" stores much longer and forms brilliant white bulbs up to 7.5cm (3in) across (both from Mr Fothergill, as before). Simpson's Seeds (01985 845004) also has a good selection, including the pungent, red-skinned Spanish 'Moraluz'. I am also trying "Cristo", the classic French-style garlic with white skin, pinkish cloves and good storage qualities. France, of course, is a great source of garlic, and nothing can compare with the juicy, long-stemmed bulbs I've seen on sale in the Quai des Fleurs in Paris. If you're ever in France it is well worth looking out for some there.

Garlic can, in fact, be planted any time from the autumn till early spring, though later plantings may form small or ill-developed bulbs. If your soil is very wet, start the garlic off in containers in a cold frame or unheated greenhouse, one clove per pot, planting the entire root ball out in spring to avoid disturbing the roots. The crucial thing is to bury it deep enough. Garlic likes to be a couple of inches underground – or, in the case of larger cloves, twice the depth of the clove. I forgot this, as I was planting mine at the same time as shallots and made the mistake of leaving the tips just protruding from the soil, as you do with shallots. After consulting my books on arriving home, I had to dash back to the allotment in the morning to dig them all up and re-plant them. I also lined the bases of the holes with horticultural grit – thus ensuring that, even if the weather does its worst, they won't sit in wet soil.

Garlic can be a useful companion crop. I have found it deters aphids when planted around the base of roses, while in an American trial there were dramatic improvements in crops of tomato plants when garlic was grown in the same bed. (Unfortunately, this pairing had the opposite effect on the garlic, so don't waste your best cloves on this.) There is also evidence that the strong smell of garlic and other members of the onion family keeps carrot fly away, so I have left spaces for rows of carrots between alternate rows of Jersey shallots and garlic. Though garlic is relatively undemanding to grow, it needs regular weeding to cut out competition for nutrients, and may benefit from a feed with a nitrogen-rich fertilizer, such as comfrey liquid or calcified seaweed, in spring. Apart from that, it's just a case of laying back and thinking of gazpacho. And aioli. And *ajo blanco*, the creamy white soup from Andalusia. And guacamole, and garlic bread, and chicken roasted with 40 cloves of garlic....

23 December 2001

A VASE OF WINTER BLOOMS

Many gardeners enjoy the challenge of picking a bunch of garden flowers for the house in the dead of winter. Some of my favourite passages in *Vita Sackville-West's Garden Book* – a great fireside read for this time of year – describe her "prowling round through the drizzle with the knife and secateurs" in search of an unseasonal posy, or "tuzzy-muzzy" as she calls it. In late November she manages to gather a bunch containing scented *Viburnum* x *bodnantense* and *Viburnum fragrans*, some sprigs of fragrant *Daphne retusa* and a few stray roses, along with lemon-scented verbena, ivy-leaf geraniums, cyclamen, gentians, polyanthus and *Abutilon megapotamicum* still defying the frost – "not a bad little bunch from out-of-doors", she concludes. By December, she is down to just a few flowers – the trusty viburnums, witch-hazel, hellebores and the winter-flowering cherry *Prunus* x *subhirtella* 'Autumnalis'.

It is something of a gardening tradition to pick a posy for the table on Christmas morning, and it would make interesting reading to compare these from year to year. This winter, with global warming and an extended Indian summer, many of us – particularly those who benefit from the added shelter of an urban microclimate – might be able to muster a festive bunch of flowers that might far surpass (in quantity if not in quality) those harvested at Sissinghurst in the Forties and Fifties. In the sheltered walled garden of our local park the other day I noted countless roses, polyanthus, evening primrose, fuchsias, malvas, the odd cranesbill geranium and snapdragon and even a swelling oriental poppy bud as well as more seasonal viburnums, chrysanthemums, hebes and sprays of yellow mahonia.

My own little garden supports a rather less impressive tally, relying as it does on evergreens in winter, but the few flowers stand out all the better for the contrast. There's a welcome flush of flowers on the *Clematis cirrhosa* var. *balearica* around the front door. This has to be one of my favourite winter-flowering plants – 'Freckles' has similar creamy bell-shaped blooms, also flecked with wine-red spots, but not its dark, deep-cut foliage. A little bunch of the nodding blooms sits on my desk as I write – they only last a day or two inside, but it is lovely to be able to gaze into their spotted faces rather than rush past them on my way in and out in the cold.

Also in fine fettle is the winter-flowering cherry. I could only ever have one or two small trees in a garden this size and though there were many potential competitors I am glad I chose this. Its pink-tinged white flowers look beautiful on the bare branches, and glow like little fairy lights against the ivy-clad wall. The flowers were late appearing this year, but the gorgeous golden foliage made patterns and pools of light on the newly mulched soil when it finally fell from the tree. It will now go on blooming till new leaves open in spring. If the tree were bigger, I would cut large sprays to bring inside, but I have to content myself with a couple of twigs in a Japanese vase.

It's my dream one day to have such an abundance of flowering trees and bushes that I can gather huge fragrant armfuls to arrange in jugs through-out the house all year. One thing I'd include in this fantasy garden would be wintersweet (*Chimonanthus praecox*), another shrub that produces its flowers on bare branches. Some find the small, waxy flowers unremarkable, but the real point is the heady scent, which will fill a room in seconds. The trick with wintersweet is to plant it where the low winter sun can shine right through it, making the cream and maroon flowers glow like church candles. It really *is* unremarkable for the rest of the year, so partner it with another deciduous shrub that comes into its own in spring.

Witch hazel is another winter bloomer that looks good in a vase – the spidery flowers, like shreds of yellow silk on the bare branches – are a star-tling sight in the garden, and some fine unusual specimens can be seen in the RHS Gardens at Wisley. Bright yellow Chinese witch hazel, *Hamamelis mollis,* is the variety most commonly grown, but there are also the rusty orange flowers of *H.* x *intermedia* 'Jelena', the coppery reds of *H. japonica*

'Rubra Superba' and the cream flowers and stunning autumn foliage of *H. vernalis* 'Sandra'. Witch hazel has the advantage of flowering from a very early age, so there's not that wearisome wait before you can start picking. The flowers last a good ten days in water, especially if you bring them in while still in bud, and the smell is delicious.

Finally, what better winter offering for the house than long wands of pussy willow (*Salix caprea*) in a tall glass vase? In the absence of any to cut, I bought a large bundle from New Covent Garden Flower Market to divide among friends. The soft silver-white buds on black stems are not only beautiful; they contain the promise of spring.

2002

TIPS FROM THE TOP

In this job, a new year means a new round of garden visits to look forward to and another set of gardeners to meet. Last year, commissions for this magazine took me from sunbaked Barbados and Beverly Hills through snowstorms in the Scottish Highlands to the depths of Dorset, north Norfolk and London's East End. I was lucky enough to meet world-famous experts such as Beth Chatto and Piet Oudolf – and even the Queen's own head gardener at Balmoral – and to benefit from their specialized knowledge and years of experience. I always come away from interviews with scribbled notes of new ideas and varieties to try. These don't always make it into the finished articles, so I'm starting this gardening year with a selection of hot tips from the gardeners I've encountered over the past 12 months, and making it my new year's resolution to put them into practice.

The year began in style in Barbados, where Todd Longstaffe-Gowan has been creating new gardens around Fustic House. He recommends the Indian sandpaper vine (*Petrea volubilis*) as a handsome substitute for the more common bougainvillea in a conservatory. It is easily raised from seed and can grow to 9m (30ft) high, sending out racemes of beautiful lilac-blue flowers all year round – those in warmer climes can enjoy it outside. Closer to home, Longstaffe-Gowan's own garden in Stepney, East London, makes use of empty oyster, crab and scallop shells as an attractive mulch around the bases of plants in pots. A more conventional mulch of leaf-mould is what Gavin Smith, head gardener at Abbots Ripton Hall in Huntingdon, swears by. Every autumn he gathers up all the leaves in the garden – mostly oak and elm, which rot down well – and leaves them in bays for a year before spreading a layer of the resulting rich mould all over the beds. As well as improving the heavy clay soil, the mulch keeps weeds down and water in – and what's more, it doesn't cost a penny.

Sometimes the smallest details can affect the entire atmosphere of a garden. Among the many subtle touches via which the designer Arne Maynard merges a new country garden with the surrounding landscape is to lay a narrow strip of grass down the centre of a gravel drive. "It dresses it down to look like a cart track," he explains, adding that the poor well-drained soil encourages wild flowers and should cut out any need for mowing (which would spoil the rural effect). Integrating local materials can have a similar effect, however unconventional their means of arrival. High on the south Devon cliffs, Naila Green made an impromptu mosaic from the pebbles her pet labrador retrieved from the beach – an idea I'd also seen at Bryan's Ground in Herefordshire, where David Wheeler and Simon Dorrell have filled the compartments in a formal parterre with sun-bleached sticks brought back by their dogs from walks.

Those who garden in extreme conditions have useful advice to pass on. In the Highlands of Scotland, where killing frosts can come in July, Balmoral's head gardener Andrew Simmons has found the lettuce 'Frillice' stands up well to extremes of temperature, resisting both late frost damage and bolting to produce beautiful crisp leaves well into the autumn. Well, if it's good enough for the Royal table.... Harsh salt winds can be a problem on the coast, where I visited Susan Campbell's garden on the shores of the Solent. She gets great results with annuals by sowing and establishing them under cover, and then setting out the sturdy young plants behind a slightly higher border perennial such as lavender, which acts as a windbreak. And in her famous gravel garden in Essex, where irrigation is banned in an experiment in drought-proof gardening, Beth Chatto finds that spreading 15cm (6in) of baled hay around the bases of trees and large shrubs keeps the soil beneath moist and cool all summer.

As our greatest living plantswoman, it was no surprise that Beth Chatto also introduced me to some beautiful new plants. I was particularly taken by her favourite euphorbia, *E. myrsinites*, whose articulated fronds of grey-green leaves sprawl around the foreground of her plantings, interspersed with creeping thymes and small spring bulbs. Another famous plantsperson, the Dutch nurseryman and designer Piet Oudolf, introduced me to the magical ornamental grass, *Calamagrostis* x *acutiflora* 'Karl Foerster', one of the restricted palette of plants he has used to such effect in his design for Bury Court in Surrey. Its stiff vertical stems form a shimmering translucent screen in autumn and winter, allowing glimpses of other plants through the bleached haze and throwing dramatic shadows on the ground.

If I had to choose, my favourite garden of last year would be Sticky Wicket near Dorchester, where Pam Lewis has created what must be the most beautiful wildlife garden in the country. A tried-and-tested expert at the tricky business of establishing wildflower meadows, Mrs Lewis recommends sowing yellow rattle to get rid of the coarse grasses that crowd out the more desirable flowers. A semi-parasite, yellow rattle feeds off the grass roots and should gradually help increase the ratio of wildflowers to grasses. Make a visit to Sticky Wicket one of your new year's resolutions – it's open from June to September on Thursdays only, 10.30am–8pm (01300 345476). And happy gardening to you all!

13 January 2002

BORLOTTI BEANS FROM ITALY

Whenever I'm in Italy, I find it hard to resist buying vegetable seed. The packets sold there under the names of Franchi or Bavicchi are not only ten times larger than those on sale back home, where it is not uncommon to find a miserly 10 or 20 tiny seeds in a £2 packet. They are also, like so many things Italian, beautifully designed – emblazoned with big bright photographs and striking graphics. Buying seed for things I need a lot of – basil, flat-leaf parsley and rocket, for instance – makes good economic sense, and it is also possible to pick up local or unusual varieties that are hard to track down over here. On a recent autumn holiday in Umbria I was pleased to find a good mixture of "cut-and-come-again" salad leaves that includes chicory, endive, several types of lettuce and herbs, and wild rocket, whose delicate, deeply-indented leaves are less likely to become riddled with flea beetle holes than the more common salad rocket. But I was most happy with the box of borlotti beans – a real bargain at just over £2 for a good 450g (1lb) of beans to share among friends.

A friend who used to live in Italy had told me borlotti beans were well worth growing over here. With their red-streaked pods and spotted beans, borlotti are a classic ingredient in many classic Italian dishes. For the gardener, they have the desirable attribute of being harvestable at three distinct stages. Picked while small and still green, they can be steamed or boiled whole like a french or runner bean. But if you wait until the pods are ripe, stiff and mottled crimson and white, the pods can be split and the beans eaten fresh – boiled for 30 minutes and simply dressed in extra virgin olive oil and flat-leaf parsley as they do in Tuscany, or to make the famous Venetian dish, *pasta e fagioli*.

Fresh borlotti beans are sold in their pods in markets all over Italy, but can be hard to get hold of over here. The River Cafe cook books recommend them for several mouthwatering recipes, and suggest using frozen beans. But how much better to be able to harvest them fresh yourself. They last on the plant for several weeks at this stage, after which the pods start to harden and eventually turn black. It is this last stage for which my friend so values his borlottis. He has to take his holidays in August when his children are off school, and has grown resigned to finding his vegetables dried to a frazzle when he gets home. Unlike the others, however, the borlotti beans are still usable. They should all be harvested before the first frosts and laid on trays for a few days to dry out completely before storing in tins or jars. They can then be used throughout the winter in hearty soups.

Borlotti beans are cultivated like runner or climbing french beans, and are just as easy to grow. Until recently, the only variety available as seed in the UK was the colourfully named 'Lingua di Fuoco' – which translates as 'tongue of fire' – from the Organic Gardening Catalogue (01932 253666). But the excellent Seeds of Italy brochure (0208 930 2516) lists three varieties, including 'Lamon', the gourmet's choice for *pasta e fagioli*. Seeds of Italy is a godsend for those who fancy growing the ingredients for Italian cooking but don't often get to Italy. Set up two years ago by Giani-Piero Franchi, a direct decendent of Giovanni Franchi, who started his seed business in 1783 selling from a horsedrawn cart, the company imports more than 380 varieties of Franchi seeds, including courgettes, pumpkins and cardoons, as well as 15 types of tomato and a wide range of flowers. Giani-Piero found he was being asked by so many people to bring back basil, rocket and other seed from his frequent family visits that he decided to launch the company here. The excellent mail order catalogue, which is illustrated with pictures of the smart and colourful packets, contains useful growing tips and recipes for using varieties such as *cima di rape* (turnip tops), yellow cornetti beans, and the black Tuscan kale *cavolo nero*. Seeds are also sold in garden centres and (in a stroke of marketing genius) at delicatessens, where people popping in for sun-dried tomatoes and pesto are proving keen to grow their own.

So successful has Seeds of Italy become that other seed companies have followed suit. Mr Fothergill's 2002 catalogue (01638 552512) includes a new "Med Veg" range, with the ridged 'Romanesco' courgettes favoured by the smartest cooks, a round violet aubergine and the attractively ringed 'Tonda di Chioggia' beetroot among its thirty-strong listing. Some might doubt that Mediterranean varieties would thrive in our colder and wetter climate. But Italy isn't just the hot south. The north of the country has winters longer and colder than our own – in fact, Britain has a longer growing season – and all the varieties imported by the companies above have been selected to be suitable for growing in the UK. So there's no excuse not to get sowing – and cooking – in the year ahead.

Seeds of Italy, 260 West Hendon Broadway, London NW9 6BE, ring 0208 930 2516 ; www.seedsofitaly.com

27 January 2002

A LITTLE LIGHT PRUNING

Pruning is one of the few jobs that can be done in the garden in the depths of winter, when the ground is too cold and hard to work. I spent a chilly afternoon at the allotment tending to my fruit bushes, which have been left to their own devices since we constructed and planted the fruit cage a couple of years ago. Currants and gooseberries can be left for two or three years, but it's good to get the secateurs to them before the plants grow too unwieldy. Any time between fruiting and late winter is fine. Blackcurrants fruit most freely on growth formed the previous summer – easy to spot as it is smooth and pale brown as opposed to the older, shaggy grey bark. The aim of pruning is to remove the less productive older wood in favour of strong new shoots. Once the plant is three years old, up to a third of the oldest wood can be pruned out close to soil level, while two-year-old wood with plenty of side-shoots can be left. You can always tell a blackcurrant from a red or white currant by the smell of the leaves. Even in the dead of winter, with just a smattering of small pinkish buds on the bare branches, the scent of black-currants hung in the air while I worked.

Red and white currants require slightly different treatment. Rather than fruiting directly from the main stems, the clusters of currants form at the base of young lateral shoots. Whether grown as bushes or cordons, plants are pruned to encourage short, stubby fruiting shoots known as spurs. Prune the main branches by up to a half each year and reduce all side shoots to two or three buds. Keep the centre of the bush open by removing any shoots that are growing inwards, and cut out entirely any new shoots that are less than 10cm (4in) from the ground. My red and white currants have been fruiting since the first year, but next summer, their third, should be their best yet. The crop increases annually to reach a peak after five years or so, and a well-managed bush could last between 20 and 30 years, so it's worth taking good care of them.

Gooseberries are "spur-pruned" like red and white currants, though the side shoots are shortened to three or four buds instead of two. To encourage air flow and prevent disease, remove excessive growth in the centre of the bush, including any branches growing inwards or crossing over other growth. A more upright habit can be achieved by pushing in four canes around the base of each bush, about 30cm (1ft) from the main stem, and tying them loosely with string at about 46cm (18in) high. Once the shape is established, the canes can be removed. Start looking for signs of mildew and aphids in early spring.

The most productive of our fruit plants so far have been the raspberry canes, particularly the autumn-fruiting varieties, which kept on cropping till the end of October. From just ten original canes, we can pick a large bowl-full or more a week – but it's my opinion that you can never have too many raspberries, so I'm adding another ten canes brought from the seaside garden I looked after last year, including a pretty golden-fruiting variety given to me by a friend. Summer-fruiting raspberries need just the tips of the canes cut off in winter, as they fruit on the previous year's growth. Autumn-fruiting varieties, however, fruit on canes produced earlier in the same summer, so the entire plant can be cut to the ground each winter. Make sure you don't mistake your summer for your autumn raspberries, though, or you'll get no crop at all.

By the time I'd finished in the fruit cage, the plants were looking pleasingly tidy. All that was letting the side down was the layer of grass and weeds sprawling across the three beds. I spent a good few hours clearing it all out – raspberries, in particular, are hungry surface-feeders and dislike any competition for nutrients. Even after a few frosts, there were an alarming number of slugs, snails and caterpillars still sheltering in the undergrowth and in the straw I'd put down in summer among the strawberries. I left the earth exposed so that the hard frost forecast for that evening could finish the creepy crawlies off. And for once, I left the door open and the netting round the sides rolled up, so the birds could come in and do the same (if you have ducks or chickens they can do this job for you from autumn onwards). When the soil starts to warm up in early spring, I shall mulch the entire bed with thick layers of newsprint, right up around the bushes and canes, and cover with a thick layer of well-rotted manure. That should keep the weeds down next summer, reduce the need to water (the fruit cage is furthest from the water tank) and ensure a good healthy crop of fruit. But summer pudding seemed a lifetime away as I crunched through the frosty grass on my way back to the gate.

3 February 2002

GROW YOUR OWN SAFFRON

Crocuses look best in large swathes beneath deciduous trees, where the low winter sun can light up their fragile yellow, mauve or white flowers. But in smaller gardens like mine, they work very well in pots. They come up year after year, as reliable as clockwork – the pallid nib-like shoots first, followed by the first pointed green leaves in January, and finally the promise of a bud within. These are the pots that I move to prime position in front of the French windows – and some even make it inside. I plant the bulbs in little terracotta pots, or old Italian painted mugs that are cracked or have lost their handles – six or seven corms of one variety per pot – and when the flowers are about to appear I put them in places where the colour of the pot or the flowers sits well with their surroundings. "Bluebird", a beautiful variety with aster-blue outer petals and creamy white insides, looks lovely in our blue-and-white spare bedroom, while the chocolate-feathered petals of 'Gypsy Girl' are a joy in an old brown tea-pot on my desk. (Both the above varieties are sold by Bloms – 01234 709099 for catalogues.)

This year, I intend to try raising the saffron crocus, *Crocus sativus*. Though its natural habitats include sunbaked southern Spain, Morocco and Kashmir, it is also grown commercially out of doors in North Wales, so the average British garden should be fine. How wonderful to have my own home-grown saffron to flavour soups and risottos! The part of the flower used as a spice is, of course, incredibly small – just the thread-like stigmas that are attached to the ovary. It takes an unbelievable 75,000 flowers – all plucked by hand – to produce about 450g (1lb) of dried saffron. And not only is it costly to buy in this country; the quality is often questionable. Saffron can keep for ten years if stored in the dark, but it is usually sold in clear plastic boxes or yellow cellophane so customers can see what they're getting. All too often, it is not true Crocus *sativus*. It's not uncommon for the totally flavourless stamens of any old crocus plant to be masquerading as cheap saffron, and the corms sold as *C. sativus* are often sub-species or *C. speciosus*.

Though commercial bulb companies do supply *C. sativus* corms (De Jager (01622 831235) sells it at £19.25 for 50), these will take several years to produce a good harvest, and it is preferable to plant mature corms. Caroline Riden, the only commercial prouducer of saffron in the UK, supplies a 'Starter Kit' of 20 large, mature corms, together with a booklet containing the fruits of her 20 years' experience of saffron growing, for £25 including p&p. It seems expensive, but the thrill of producing my own crop of this ancient, most precious spice will be worth it. Each corm produces three to four flowers, and each flower has three stigma strands, so at my reckoning, twenty corms should give a total of around 210 strands – an ample year's supply given that you might use just ten to 20 strands for a risotto milanese and fewer for soups and sauces. I'm already looking forward to my first harvest.

Crocus sativus is one of the autumn-flowering varieties, and isn't planted till the summer. But such is the demand for Mrs Riden's corms that it is worth putting in an early order. They are despatched in June and can be planted until late August, but it's worth preparing a bed now. A sunny, sheltered position is where they will thrive, the soil enriched with well-rotted farmyard manure or compost. When the corms arrive, plant them 15cm (6in) deep and 15cm (6in) apart – they are apparently fine in large pots, which is how I shall be growing mine. Then it is just a few weeks to wait until October, when the glorious flowers appear – the petals subtly streaked and feathered in lilac, mauve and white, and the interiors set alight by the orange-red stigma and bright yellow styles. For the best flowers, you have to hope for a five-degree temperature drop in early October – the plants may be sluggish to start if the weather stays warm. Harvesting and drying relatively small amounts of saffron is not difficult, especially with Mrs Riden's leaflet, which is full of helpful and detailed advice. For an information sheet on Crocus sativus and how to order the Saffron Starter Kit for £25, send an sae to Mrs Caroline Riden, Caer Estyn farm, Rhyddyn Hall, Caergwrle, Wrexham, North Wales LL12 9EF.

10 February 2002

SEA KALE IN THE CITY

It is heartening to see the first signs of spring at the allotment. The purple sprouting broccoli is finally showing edible shoots – all the more welcome because we had to do without last year. Those first dark purple sprouts from the centre of the plant are the most delicious. I award them all the ceremony of the first asparagus, steaming them gently and serving with melted butter and ground pepper. Later in the season the smaller side shoots can be piled high on a plate, perked up with garlic, lemon juice and olive oil. I've made a note in my diary to sow next year's crop in good time – it's easy to forget in the hurry to get this summer's crops going. Sow in April or May in seed trays or small pots – the young plants can be put in their final positions in late summer, when space is freed up after earlier crops, such as peas or broad beans, are over. A variety named 'Rudolph', has been bred to crop from October onwards, but for me the point of purple sprouting broccoli is its seasonality – so welcome in that early spring gap.

My couple of sea kale plants brought back from the seaside house we rented last year are also showing their first dark purple shoots above the soil. Sea kale still grows wild in unpolluted shingle along England's south coast, and here at the allotment, in a neat raised bed among rows of broccoli, curly kale and cavolo nero, it looks slightly incongruous – but it seems happy enough. I remember panicking last year when I couldn't see any sea kale along the beach – convinced that its new fashionableness had brought a fleet of lorries from London to dig it all up for the restaurant trade. But as the warmer weather and longer days arrived, the shingle was splashed with small purple blotches that grew larger and paler as the shoots opened into glaucous grey cabbage-like leaves. To be eaten at its best, sea kale needs to be forced in the dark, producing long blanched shoots. You need a large bucket or, better still, a custom-made forcer with a lid. Luckily, my seaside landlord the potter, was able to sell me one of his own beautiful hand-thrown terracotta models before I left. You can find them on sale at the shops at Great Dixter in E. Sussex (01797 253107) or West Dean Gardens in W. Sussex (01243 818279) strictly no mail order.

Also emerging is a patchy carpet of self-sown rocket. It's a sign that the soil is becoming warm enough to sow the first salad crops – best covered with cloches or low plastic tunnels to protect from the last frosts. And in our spare bedroom at home, dozens of seed potatoes are sprouting like mad. Potatoes grow better if you 'chit' them for six weeks or so before sowing. Place them in a cool room with plenty of light so they send out strong young shoots from the 'eyes'. I save old cardboard egg-boxes for the job as they make it easier to ensure that the tubers remain with their 'rose' end (the blunt end with the most potential sprouts) uppermost. The traditional time for planting new potatoes is St Patrick's Day, 17 March – any earlier and there's the risk of frost damage as the first leaves emerge. Very early varieties, such as 'Concorde', can be planted as soon as the soil is thawed out and dry enough – but in frost-prone areas it would be wise to cover the rows with low polytunnels or fleece for the first few weeks.

It's tempting to use old potatoes that have sprouted in the vegetable basket, but these may not be virus-free, and the shoots will snap off easily. It is recommended to buy only certified virus-free seed potatoes from a reputable supplier. If, like me, you find the many varieties – divided into 'earlies', 'second earlies', 'early maincrops' and 'maincrops' – overwhelming, Alan Roman's *Guide to Seed Potato Varieties* (HDRA) explains how to grow and cook more than 100 of them. Or let someone else do the legwork and go for one of the collections in the Organic Gardening catalogue (01932 253666) which comprise 1kg (2¼lb) each of five selected varieties. 'The Cook's Choice', 'Blight Resisters', 'Early Bird' and 'Waxy Salads' are all well-chosen mixtures – the last includes 'Charlotte', 'Maris Peer', red-skinned 'Roseval', 'Nicola' and my all-time favourite, 'Pink Fir Apple'.

HOUSEPLANTS BACK IN VOGUE

I used to think that houseplants were naff – a prejudice that was reinforced when the editor of a glossy interiors magazine I worked on used to ban them from photo shoots. But there's a lot more to pot plants than studenty-spider plants and dusty old yuccas. Like anyone who loves gardening, I have admired and acquired plants over the years until, almost by stealth, our house has grown very leafy. There are plants in almost all the rooms, ranged along mantelpieces or clustered in windows where their massed leaves provide privacy from passers-by. So I was relieved to read that house plants are back in vogue – this month's edition of *Vogue*, to be precise, where the cult home column "Rita Says" pronounces potted gardenias "delicious", and recommends maidenhair ferns and even stuffy old aspidistras as the new gardening "must-haves".

One of the unexpected pleasures of being back in London again is that I have the time really to enjoy the plants in the house. Last year, when we were dividing our time between here and the house by the sea, they were more a source of guilt than of joy – a nagging worry at the back of my mind as I sped up and down the motorway from one place to another. With two gardens to look after, it was as much as I could do to give the indoor plants an occasional slosh of water. They survived – bar one or two exotic and expensive exceptions – but most plants, indoor or out, need more than the minimum of care in order truly to thrive.

In their Seventies classic *The Secret Life of Plants*, Peter Tompkins and Christopher Bird claim that plants are sensitive to our feelings towards them and will respond to impulses to kill or harm them, even from a distance, by withdrawing their "life energy" down into the roots. It's hardly surprising that loved plants should do better than those that are merely tolerated – a cherished plant is more likely to be looked at and fussed over, and I've always known that much of good gardening lies in the looking: you see what needs doing before the plant starts to suffer. But to my mind there is a further, hidden, mysterious ingredient. Is it so silly to think that plants, just like human beings or a cats or dogs, could thrive on affection? I was wondering about this as I looked at the splendid furry-leafed pelargonium (*P. tomentosum*) that fills an entire window in our bathroom. I swear it has grown more in the three months I've been back in full-time residence than it did under the care of our non-gardening lodger all year while I was away – and it ought to be dormant in winter. I haven't given it any special care. Nor have I been feeding it. But every time I go into that room I wonder at its soft fuzzy leaves, a soft greyish green in the mornings, when its millions of tiny hairs create a luminous halo around every leaf, and brightest lime in the afternoons as the sun swings round to back-light it. I really love that plant, and I like to think it knows.

I bought a lot more scented pelargoniums last year, and they now fill two of my skylight shelves – the smell of their leaves and the shadows they cast are a joy whenever I pass them on the stairs. A couple of last year's casualties have made room for more of my other favourite and most accommodating group of plants: succulents. I love the subtle shapes and colours of their leaves – the glaucous grey-green echeverias; the fat fleshy growth of the crassulas and kalanchoes; the dramatic black-red rosettes of *Aeonium arboreum* 'Schwartzkopf (all of which can go outside for the summer).

At last month's Royal Horticultural Show in Westminster, I hung for ages around Brian Hiley's stand, admiring some of the more unusual succulent varieties. There was a splendid specimen of *Aeonium tabuliforme*, so-called because it grows completely flat – this one was a perfect green rosette at least a foot across; and a huge *A. canariense*, rather like a great cabbage with its green and cream-streaked leaves. The echeverias were fascinating: some with their grey leaves tinged pink all over, like the fashionable *E. peackockii* 'Perle von Nurnberg', some with bright rosy tips to the leaves such as *E.* 'Gilva's Red', and some with attractive purplish points like *E. colorata* 'Brandtii'. The latter's leaves curl up at the ends like pantomime slippers; those of *E.* 'Phyllis Collis' sit flat in the pot, while *E. glauca cristata*'s are creased and crimpled, almost appearing diseased. I succumbed to the crinkly-edged leaves of *Kalanchoe pumila*, with its purplish grape-like bloom, and a lovely blue-green echeveria called 'Gilva's Blue Surprise' – precisely what the surprise is we shall have to wait and see. I also bought some aloes to add to my burgeoning collection. But they deserve a column to themselves.

3 March 2002

CYCLAMEN FOR BEGINNERS

If, like me, you were given a potted cyclamen for Christmas, now might be the time when you're thinking of throwing it on the compost heap. They are lovely things throughout the winter, sending up a succession of tiny new buds from the centre of the plant so long as you keep the compost moist. But once the flowers stop and the leaves start turning yellow, it's easy to think their days are over. In fact, cyclamen are easy to keep going year after year, as I found out last autumn, when a couple of plants I had slung out in the garden without much thought were discovered just coming into bud. Inspired by this success, I have done some research into the best way of caring for cyclamen.

So long as your plant continues to flower and carry leaves, keep the soil moist – set it on a saucer of gravel and water from the bottom so the crown is never in danger of rotting in waterlogged compost, and never leave the pot standing in water once it has taken up all it can. (Garden lore has it that cyclamen should be watered with weak tea, but I've never tried this.) When the last flowers have faded, let the plant dry out by degrees, keeping it inside or in a frost-free place during the remaining cold weeks. Stand it outside in a shady place through spring and summer, sheltered from heavy downpours – there is no need to water, no matter how hot it gets; cyclamen's natural habitat is the Middle East, where the crowns get a good baking in summer. Start watering gently again in late July or August to coax your plant back into life. New buds should appear quite soon, but to get the best from your plant you should repot it at this stage. Cyclamen like a loosely-structured fibrous loam (or peat-substitute compost) and sharp-sand mix, with a handful of bonemeal added. Don't make the mistake of burying the tuber – it should sit on the surface, three-quarters visible. Increase watering gradually into autumn, then bring the plant back in – either into a warm greenhouse or on to a sunny windowsill. Be careful not to over-water – yellowing leaves are the first tell-tale sign.

I've never tried growing cyclamen from seed, but have long been intrigued by their habit of drawing back the seed heads by coiling the spent flower stems around the crown like springs. I'm not quite sure why the plants do this (all except for *C. persicum*) – you might imagine that they release the ripened seed with a sudden ping! to spread it as far from the parent plant as possible, but this does not seem to be the case. The seeds are gently released close to the crown, not flung suddenly far and wide. Outdoor colonies of cyclamen increase steadily but gradually, relying on distributing agents, such as birds and ants, to carry the seeds away. If you are lucky, I guess you might find tiny seedlings growing around your plant in its pot, but this has not so far happened to me. For best results, ripe seed should be soaked overnight and sown in a mix of equal parts seed compost and sharp sand, and the pots sealed in clear plastic bags and kept at 16°C (61°F) minimum till germination has occurred.

Most of the cyclamen grown as pot plants are the larger-flowered Persian cyclamen, but I must confess a preference for the fragile fluttery flowers and tiny marbled leaves of the smaller varieties. The hardy outdoor varieties are small too, and like their indoor cousins, long-lived if the conditions are right. They are one of those obliging plants that actually prefer to grow in the shade of trees, where the leaf canopy should protect them from water-logging. And it is here that they look most beautiful, flowering – if you choose the right varieties – not only through winter, but on through spring and summer into autumn. Planting ten or so small plants of different types should result in a subtle patchwork of the patterned round or heart-shaped leaves and flowers in all shades from white to sugar-pink, cerise and mauve. *Cyclamen coum* is the classic winter-flowering variety, and is totally hardy. To prolong the flowering season you could also include *C. hederifolium*, whose delicate pink flowers precede its pointed silver-streaked leaves in late autumn – the white variety 'Album' is even prettier – or *C. persicum*, which, in a sheltered spot, should flower from February to April. The rarer

C. balearicum, *C. repandum* and *C. purpurascens* will then offer a succession of flowers from spring right through to early autumn.

10 March 2002

THE ACCEPTABLE FACE OF BIOLOGICAL WARFARE

It's that exciting time of year when new growth seems to double by the day. Herbaceous plants are reappearing in the form of leafy rosettes around the remnants of last year's dead stems – frilly green whorls of aquilegia, and tiny pinkish hands of cranesbill geraniums reaching up to the sky. The euphorbias are at that delightful stage when they lift their bowed heads to unfold their showy chartreuse flowers, green swords of iris are poking above the soil and my *Clematis montana* is covered in buds – a promise of the rosy pink bunting that will be strung around the garden in May. Each time I go outside there's more to look at and admire. But there is also more to worry about – the warmer weather is good for pests as well as plants, and tender new growth is especially vulnerable. I've spotted the first aphids and caterpillars already, and slugs and snails are leaving tell-tale trails across the soil.

Painful experience has taught me not to pussyfoot about – delays can lead to severe and irreparable damage. Sap-sucking aphids not only cause yellowing and distortion of leaves and stems, they can also spread viruses. And caterpillars will munch through leaves in a matter of minutes, delaying new growth and permanently disfiguring some plants.

Last year my young hollyhocks were repeatedly razed by caterpillars while I ranted in error at the slugs. If a plant is being nibbled and you can find no traces of slime, the culprit may well be a caterpillar; check carefully among the buds and on the undersides of leaves and you may well spot them – small at first, but getting fatter and juicier by the day. There is a particular bright green caterpillar that hatches from a cocoon formed in the new unopened leaves of shrubs such as hebes. By the time the creature emerges it will already have done a lot of damage as it eats its way out into the world, and those new leaves – so pretty and purply in the case of my poor hebe – will be riddled with holes and will never recover. When it comes to holey leaves, however, nothing compares to the damage wreaked by slugs and snails on hostas, whose voluptuously curved and ribbed foliage is their whole point; once that gets damaged the plant can be ruined for the entire growing season.

But before reaching for the spray gun or slug pellets, *please* consider the organic options that are harmless to birds, pets, humans, worms and beneficial insects. Biological controls – using nematode worms or other organisms that prey on specific pests or cause them to stop feeding – can be used now the weather is getting warmer. Panic use of chemicals early in the year rules this option out, as residues may remain for up to two months, preventing the nematodes and beneficial insects from doing their job.

Biological controls come in sealed packs and are either mixed with water and sprayed or watered on, or simply released around affected plants. For aphids in greenhouses and conservatories, *Aphidius*, a wasp larva (or *Aphidolotes*, a midge larva, for large infestations), can be applied once temperatures are above 10°C (50°F). In open ground, you have to wait until May for ladybird larvae, so use a soft soap spray and/or pinch insects off by hand until then – I used to be squeamish about the latter but have become quite heartless. Dipel, an organic-approved spray, stops caterpillars feeding and is harmless to other wildlife. It is mixed immediately prior to use and can be used all year round.

For slugs, the nematode preparation sold as Nemaslug can be watered around plants once the soil temperature is above 4°C (40°F) I've found it very effective in reducing the slug presence, but it's worth doubling up with barrier methods such as copper tape around pots (which deters snails too) and 'snail mats' – discreet black discs which contain a copper element that slugs and snails find aggravating. These mats, which sit around the bases of plants, were until recently only used commercially, but are now available from Green Gardener (01603 715096), a family business that specializes in biological and organic pest control and can provide all the products mentioned above. Their website www.greengardener.co.uk is full of useful information, while their excellent helpline (same number) is manned by the owners, Annie and John, daily from dawn until dusk.

17 March 2002

ALOE VERA, THE MEDICINE PLANT

Aloes, like many other members of the succulent family, possess a pleasing combination of fleshy glaucous leaves and a geometric growth habit. Most have long pointed leaves arranged in an open rosette – similar in pattern to the agave, but fleshier, and without the needle-sharp terminal spines. Some, such as *Aloe aristata*, often grown as a houseplant, have horny leaves ending in transparent wisps; others, like *A. brevifolia*, are attractively squat, with little white teeth edging the foliage. There are more than 350 varieties of aloe, many of which make very good indoor or conservatory plants, but the best-known by far is aloe vera, often called the 'medicine plant'.

These days, aloe vera may be most familiar as an ingredient in shampoos or beauty products, but scientific research is proving what many ancient civilizations knew all along: that the plant has impressive healing powers. The ancient Egyptians called aloe vera 'the plant of immortality', while its other folk names from around the world include 'wand of Heaven', 'miracle worker' and 'silent healer'. The clear greenish gel inside the leaves not only has anti-inflammatory and anti-microbial properties, which help prevent infection in wounds, it also contains a growth-promoting factor, which enhances and speeds up healing. This unusual double action helps explain aloe vera's reputation as a heal-all for everything from minor cuts and scratches to major wounds, acne, eczema, athlete's foot, ulcers, sunburn and serious burns.

I first became aware of the plant's powers while on holiday in the Caribbean, where local women wander up and down the beaches, offering aloe vera massages to pink-tinged tourists. Once I'd experienced its soothing effects for myself – and its additional efficacy as an insect deterrent – I copied the locals and bought my own supply of leaves from roadside stalls. When I got back home to Brixton, south London, I soon spotted aloe leaves, half-wrapped in newspaper, among the mangoes, yams and paw-paws in our lively Afro-Caribbean market. And I was delighted when my husband bought me a plant as a present at the 'Lambeth Country Show' – an annual event where our local park is taken over by music stages, ethnic food stalls and fruit flower and livestock displays.

That was four years ago, since when my little plant, just 13 or 15cm (5 or 6in) tall, has grown into a monster, with leaves 0.6m (2ft) long and a good 7.5cm (3in) across. At first, I was loth to cut leaves for my own use, and left the young plant to establish itself – but I've since found out that the full medicinal value of the plant does not manifest until it's three or four years old, so I did well to hold back. Over the years, I used the odd leaf that was knocked off while moving the plant or watering, and I've now begun to harvest a leaf every few months to heal all manner of minor wounds – most of them, ironically, sustained while gardening. I was recently overjoyed to find five or six young aloe "pups" clustered around the base of the central stem – this is how the plants propagate themselves. Some of the youngsters have been potted up for friends and family, but I'm priming the largest for a place in the kitchen, where its soothing gel would be handy in case of burns. I think every household should have an aloe vera plant.

Aloes are increasingly available at garden centres, but they are not always reliably labelled. Almost all the varieties are attractive, but if you want to use the plants medicinally, it's vital to get a true *Aloe vera*. *The RHS Plantfinder* lists twenty or so nurseries that provide it, some of them mail order. Buy as big a plant as you can find, and pot it up in good quality compost mixed with sand or grit, with plenty of crocks or pebbles at the bottom to ensure good drainage. Over-watering is the main danger, so water the soil only when it starts feeling dry – once every one or two weeks in an average summer, and every two to three weeks in winter. Make sure the plant has plenty of light; when deprived of light its leaves, usually upturned and perky, will start to fall flat. And in severe drought, they will absorb their own water, becoming thin and somewhat shrivelled. They can be moved outside for summer, but need to be brought back inside before the frosts.

When your plant is mature enough to harvest, take only outside leaves from the base of the plant. The leaf can then be split to release the gel, either

directly onto flesh, or scraped out and liquidized and kept for up to four weeks in the fridge. For a health-giving drink, slice the leaves into spring water and leave in the fridge for a day before straining and adding to fruit juice. I can't promise miracles, but I think you'll be pleasantly surprised.

24 March 2002

CULTIVATING PATIENCE

March is the month when my natural impatience – not a helpful characteristic in a gardener – comes to the fore. Spring seems to be springing all around me: the allotment is ablaze with daffodils and on warm days I can even eat my lunch in the garden. Like the plants and birds, I can feel those tiny daily increments of light and heat, and am rising earlier, full of energy to get outside and get gardening. Of course there is lots I can do – planting seed potatoes, hoeing the first weeds, preparing beds for later crops. What I am really itching to do, though, is sow seeds: for me this is where the true alchemy and excitement of gardening lies. But experience has finally taught me to hold back.

It is so easy in one of the warmer spells, when birds are singing, buds are bursting and sunburn seems more than a remote possibility, to tear open a few packets and start sowing seed. Spring, however, comes to the birds and flowers sooner than to the soil. The nights are still cold, and nocturnal temperatures need to rise in tune with the day's increases in order for the soil to warm through and dry out sufficiently for most seeds to have a chance. Seed sown in cold, wet soil rots in the ground; and many of the seedlings that do surface will be stopped dead in their tracks by cold winds or a late frost, frozen into immobility. For too many years the allotment has been littered with redundant plastic plant labels, each marking the grave of some over-optimistic planting that came to nothing: "Peas 'Pilot' 28 Feb" they say; "Fennel, 15 March". So this year I have been the model of restraint.

Many of the old traditional herbals advise sowing seed while naked, beneath a full moon. Though this conjures up images of strange pagan rites, the truth may actually be tied up with the weather: if it is warm enough to go naked, the ground will be warm enough to sow. In medieval Lincolnshire, to test whether the soil was in the right condition for sowing barley, farmers apparently used to take off their trousers and sit on the ground: if it was comfortable for them it would be comfortable for the barley. A less flamboyant alternative – and one more likely to find favour with the authorities down at my allotments – might be to test the soil with a bared elbow, as a mother does the water for a baby's bath. I have done this several times at different hours of the day, and so far it has always resulted in muddy arms and a shiver. But it shouldn't be too long now.

There are a few short cuts that avoid the wait. One is to cover the soil with horticultural fleece for a few weeks prior to sowing or planting. The fleece acts like a woolly blanket, protecting the soil against sudden changes in temperature, while its tiny perforations (it is not unlike the stuff from which teabags are made) let air and moisture through. With carrots, it can be left in place after sowing, to keep the soil warm and flummox carrot fly. The only problem with fleece is that it can look rather unsightly. Even on an allotment, where mouldy old carpet and black plastic are the order of the day, a fluttering expanse of snowy white fleece, to me, looks somewhat out of place. Maybe it's the fact you have to buy it new: it goes against the make-do, makeshift allotment grain.

The other way to satisfy horticultural impatience, of course, is to sow under cover in seed trays, pots or "cells" – those sheets of individual planting compartments, rather like plastic eggboxes. This will usually ensure a head start over crops sown straight outside, provided the seedlings are hardened off properly (gradually acclimatized to outside temperatures) and the delicate young root systems are not disturbed. One way to guard against the latter is by sowing in root trainers – packs of planting cells with vertical grooves in the sides that train the roots straight down to give the plants a good start in life. Unlike many other individual planting units such as peat plugs, they can be used again and again, as one side can be opened like a book to allow roots to be examined and the plants to be taken out with the minimum disturbance. They are particularly useful for deep-rooted plants such as beans, and can even be used for carrots and parsnips, which are usually impossible to transplant. I've never tried root trainers before, but am giving them a go this year for my carrots, sweetcorn and runner beans. I'll let you know if I become a convert.

"Rootrainers" are available in three sizes: 7.5cm (3in) deep for annual herbs, flowers, salads, etc (£12.50 for two packs of 32 cells each, with tray and propagating lid); 13cm (5in) deep for carrots, sweetcorn, plug plants, two packs for £13) and 18cm (7in) deep for parsnips, sweetpeas, runner beans (two packs of 40 cells and tray, £15) from Rootrainers, Kersquarter, Kelso, Scotland TD5 8HH (01573 225757).

BIRDS IN THE GARDEN

It's hard to get any work done at the moment, so captivated am I by the theatrical show outside my window. A blue tit has fallen in love with his own reflection in the large mirror on the rear wall of our garden and spends the entire day fluttering to and fro, and flirting with himself in the glass. I recently gave the mirror a good clean and cleared some of the foliage that was threatening to obscure it, so it appears once more to form a window through to another leafy world. The illusion is obviously as convincing to wildlife as it is to the person who once asked, "Is that your garden through there, too?" – and luckily the small dimensions of this space mean there's no danger of birds flying into the glass and stunning themselves. This little blue tit certainly seems to be enjoying himself. The spiralling branches of a jasmine plant provide a springboard for an impressive display of aerial gymnastics, while the frame of ivy leaves around the edges is perfect for playing peek-a-boo, and he's happy to sing to his own reflection for hours, like a budgie in a cage. This morning another blue tit was trying to attract his attention, tweeting impatiently and bouncing up and down on a nearby branch, but he only had eyes for himself. If this catches on, I could be responsible for a serious depletion in the blue tit population.

The birds in this garden are a real joy, but I have had to wait for them. It takes time to attract birds to an urban garden – particularly one that was created from bare concrete and so held no previous attractions. For a good year or two my offerings of sunflower seeds and bacon fat went largely untouched, or were seized in dawn raids by squirrels. But then my father made me a clever squirrel-proof bird table, with a caged-in upper storey that enables smaller birds to slip through and eat unhindered. And the galvanized metal arch I designed to train climbing plants around the french windows is also great for hanging smaller feeders and seed balls. Finally, my garden has become the haven for birds that I'd dreamed of – tits and sparrows mainly, a few chaffinches and goldfinches, and lots of blackbirds who hop around the flower beds scavenging for worms and, I hope, slugs. The odd unwieldy pigeon or jay sometimes flaps its way in, looking comically oversized in this tiny space as it threatens to tip the bird table off balance. By far the biggest thrill was when what I can only describe as a swarm (a charm?) of six or seven goldcrests descended on the garden one afternoon last summer, the bright orange flashes on their heads creating fireworks as they flew.

I'm hoping that the little nesting box hanging on the house wall might be used this spring – even if it's not by my narcissistic blue tit. Last year we had a robin's nest in an old terracotta teapot in the yard of the seaside house we rented – truly the stuff of fairytales – and it was a joy to watch the parents fly in and out with food and the fledglings embark on their first flights. My husband said they'd be too fat to fly, as I'd been leaving them snacks of hot cross bun and *panettone* crumbs, but they were soon swooping round the yard and in a day or two were gone. It would be lovely to have a nest here some day.

Down at the allotment, we also encourage birds, with feeders and tables that are kept well-stocked throughout the year. The help they provide there by eating slugs and snails and other pests is invaluable – and when I see them rootling through the soil for food it makes me glad we've never used slug pellets. We have to be mindful of the damage birds can cause to crops, though. Birds don't often eat leaves, as they find them hard to digest, but woodpigeons are an exception, and brassicas are their favourite. It's advisable to cover all cabbage, kale and broccoli plants with netting to keep birds off – even my perpetual spinach was stripped down to the central ribs this winter. And of course a protective cage is necessary if you are growing soft fruit.

We've not so far had a problem with bird damage to other crops, but my fellow plot holders employ any number of ingenious scaring devices. One stretches the strong plastic tape used for packing parcels among his runner bean poles, where it strums and flashes in the wind – a 30m (98ft) roll of "Buzzline", which works in a similar way, costs £4.50 from The Organic Gardening Catalogue (01932 253666). Another, who may possibly work in the music business, has strung unwanted CDs on a clothes line, which makes his plot look like a contemporary art installation. My favourite deterrent, though, and a method which is apparently centuries old, is the imitation bird of prey made from an old potato with feathers stuck into it, "hovering" most realistically from the bough of a tree.

7 April 2002

SOWING NEW POTATOES

We had one of those fantastic days at the allotment recently – the sort of day that reminds us why all the hard work is worth it. The sun shone for hours, with a lovely warm breeze tossing the daffodils I planted years ago along the length of the layered hedge that forms our western boundary. There were catkins on the hazel, a cloud of white blossom on the blackthorn, and dozens of blue tits, great tits and finches fluttering around the feeders that hang from the old oak tree in the corner. As usual, we spent the first half-hour wandering round the beds and getting excited about the new growth brought on by this spell of warmer weather: rosy pink nibs of lovage, sprinklings of green where we'd sown the first rows of radishes and rocket a few weeks earlier, and ghostly pale shoots on the sea kale we are forcing beneath a splendid terracotta dome. By far the best surprise, though, was that for the first time the pond was full of frogspawn – four huge glittering masses of the stuff, guarded by a pair of very vocal frogs. We couldn't work out whether they were protecting their progeny or revving up for yet another round of courtship.

Finally we got down to work. We sowed more of the hardier vegetables in situ: another line each of rocket and radishes to try to stagger our yield, some 'Boltardy' beetroot, and the reliable perpetual spinach. We put in some 'Red Baron' onions, as organic red onions are still relatively expensive (and rare) in the shops, and made our third sowing of broad beans, which should keep us in this most delicious of vegetables well into summer.

Most of our efforts that day were devoted to potatoes, however. Having said we'd limit this year's crop due to pressure on space, I realized there's time to sneak in a sowing of new potatoes in time to clear the ground for later summer vegetables such as courgettes and squashes. As I was more efficient than usual with chitting the tubers in old egg boxes in the spare bedroom, we were able to meet the traditional planting date of Good Friday for new potatoes – and as Easter was quite early this year, it gave us a head start. We filled the raised squash patch with 'Colleen', an Irish 'first early' variety with waxy light yellow flesh, and dug three trenches elsewhere for 'Roseval' (an attractive dark red salad potato much favoured by the *River Cafe Cook Book*), which, being one of the 'early maincrop' varieties, will go in a couple of weeks later. The rest of that bed will be devoted to my favourite 'Pink Fir Apples', a 'late maincrop' that is planted last of all. First earlies take 12 to 15 weeks to mature, second earlies 16 to 18 weeks and maincrop varieties around 20 weeks, so that should supply us with a good mixture of potatoes right into autumn. Last year we sowed far too many of the same type and were somewhat over-run. One forgets that a single tuber can produce 1.8kg (4lb) or more of spuds if given plenty of space, rich moist soil and sun.

It is, however, very easy to grow potatoes in containers – great if all you have is a small garden or balcony. We'd never tried it before, but as there were some leftover tubers of 'Colleen' that we couldn't find room for, we decided to give it a go. You can plant them in pots – 30cm (12in) wide and 0.6m (2ft) deep is the smallest feasible size – but we are also experimenting with tall, sturdy cardboard boxes. Good drainage is vital so check the holes and spread a 5cm (2in) layer of gravel in the base. Then put 15cm (6in) of compost in the bottom, space as many tubers as will fit, allowing a good 20cm (8in) between them (just two in a 30cm [12in] pot), cover with a further 15cm (6in) of compost and water well. When the leaves grow through to about 20cm (8in), add another 15cm (6in) of soil so just the tops of the leaves are visible, and repeat till you reach either the top of your pot or a height of 1m (3ft). Some people use a stack of old tyres, adding a new one with every layer of compost – not the most elegant of methods but reputedly effective. The important thing with container potatoes is to keep them well watered, so I hope our cardboard will hold up. Feeding once the flowers have formed should ensure a better yield.

There are few things more delicious than sweet new potatoes freshly dug from the garden – like sweetcorn, they dehydrate quickly, converting their sugars to starch. Plant some now and you could be enjoying your first crop on Midsummer's Day. And if you save a few tubers for chitting, you could do the whole thing over again and have some more with your Christmas dinner.

FRITILLARIES

April is the month for fritillaries. First to emerge is usually our one native variety – the snake's head fritillary *F. meleagris*, with its fragile drooping bells in murky chequered purple, pinkish mauve or white. Vita Sackville-West, who loved all fritillaries, called this "a sinister little flower, sinister in its mournful colours of decay" – and it has a host of slightly macabre nick-names including 'Sullen Lady' and 'Leper's Bell'. Perhaps, individually, they may possess a mournful air, but for me the sight of a meadow full of fritillaries with the sun shining through those subtly patterned petals can only be uplifting. This is where they grow best, of course – and preferably in a water meadow which is well-drained in summer. They look beautiful, too, in small orchards, sharing the grass beneath fruit trees with buttercups and cowslips. But even in my small London garden I cannot be without these exquisite flowers, and grow them in pots so I can bring them inside on to my desk when they're in bloom. I keep meaning to try to establish a "portable meadow" – a patch of delicate grasses and wildflowers in a low trough which I could study at close-quarters. But I wonder if it would be too like keeping a canary in a cage?

Next up – or often dead-heating – are the stately coronets of the crown imperial, *F. imperialis*, their rings of yellow, burnt orange or bronzy-red flowers topped by pineapple-tufts of foliage. From the moment their great thick shoots emerge from the soil in early spring there is an inescapable whiff of fox about. The smell of every part of this plant is decidedly pungent, and to many people unpleasant, but for me it's a sure sign of spring, and as powerful as cut nettles in evoking childhood memories. Crown imperials shoot up fast – on warm days you can almost count the inches – and can reach 1m (3ft) high. I once grew *F. imperialis* in large pots with great success the first year, though they failed to show the second; feeding the crown with a dressing of well-rotted manure, or digging up the bulbs and improving the soil is supposed to help coax recalcitrant bulbs back into bloom. Traditionally they are woodland plants, and tolerant of a fair amount of shade, yet their symmetrical, upright growth habit also lends them to more formal situations: they provide a dramatic spring infill for the compartments of a box parterre, or ranged in ranks along a formal border. In her excellent book *The Bold and Beautiful Garden* (Frances Lincoln, £25), Sarah Raven recommends surrounding crown imperial fritillaries with dark wallflowers or the crimson foliage of *Euphorbia dulcis* 'Chamaeleon' – which is helpful, as the bright reds and oranges can be hard to place in the garden. One can only imagine the thrill of discovering a clump of these torch-like blooms in a woodland ravine in their native Persia.

There are many other types of fritillary, in gloriously off-beat colour combinations. *F. graeca*, a lot like its snake's head cousin, but with verdigris-green bells strongly chequered with purplish-brown, grows just 10cm (4in) tall and flowers into May. Its fetching colour combination is repeated in *F. acmopetala*, the beautiful clear enamel-green lining of its dark matt chocolate bells showing at the edges where the petals curl upwards slightly. Reaching 30cm (1ft) high, they are reputedly easy to grow in sunny, rich and well-drained soil. *F. pallidiflora* has soft chartreuse bells and glaucous green foliage, reaching 46cm (18in) tall, while *F. verticillata* is remarkably pretty

with up to 15 green-tinged white bells per two-foot stem. In the past I've fallen for the dusky charms of the near-black *F. camschatcensis* with no success at all, but I may have pushed its degree of shade-tolerance to the limit. *F. assyriaca*, whose chestnut brown flowers are edged with yellow and tinged olive green in the centre, is supposed to be easier.

My favourite fritillary – its tall spires of flowers somewhere between plum-purple and chocolate – is *F. persica*. *F. persica* 'Adyaman' is the one to grow; it has an RHS Award of Garden Merit and is reliable given enough space in sun or light shade. If cramped, it will shoot up with a whorl of attractive leaves but no flowers. *F. persica* is one of those plants that is just as mesmerizing to watch while it is growing as it is to admire in flower – I've been checking the one by my front door every day for weeks. The growing point noses through the soil like a huge green snout in February, becoming a swollen rosette of leaves come March. These gradually start to feather open to reveal a cone of pale clustered flower buds that space out and darken as flowering-time approaches. The ravishing dark flowers last a good three weeks or more and are a guaranteed talking point among visitors.

Bloms Bulbs (01234 709099) and De Jager (01622 831235) are good sources of fritillary bulbs.

5 May 2002

SPRINGTIME IN MANHATTAN

This column comes from New York, where I have been enjoying a week's holiday in bright spring sunshine. The warm weather has coaxed all the flowers into bloom – Central Park is a cloud of pink and white blossom and there are spring flowers in all the tiny neighbourhood parks and verges. Even if the Downtown sky seems sadly and strangely empty, the flowers do seem like a symbol of hope in a city that is still licking its wounds. And none are more beautiful than the million daffodil bulbs, sent as a gift from the Dutch government in the aftermath of the terrorist attacks, and planted throughout the city by teams of volunteers last autumn.

Manhattan has a strong tradition of public and community gardening. In a city of apartment dwellers, where only the very wealthy can enjoy the luxury of a private back garden – or "yard" as Americans call it – every square foot of cultivatable land is prized and exploited. There are gardens on sunbaked rooftops, on shady strips of land behind office blocks, central reservations and derelict plots between buildings. On a previous visit to New York I made an extensive tour of the colourful community gardens of the Lower East Side, where scruffy Spanish churches and graffiti-spattered shop fronts look out on gardens of great beauty and ingenuity – neat patchworks of pebble- or brick-edged flowerbeds interspersed with impromptu sculptures, neighbourhood composting schemes and al fresco shrines to the Madonna. There are long waiting lists for individual plots the size of a kitchen table, while communal areas are used for local meetings, workshops, wedding receptions and concerts.

This time my attention has been caught by the 'Viewing Gardens' – fenced-in parcels of land that range from sizeable triangles between streets to tiny roadside strips and traffic medians, all planted up to be enjoyed by passers-by. Each garden bears a sign proclaiming it part of the Greenstreets scheme begun in 1986 by the City Parks and Recreation Department and revived in the Nineties by then-Mayor Rudolph Giuliani in his often controversial crusade to clean up the city. From the elegant Jefferson Market Garden at Greenwich Avenue between 6th Avenue and West 10th Street, with its shady yellow-wood trees encircled by hostas, to some small circles at the south end of Hudson Street planted with evergreen shrubs in a pattern of pebbles, these are well-designed spaces that enhance the paved street areas for everyone. Pledging to use a segment of the capital's budget to "plant trees and shrubs in the city's barren streetside places", Greenstreets has created hundreds of such gardens with the aid of local volunteers who, often lacking gardens of their own, are happy to help with upkeep. These gardens are immaculately kept, and often sport signs that tell something of the history of the area before it became a garden.

If you are walking along Houston Street and think you have stumbled upon the one untidy viewing garden in the city, the chances are you have come across the Time Landscape – a tangle of seedling trees and weeds that has sprung up as the result of an environmental artist's attempt to revert a corner of the city's grid to what Manhattan might have looked like before white settlers arrived. On a small rocky hummock he planted oaks, hickory, maples, junipers and other native trees, which over 15 years have grown into an impenetrable tangle underplanted with self-sown weeds and the odd ornamental plant blown in or carried in by birds. Only the poetry of the idea distinguishes it from an everyday vacant lot. But like those splendid outcrops of rock in Central Park, wild nature in the city reminds you of the elements on which urban civilizations are built – and to which, with surprising speed, they might one day return.

I think about such things as I contemplate the overgrown garden of the little apartment I'm renting in a West Village brownstone. At first I was unnerved by the untamed jungle of self-seeded Bradford pear trees and unpruned privet almost 6m (20ft) high. I longed to prune the trees and l iberate the concrete lions and cast iron tables and chairs from the rising tide of ground ivy that threatens to engulf them. I fantasized about the building's owners letting me return rent-free for a month or two, to tidy things up. But the longer I've stayed here, entranced by the spotted woodpeckers and bright red cardinals, and the family of squirrels that plays in the branches, the more I've fallen in love with this wild patch of woodland in the city. Perhaps my task is not to transform this garden, but to try to bring something of the courageous and companionable spirit of New York to the streets of London on my return.

19 May 2002

THE ART OF INTERCROPPING

The allotment at this time of year is like a jigsaw puzzle when all the final pieces are falling into place. The tomatoes, sweetcorn and courgettes sown in pots are now ready for planting out, and the recent outdoor sowings of peas, beans and salad greens are frilling out in ever-expanding patches of green. We need to consider very carefully where all our crops should go. Even though we have two adjoining plots – a total area of something like 9 x 37m (30 x 120ft) – there often seems to be a shortage of space in early summer. But with clever planning and what is known as "intercropping", it's usually possible to find a spot for everything.

The idea of intercropping is that slow-growing vegetables such as brassicas and onions can be inter-planted with rows of rapid-growers such as radishes, salad rocket or smaller lettuces. The fast growers or "catch crops", which should only take a few weeks from sowing to harvest at this time of year, will be ready long before the larger plants mature and take up the full surrounding area of soil. We've done this in the past with lettuce seedlings between onions or shallots, or radishes sown in the centre of runner bean teepees before the beans grow high enough to shade them out. There's plenty of room for a low-growing catch crop at the base of sweetcorn stalks – the canopy of the corn lets in enough light for oriental leaves such as mizuna or mustard greens to grow quite happily, while keeping down weeds into the bargain. A ground cover crop will also cut down the need for watering in high summer – a welcome bonus at our allotments, where hosepipes are banned and all watering must be done by hand.

Intercropping with the right sorts of vegetables can even help deter pests. For instance, we have tried to evade the attentions of the carrot fly this year by sowing our carrots and parsnips between rows of garlic and shallots. The strong scent exuded by members of the onion family is said to smother that of the root vegetables, leading the carrot fly to hatch its root-nibbling grubs elsewhere. Research is still being carried out as to the precise effects of companion planting, but the organic gardening organization HDRA suggests that mixed planting can cut down on pest damage simply by reducing the chance of a pest landing on a suitable host. Certainly, brassicas sown among french beans do seem to suffer less from aphids and cabbage root fly, while basil and tomatoes make as great a combination in the garden as they do in the salad bowl, both plants growing more healthily together than when apart. Sometimes, a pairing of plants works so well for each other that it seems silly to grow them any other way. A particularly satisfying combination is dill and chervil which, once established in the same spot, will self-seed and co-exist in tandem. Chervil germinates naturally in autumn, remains green all winter and runs to seed in late spring, just when the dill seedlings appear and take over. The strong scent of such herbs may also protect neighbouring plants from pests.

Not only is intercropping useful; it can also look extremely pretty. Joy Larkcom's book, *The Organic Salad Garden* (Frances Lincoln £16.99) has pictures of frilly 'lollo rosso' lettuces interspersed with early summer cabbages, and squares of cress or parsley framing blue-grey broccoli seedlings. We often try to squeeze a catch crop of oak-leaf lettuce or radishes as an attractive edging around an entire bed, and this year I've sown borders of the poached egg plant, *Limanthes douglasii* to attract beneficial insects such as hover flies, whose larvae feed on aphids. Marigolds – in particular the frilly French variety, if you can bear them – are among the most helpful flowers you can grow in a vegetable patch. With planning and a little i magination a functional vegetable plot can be turned into a colourful, yet highly productive patchwork.

2 June 2002

FOX AND THE CITY

Far from being starved of wildlife here in the city; we have had our fill in recent weeks. We have nightingales in our local park, a pond swarming with tadpoles at the allotment, and blue tits nesting in our back garden. The latter is particularly gratifying, as regular readers may remember that the male had previously been engaged in a narcissistic (and, I feared, terminally celibate) love affair with his own reflection in the mirror in our rear wall. But nothing can compare to the thrill of finding a tiny fox cub sunning itself at the allotment the other day. Just 20cm (8in) long and covered with pale brown fluff rather than fur, it can only have been a few weeks old. When I first saw it, sprawled on the grass bank, I feared it might be dead, but then I saw its ribs rise and fall, and realized it must be sleeping. I couldn't resist picking the cub up, and played with it for a while before I remembered that its mother – wherever she was – might not appreciate my scent on her return. By this time, however, the cub had clearly decided I would make just as good a mum in her absence, and started to follow me around the beds. Whenever I stopped, it sat on my feet and started playing with my laces. I had to wait till it fell asleep again to avoid being followed all the way to the gate. I returned in the evening to check on it, and was pleased to see both the mother – who was carrying a dead bird in her mouth – and the cub, sheltering this time in the brush behind our compost heaps.

Foxes have become increasingly common in urban areas, lured – like other originally rural creatures such as pigeons and squirrels – by warmer temperatures, ready food supplies and safe breeding places. According to a recent survey, 75 per cent of urban fox cubs are now born beneath garden sheds rather than in traditional underground dens. No matter how thrilling it may be to see one saunter along the street at night, or steal across your lawn, foxes don't tend to be favourites with gardeners, however. By far the majority of calls to The Fox Project (01732 367 397) are from gardeners fed up with ransacked vegetable patches, holes in their lawns and unspeakably smelly droppings all over their gardens. Describing itself as a "fox advice bureau", the Fox Project offers advice to fox lovers and haters alike, aiming "to help people to understand foxes and find ways to live with them". Their own publication *Unearthing the Urban Fox* (£5.50 inc p&p mail order) recommends several non-toxic or low-toxic deterrents for foxes, which include the standard repellants Renardine and Get Off My Garden, available from garden centres. John Bryant, whose book *Living with Urban Wildlife*, (Centaur, £9.95), was published last month, offers a philosophical approach to those who have a genuine problem with wildlife – whether it be foxes, pigeons, rats or squirrels – and who want to solve it without harming the culprit. "Animals are individuals, so you may have to try a number of deterrents before you hit on the one that works," he says. "Culling doesn't work, because as soon as there's a vacancy in nature, something else will move in. The trick is to leave the creatures in their territory, but try to educate them as to where they are welcome and where they are not." His top tip for foxes is a device called "Scarecrow", designed in Canada to keep herons out of ponds, but just as effective against foxes and other unwanted animals. It works by detecting intruders to the garden and squirting them with jets of water – a nice modern twist on the watery practical jokes in Renaissance gardens, and understandably rather popular with children, too. Scarecrow covers a 130m² and costs £64.95 mail order from aquatics-online.co.uk (01656 651149). One word of advice: set it to come on at night time to avoid getting drenched yourself.

9 June 2002

ALL CHANGE IN THE BACK GARDEN

In Stephen Lacey's excellent new book, *Real Gardening* (Penguin/Michael Joseph, £20), he recalls overhearing one gardener remarking to another at a nursery, "Isn't it lucky that plants die on us occasionally!" I felt rather like this recently, as I spent a sunny Saturday re-planting two of the old galvanized dustbins that are ranged in a line along the sunny south-west facing wall of our house. One plant had died – a young wisteria that I'd put in three years ago and which had never flowered well. The other had to go because it had finally outgrown my tiny garden. A small ceanothus that I'd potted up by the back door in the winter of 1998 had become an unwieldy brute – a beautiful one, albeit only for the few months of the year when its tight green buds unfold into bright blue puffs – and was beginning to block the way out into the garden. Some rather inexpert pruning cleared the access, but left ugly bare limbs in its wake. I knew I'd messed up when my husband, never one to make anything but favourable comments about the garden, asked: "Are you going to do something about that shrub? It looks awful." Extracting the ceanothus from its pot was one of our rare joint efforts in the garden – it needed one person to lever the plant and its enormous root ball up into the open and another to hold the plastic bin liner out below. Guess which job I did? The shrub was sent to enjoy a pleasant retirement in a sunny corner of the allotment, while I contemplated what to do with my pair of empty pots.

The soil was good, as I had mulched with 7.5 or 10cm (3 or 4in) of well-rotted horse manure last autumn, but I took the precaution of watering in some Nemasys solution – the biological control for vine weevil – in case the evil cream grubs had been behind the wisteria's demise. It's never a great idea to plant a straight replacement where a previous plant has died, so I chose a passion flower vine and the dusky purple clematis 'Arabella', which should flower from July to October. I trained the passion flower's pair of branching stems along the parallel vine wires that run at 0,6m (2ft) intervals up the back wall – it will be in full sun all afternoon against a white-washed wall, so we might even see some fruit. In the front of the tub, where I have always had 'Spring Green' tulips, followed by a tee-pee of sweetpeas, I decided to make a permanent planting of bearded irises. I've never grown irises successfully before, as I've always unwittingly given them too much shade, but it suddenly struck me that this sunny, well-drained spot could become an iris bed in miniature. The fashionably dark 'Black

Knight' is now flanked by a pair of lavender-flowering 'Bedtime Stories' – their rhizomes exposed so they can get a good baking in summer. (Another way to fail with irises is to bury them too deep.) The sword-like leaves look great emerging from a ground cover of soft silvery lamb's ears (*Stachys byzantina*), whose leaf cover should be open enough to allow enough sun and air through to the roots.

For the other bin I found a large wisteria already in flower (a rich violet variety called 'Amethyst') whose half-inch-thick woody stems seemed miraculously ready-moulded to grow around our back door. A cloud of bronze fennel, purple sage and *Cerinthe major* 'Purpurascens' should soon be filling out in front, with the electric violet heads of *Verbena bonariensis* swaying above. The new planting was completed in the nick of time for our garden's second opening in aid of charity through the National Gardens Scheme, and it was good to meet so many readers of the column who came along. Thank you all very much.

16 June 2002

CULTIVATING LOCAL DISTINCTIVENESS

It's become a cliché to moan about the "homogenized High Street", with its identikit supermarket and Starbucks on every corner. Yet the same process has been at work in our residential streets and gardens. When people still gardened with what they could beg, steal or borrow from their neighbours, gardens in different parts of the country were literally and aesthetically rooted in place. Now that the latest "must-have" plants and slate chippings can be bought up in one job lot from the Superstore, our gardens are beginning to look similar. This, for me, is the real problem with the "makeover culture" of gardening: I never knock it outright – at least it gets people started – but the notion that a garden can be bought in, lock, stock and barrel, does divorce it from its surroundings. Want a replica of Derek Jarman's seaside shingle garden in your back yard in Birmingham? Lay in the bags of beach pebbles and driftwood. Fancy a wildflower meadow for your roof terrace in the City? We have the technology. Given the fashionability of wild planting at this year's Chelsea Flower Show, I wonder whether trendy urban gardeners will be ditching the decking in favour of grassy knolls and layered hedges – even more incongruous in their way. Alexander Pope's famous plea to "Consult the genius of the place in all" has all but been forgotten.

Several years ago the arts and environmental charity Common Ground published a thoughtful little pamphlet called *The Art of Gentle Gardening: Thoughts on Linking Plants, People and Places* (£3 inc p&p) in which it suggested how to tap into local potential in our gardening, from the materials used for paths and boundaries to the types of plants grown. In the countryside this can be a relatively simple matter of observing the traditional local way of building walls or constructing fences – and perhaps giving them a contemporary twist if you feel so inclined – or choosing plants associated with the area, such as rare Worcester black pears in Worcestershire, the saffron crocus in Saffron Walden, or the mazzard cherries brought in by the Huguenots to the south Devon estuaries. Town dwellers may have to delve a little deeper, into history as well as their imaginations, but inspiration is all around us – when wheelie bins replaced galvanized dustbins outside London houses, I collected them up and now use them in my garden as planters. My own area, Brixton, is one of the many parts of the UK where ethnic diversity has made for a vibrant and colourful local culture – the people in my street who came over from the Caribbean in the Fifties were painting their front garden walls bright green, blue and white long before the guys on Ground Force. And some of the Bangladeshi community gardens in the East End are a riot of colour and unusual ingredients for curries. Planting in towns can also make a nod to the history of the area. Shirley in Croydon would certainly be brightened up by sowing more Shirley poppies in honour of the Rev. William Wilks, who first bred them there in the 1880s. Or what about planting 'Crawley Beauty' apples in Crawley, or 'Pershore Yellow Egg' plums in Pershore?

The key to tapping into your locality's potential lies in noticing the details that make your area look and feel different from others – even within the same city. Common Ground's new website, www.england-in-particular.com, aims to celebrate this "local distinctiveness" by gathering and documenting "the particular weave of places with ordinary culture, everyday nature, commonplace buildings, gardens and landscapes". They need contributions, particularly from city dwellers, as they work towards publishing a book – "a kind of encyclopedia of the local"– in a couple of years' time. Send stories, details and photographs illustrating the local distinctiveness of your area to Common Ground, Gold Hill House, 21 High Street, Shaftesbury, Dorset SP7 8JE (01747 850820) or visit www.england-in-particular.info.

30 June 2002

A FACELIFT FOR THE GARDEN

Summer solstice has come and gone; the year is at its turning point and many plants in the garden have reached their peak. This is the time in the gardening year when the pace suddenly seems to slow down once more. The spring and early summer frenzy of sowing and planting out has subsided, and our labours are beginning to bear fruit. We enjoyed our first harvest of broad beans from the allotment the other day, eating the small young beans raw in the typical Italian way, accompanied by Parma ham and chunks of grainy parmesan.

As summer settles into itself, there is the sense in which gardeners, too, have to sit back and accept that what they haven't got round to sowing or growing this season will have to wait till next year. It's a bit like being my age – 40 – and realizing that certain childhood dreams (being one of Pan's People, having seven children like Ma Walton) are *probably* not going to happen, in this lifetime at least. But this is not to say that all there's nothing to be done. Now is your absolute last chance, for instance, to sow purple sprouting broccoli for early next spring. I sowed mine last year on 3 July (it's meant to go in in May) and still got a crop, albeit not until April, when you really want it earlier. And one or two more sowings of salad greens, if it's not too hot, should see you through until September.

In the flower border, regular dead-heading will do much to help your garden defy the late summer tendency to straggliness. Roses obviously spring to mind, and with the repeat-flowering types you will really see the results. Use sharp secateurs and cut at a slant just above a side shoot, being careful not to take off too much leaf. Many of the herbaceous perennials will also benefit from having their old flowers cut or trimmed. Pinks, aquilegias, delphiniums and penstemons should all put forth a second flurry of flowers, though these are seldom as impressive as the first. Herbs such as rosemary and purple and variegated sage, which are desirable as foliage plants as well as for their culinary uses, should really be trimmed before they flower, to keep the leaves in peak condition.

Some plants respond well to more drastic action. In the vegetable patch, parsley, sorrel and perpetual spinach can be cut right back to the ground, watered well and left to regenerate – my landlord at the seaside house we rented last year used to make huge quantities of something called 'Homity Pie' with the shearings. And in the garden, you can be similarly severe with *Alchemilla mollis,* cranesbill geraniums and galegas, whose leaves will soon look tired. Only the geraniums are likely to flower a second time, but all should produce fresh new mounds of foliage which will last into autumn. With lavender, a hard pruning after flowering will save plants from growing leggy and woody in the middle. Here it's important *not* to cut right back, since the plant won't re-sprout from dead wood. Leave just a few live leaves where you cut, and the plant will soon put out an attractive coat of new paler green foliage.

The only disadvantage of such severe pruning and cutting back is, of course, that your borders will look rather shorn and patchy while the plants are growing back. Why not turn this to your advantage and do it just before you go on holiday? Water and feed well – and ask a neighbour to come in and water once a week or so, depending on the weather. Then, all the while that you are relaxing on the beach and re-charging your batteries, your garden, too, will be renewing itself. You should both be rejuvenated on your return.

PURPLE HAZE

This seems to be the year of purple vegetables. The plant of choice in many stands in the floral pavilions at this year's Chelsea Flower Show was the purple tree spinach (*Chenopodium giganteum*), whose attractive spires of purple-splashed leaves graced flower and vegetable gardens alike; the Cottage Herbery (01584 781575) has seed and plug plants. Red orach (*Atriplex hortensis rubra*) and the frilly leaved Japanese basil 'Purple Shiso' made pretty borders on the Jekka's Herb Farm (01454 4188780) stand, while Sarah Raven was selling packs of "Weird and Wonderful Vegetables", including the blue-purple leek 'Saint Victor' and crimson-black 'Purple Teepee' dwarf french beans on her stand in the main shopping avenue (£15 for eight packets of seed, 01424 838181 for details). But for the best display of dark-hued veg, you couldn't beat Medwyns of Anglesey (01248 714851), who were displaying a new purple carrot called 'Purple Haze' (not often that Jimi Hendrix is linked with root vegetables) alongside the purple-fleshed potato 'Shetland Black', the runner bean 'Purple King' and its French consort 'Purple Queen', a glossy black pepper called 'Blue Jay' and some so-far un-named purple parsnips and peas (only the pod is purple) from their own collection.

Purple vegetables also figure in one of the best gardens at the new Westonbirt Festival of Gardens (at Westonbirt Arboretum in Gloucestershire from June to October, ring 0800 093 4075 for details). The "Journey with Butterflies" garden, which takes its inspiration from the life-cycle of the butterfly and leads visitors through an edible vegetable patch, into a giant silver chrysalis and out into a butterfly-friendly flower garden, includes some lovely curly purple kales (crinkly 'Redbor' and red-veined 'Red Russian') alongside the glaucous mauvey-green leaves of purple-sprouting broccoli, Roman artichokes and sea kale (*Crambe maritima*).

Some of the loveliest purple hues in the vegetable garden do belong to the brassica family. Even if I didn't like cabbage, I would still grow them for their beautiful leaves in all shades of green through bluey-mauve to deepest purple – they look beautiful with the low sun shining through them at the end of the day, or outlined by a thick white rim of frost in winter. 'Colorsa' from DT Brown (0845 6014656) is a Savoy-type with stunning magenta-veined bluey leaves. The younger leaves can be eaten in salads. Purple-sprouting broccoli looks beautiful at all stages of its growth, but I also enjoy red cabbage ('Christmas Drumhead' from The Organic Gardening Catalogue (01932 253666) can still be sown now if you hurry) and got an excellent crop from the purple Brussels sprout 'Falstaff' (from Thompson & Morgan, 01473 688821).

For all their exotic beauty while growing in the ground, many purple vegetables – the beans and sprouts, for instance – rather disappointingly turn green on cooking. Which is where salad crops come into their own. I love the sight of rows of fresh green lettuce leaves interplanted with the darker varieties such as 'Red Salad Bowl' or 'Rossa Ricciolina' (both cutting lettuces from Seeds of Italy (020 8930 2516). I've no time for the floppy frills of 'Lollo Rosso', which have an annoying habit of holding water, but am a convert to the purple-edged leaves of 'Quattro Stagioni' and the big-hearted deep red and green 'Maravilla de Verano Canasta', both of which can be sown through till September (again from Seeds of Italy). Their good looks apart, I've repeatedly found that red and purple-leaved lettuces are less prone to slug and snail damage than the plain green types. Spicy mustard greens are another they won't touch: 'Giant Red' from The Organic Gardening Catalogue (01932 253666) has deep purple leaves and can be sown in late summer for winter use.

Lastly, don't miss out on black tomatoes! Simpson's Seeds (01985 845004) sells 'Black Plum', which looked (and tasted) great in my garden last year, and the glamorously named 'Noire Chambonneuse' (sold as plantlets), both of which would look wonderful in pots planted with a fringe of purple-leaf basil and golden tagetes to deter the aphids.

14 July 2002

GARDENING AGAINST THE ODDS

Why do we garden? And why does the passion with which we garden so often seem to be in inverse proportion to the conditions in which we do it? This is a question over which I often ponder while weeding the allotment or cycling down London's sooty, smelly Brixton Road. This last month, three instances of what I call "gardening against the odds" have made me ponder even more. Number one is a balcony in a concrete council block that I pass on my bike on my way into the centre of town. Every summer, this tiny, unprepossessing space – it can't be more than 1.8 x 1.2m (6 x 4ft) and overlooking a busy road – is a riot of sweetcorn and sunflowers. I've never once seen the owner, but like to fantasize it's one of the many local residents, who came over from the Caribbean in the Fifties and Sixties, for whom beans and corn in the back yard still mean independence. Anyhow, it always cheers me up as I ride past.

The second is a roadside verge down near the south coast, in the village where we spent much of last summer. On a turning off the busy sea road into a modern housing estate, someone has taken the trouble to plant a narrow strip of "no-man's-land" land with bearded iris, sisyrinchiums, white astrantia and low-growing grasses and campanulas. It's such a beautiful piece of planting, I'm surprised it doesn't cause traffic accidents. And it seems to me all the more beautiful for being completely selfless – it reminds me of that old hippy tenet to "practice random kindness and senseless acts of beauty". The last instance, and one it makes me sad to write about, concerns the father of a close friend of mine, who recently died from cancer. Some weeks ago, having just been told the worst by the hospital, he became agitated that he hadn't been able to order and sow seeds of the balsam flowers (*Impatiens balsamina*) that he and his wife have always loved to grow in their garden. You could call it displacement anxiety, but I could understand this gnawing concern about his favourite seeds, which were no longer offered by the mail order company he had habitually used. I could sense the comfort he would have in knowing that the garden would be full of these sweet-smelling flowers all summer, even if he might not be there to see them. I helped to track down the seeds, he sowed them, and his wife sent me a small tray of seedlings to plant in my own garden.

So what is this human urge to garden – to fill our living space, no matter how small, with living plants – to embark on this passionate collaboration with nature, no matter how seemingly inauspicious the circumstances? After 20 years of travelling to write about gardens, it is by no means just the great and grand gardens and their owners that remain in my memory – if anything, I remember all the more vividly the hundreds of tiny patches – on strips of rooftops, sun-baked shingle, even the tops of narrow boats or travellers' converted buses – all conceived and tended with the deepest love and care. I remember the nonogenarian who was still planning (and did, in fact, finish) an ambitious water cascade in his garden in Oxfordshire; the front garden fashioned from blue-and-white painted breeze blocks and car tyre-containers in rural Barbados; the miniature Versailles behind a modern housing estate in Holland; the woman who raises home-grown vegetables, including 20-odd types of basil, on a tiny roof terrace in Chelsea. It is in honour of these and all the many other "gardeners against the odds" that I am planting out John Bloom's balsam in my garden this afternoon.

21 July 2002

SUCCESSIVE SOWING

A crucial aspect of vegetable gardening, and one I'm only just beginning to get to grips with after seven years on the job, is growing the right amount for one's needs. A forgetful spell in early summer meant no purple sprouting broccoli the following spring, while the time I put in too many runner bean plants, even family and close friends were turning them away and I had to make even more chutney than usual. It's difficult to offer hard and fast advice on this topic as so much depends on personal preference, but with careful planning you can avoid too many gluts – or at least make sure they include your favourites.

On our allotment, we never have *quite* enough broad beans for my liking, in spite of making two mass sowings – one in November, which lasts us from late May to mid-July, and one in March, which takes up the baton and continues till the runner beans are ready. I really must allocate a larger bed for broad beans next year. And it never ceases to amaze me how many pea plants you need to pick enough for supper on a regular basis. It's all very well having a sprinkling of peas or broad beans in a salad or pasta sauce, but every so often I want mounds of the things to eat unaccompanied and unadorned. This year's pea crop may look ravishing climbing up a pair of hazel wigwams ('Kelvedon Wonder' and 'Hurst Greenshaft' up one and sugar-snaps up the other), but it soon dawned on me that the crop was not going to feed our longings, so we made a later sowing in mid June, filling the 1.5 x 2.4m (5 x 8ft) bed recently vacated by over-wintering brassicas. Feeding while the flowers and pods are forming should encourage a good crop – I swear by a murky brown mixture made by steeping rough-chopped comfrey leaves in water in an old rainwater butt, and diluting it with ten or more parts water before use. It may seem late for sowing peas, but the seed germinates well in warm soil – and anyway, it was with a similarly late crop that we won first prize in the Lambeth Country Show a few years ago (probably because most other people's peas were over). I wonder if we can repeat our triumph in a few weeks time?

We've also managed to make successive sowings of french beans this year – both dwarf varieties, such as the colourful 'Purple Teepee' and 'Beurre de Roquencourt' (yellow), and the attractive climber, 'Blue Lake'. Borlotti beans I brought back from Tuscany should prove useful in terms of spreading the crop, as they can be harvested at three different stages: early on, when the pods are still greenish and can be enjoyed whole; later, when fresh beans can be popped from their red-streaked pods and boiled up in minestrone and lastly at the end of the season, when the pods are dark and withered, and the dried beans can be stored through the winter. Another crop we shouldn't run short of is courgettes. Four healthy plants are usually enough to feed a family, and we must have twelve, including gourmet varieties such as the dark glossy 'Black Beauty', ridged and flavoursome 'Romanesco', bright yellow 'Goldneck' and the oddly spherical 'Tondo di Nizza'. Picking them small – they're at their tastiest between 5–10cm (2–4in) long – should help us keep pace with what promises to be a bumper crop.

The tomatoes are also looking good, but I must be careful not to speak too soon. Last summer I arrived at the allotment to discover that all of them had succumbed to late blight – the killer disease that was the cause of the great Irish potato famine of the 1840s. More on the dreaded blight, and how best to avoid it, next week.

28 July 2002

GETTING THE BETTER OF BLIGHT

Tomatoes are by no means the easiest crop to grow, but the reward of all that painstaking pinching out and tying in should be juicy and flavoursome fruit that far surpasses any you'll find in the shops. Each year I look forward to the first harvest, and can never resist popping a few 'Gardener's Delight', still warm from the sun, into my mouth as I pick. But last year, that one first harvest was all we had. One fine evening I was picking a couple of pounds of plump shiny tomatoes to bring home, happy to see so many more small fruits still to ripen. Three days later I returned to a scene of unbelievable devastation: bedraggled plants with floppy brown leaves and soggy discoloured fruit. I knew this must be the dreaded Late Blight that I'd read about in books and that there was nothing that could be done. I pulled up all the plants and burned them, and paid a rare summer visit to the greengrocer.

Late blight (or *Phytophora infestans*) attacks potatoes and tomatoes, and is spread by wind-borne spores. The prime cause of the great Irish potato famine of the 1840s, it is a killer that can destroy an entire crop in just a few days. The first signs in potatoes are dark blotches on leaves and stems, with white mould developing in humid conditions. The whole plant may collapse quickly and lead to dry or rotting tubers, but if you spot it early enough, remove all affected foliage and earth up well around the stems, you may manage to save the crop. You may not be able to stop it spreading to nearby tomatoes, however, where blight is almost always fatal. The unmistakeable early signs are brown patches on the tips and edges of leaves, followed by dark brown streaks along the stems and a red-brown discoloration on the top half of the fruit, around the stem. If left, the fruit will rot and stink. It is all most disheartening.

None of my organic gardening books offers any effective measures against tomato blight – save using certified seed from a reputable source and avoiding planting potatoes and tomatoes too near together. On allotments like ours, the latter is not always possible, and blight can spread like wildfire from one plot to another, particularly if there's a breeze to carry the spores. With the prevailing wind blowing in our direction, our two plots at the lower end of the site are particularly vulnerable to attack. Blight *can* be anticipated, however, and dealt with accordingly. It thrives in hot, humid conditions – when the temperature has not fallen below 10°C (50°F) (nights included) for 48 hours and humidity is around 90 per cent for much of the day, then late blight is almost inevitable. This is how the Simpson family of the tomato specialists Simpson's Seeds cope with the disease, having learned the hard way. From early June, they spray fortnightly with copper fungicide (organic gardeners use Bordeaux Mixture), making sure to cover the undersides of the leaves as well. To avoid contaminating the flowers, they protect the trusses by holding an empty glass jar over them. In late July – when plants are most at risk – they switch from copper fungicide to a chemical called Dithane 945, which coats the leaves with a film of fungicide that is lethal to any spores that might attempt to settle. This would be the stuff to buy, should a hot humid spell be forecast – Mr Simpson says they have found it effective in the early stages, even *after* blight has struck. This is not an organic remedy, and it is advisable to wait till at least seven days after an application to harvest your tomatoes, and then to wash the fruit well before eating or storing. I'm loth to use chemicals – but when the alternative seems to be losing the entire crop all over again I might make an exception, just for the tomatoes.

11 August 2002

DREAMING OF OLIVE GROVES

It was Pliny the Younger who first drew literary attention to the way olive trees flutter the silvery undersides of their leaves in a light breeze. That was nearly 2,000 years ago, but I was struck anew by the effect on a recent holiday in Greece. Our terrace looked out over what must once have been a large olive grove, planted between the mountains and the sea. Some of the trees, with gnarled and hollowed trunks a couple of feet wide, may even have been seedlings when Pliny was alive; the latest research suggests that the oldest olives may be many hundreds – even thousands – of years older than previously believed. They were underplanted with *Iris unguicularis,* which must make a wonderful sight in early spring, the pools of blue petals echoing the colour of the sea beyond.

I was interested to find that this was one of the plantings recommended beneath olives by Russell Page in *The Education of a Gardener* (Harvill Press, £12) – his classic autobiography, which was part of my holiday reading. Page created as many Mediterranean as British gardens in the latter part of his life, and often found himself designing around ancient olive trees. White freesias, wild scarlet and blue anemones, small white Roman hyacinths and white jonquils were other plants he suggested for a natural look on the outskirts of a garden, while nearer the house he might go for a more formal combination of bay laurels, choisyas, late-flowering *Lagerstroemia indica,* agapanthus and tree peonies. In another scenario, he recommends making a lawn beneath the trees and then planting mauve wisteria, yellow and white Banksian roses and the free-flowering, fast-growing rose 'La Follette' to "ramp about among the branches and make swaying garlands of scent and colour". This is an extremely seductive picture, and in a rose-tinged future when I've written my bestseller and retired to a villa in Tuscany or Greece, I plan to do the same.

Those of us without sun-baked acres, however, need not deny ourselves the odd olive tree. *Olea europea* is hardier than one might imagine and can thrive in this country, given the right conditions. In Cornwall or the sheltered microclimate of a walled London garden, small trees can grow outside all year; in other situations it is best to plant in a pot and move them inside for winter. "I know people who keep olives outside in less favoured areas, but by the end of the winter the trees are thin and unhappy and barely hanging on," says Sarah Chandler at Architectural Plants in W. Sussex

(01403 891772), where the olive trees on sale range from £21.50 for a small bush and £82.50 for a lollipop standard, to £350 for a mature tree. Aged, gnarled specimens, such as those I saw in Greece, go for about £2,350, but would only be sold to those with ideal conditions. "Cold, wet soil is what they don't like," says Ms Chandler. "Survival is one thing, but flourishing is another, and if you can't give a plant the conditions it needs, it's best not to grow it." Olive trees grown in conservatories are happiest when moved outside for the summer, to avoid pest damage and temperature swings.

If I were to grow an olive tree in the city, I'd find one six foot or so high and plant it in an old dustbin. Galvanized metal would pick up on the subtle colours of the leaves, and this could be continued with underplantings of silvery cistus, artemesia, santonlina, grey-leafed teucriums and the beautiful white-belled *Convulvulus cneorum*, all of which would thrive in the sunny corner the tree would require. But you can forget about making your own olive oil. Even large trees don't fruit well in this country – though I do know a couple whose annual London olive crop gives them the garnish for a few dry martinis.

18 August 2002

RETURN TO THE SHOW BENCH

Two summers have passed since we exhibited our allotment produce at the Lambeth Country Show – a glorious annual event that transforms our local park into an unlikely mixture of traditional county fair and raucous Rasta festival. This may be the early twenty-first century in one of London's grittiest inner-city boroughs, but you'd never know it inside the hallowed white interior of the Flower Show marquee. To enter is to step back into 1950s rural Britain, with rows of gingham-topped jars of jam and hand-knits ranged up alongside the flower, fruit and vegetable exhibits. Presiding over the judging is the Lambeth Horticultural Society, whose members are experts in presenting produce for competition. Woe betide you if your shallots aren't polished to a sheen with their tops neatly trussed, or your peas and beans not of uniform size with the bloom still intact.

Back in 1999, we'd been thrilled to win first prize in the pea category (Class 51: 'Ten Pods') and third for our potatoes (Class 43: 'White, Four of Any One Variety') and red onions (Class 52: 'Five, to be Shown as Grown'). Once they'd got over the sight of us cleaning our potatoes with spit and a hankie, the organizers had been very kind to us, advising on presentation (one even offered us a paper doily). Our excitement at winning first prize had been only very slightly dampened by the realization that two of the venerable old-timers, Mr Lamothe and Mr Dare, who had won every other category hands down with their immaculately presented vegetables, hadn't exhibited any peas.

This year, making a preliminary inspection at the allotment in the week running up to the show, I was dubious about repeating our past success. The first crop of peas was over while the second sowing had yet to bear fruit. The broad beans had reached that knobbly unattractive stage, and there were no runner nor french beans to speak of. Potatoes were a possibility – though rather a dull one – but the courgettes looked in good shape. I searched for them in vain in the show schedule before realizing that, along with aubergines, artichokes and the like, they were considered much too 'Johnny-come-lately' to have a category of their own, and came under 'Class 57: Any Other Vegetable Not Classified in the Foregoing Classes'. On the spur of the moment, I rashly signed up for sweetpeas ('Class 9: One Vase of') and two of the succulent plant classes. I handed the form in the day before the show, and was touched when the organizers greeted me like a long lost friend.

The day of the show dawned, and Simon, Clarkey and I met up early at the allotment, feeling slightly grumpy and not at all confident. A week of warm wet weather had swollen all the courgettes into mini-marrows – bar three of the round variety 'Tondo di Nizza', which we picked although we thought they were probably too small. The potatoes didn't look up to much, but some dwarf french beans had appeared from nowhere and we *just* managed to find ten pods of the same size. With only half an hour till judging, there was just enough time to pick some sweet peas and head off in the camper van to the show, where we switched our potato entry to beans and laid everything out in a hurry.

Two hours later, we could scarcely believe our eyes. *Four* first prizes – for the sweetpeas, both my succulent plants *and* the courgettes, and a second for the beans! It was only when I returned the next evening to collect our produce and claim our prize money (£2 for first, £1.50 for second) that I learned the sad and somewhat humbling news that both Mr Dare and Mr Lamothe had died earlier in the year. While last time's winnings bought us a round of ice-creams, this year we could stretch to a pint each of 'Chuckle-head' cider in the beer tent. It seemed only fair that we should raise our glasses to them.

25 August 2002

THE WEDDING GARDEN

I went to a wedding last weekend where the bride and groom, both keen gardeners, had made it known that they'd like to receive plants for the garden as presents. This struck me as a very suitable and sensible idea: most of my friends have married well into their thirties, by which time they already own all the saucepans and salad bowls they are ever likely to need, and often twice over at that. Rather than the traditional "wedding list", you could visit a website with a list of the couple's most desired plants, and choose whether to pick out individual plants as gifts, or send a cheque as an overall contribution. This inspired idea not only ensures that this couple will, unlike so many others, actually get what they want for their wedding presents; it will also provide them with lasting enjoyment and memories of their wedding long after many of the more usual gifts might have got broken or lost. They are creating an entire new section of the garden for these plants, and the planning and planting of this 'Wedding Garden' will be an exciting project for the autumn; the delivery of the plants has been timed to coincide with their return from honeymoon. It's an idea that translates well to other events or parties to which guests like to bring a present. Why not make a 'Fiftieth Birthday Border', for instance, or a 'Silver Anniversary Bed' using predominantly silver, grey or white plants? The possibilities are endless, but the recipients really do need to be people who will be sticking in the same spot for a few years.

This got me thinking in general about weddings and such events – we've been to quite a few big parties this year and I've been asked to help with flowers for another. I loved planning the flowers for my own wedding in the depths of winter, and there is so much more scope in the summer and autumn months. One thing that got me down was the waste, however. Much though I'd have liked to, we weren't able to give all of the cut flowers away, and many of the arrangements that decorated the tables ended up being thrown away. How much better, I'm now thinking, inspired by my friends' example, to use potted plants or flowers that could be incorporated into your garden following the event. Again, there's a host of options. Small blooming lavender bushes would look beautiful, and their scent could fill an entire marquee; their starring role over, they could be planted out as a commemorative hedge. Box plants could be decorated with fake flowers or fairy lights and then used to make a maze or formal garden – you could use larger, topiarized pieces on the day to flank entrances and so on. For a winter wedding, what could look prettier than small pots of snowdrops in the centre of the tables? Or, depending on the timing and the colour scheme, other early spring-flowering bulbs such as bright blue muscari or *Iris reticulata*?

All of these would have a future life that would add to the garden – and to the memories of the event – for many years to come. I'm sure you can think of ideas of your own. The important thing with table decorations is, of course, to keep them low. Your guests don't want to be peering at one another through impenetrable foliage. Sarah Raven of The Cutting Garden once used a reverse version of the above idea for a spring wedding – she cut strips of turf from her wildflower meadow, complete with buttercups, harebells and daisies, and ran them right down the length of the long tables (in trays to keep them moist). After the party, they could be restored to their original habitat with the minimum of disturbance.

1 September 2002

HIDDEN GARDENS OF NEW YORK

When I first went to New York, I wondered where all the gardens were. Central Park aside, the city seemed devoid of the green squares and neighbourhood parks that one takes for granted in London. It turns out that I was looking in the wrong places. Squeezed between skyscrapers or down quiet residential streets, hidden inside museums, perched high on rooftops or languishing in some of the less-fashionable boroughs, are some real treats. You just need to know where to go.

On my first trip, I did discover the garden at the Frick Collection, the 1900s Upper East Side mansion that houses an impressive array of paintings while still retaining the atmosphere of a grand house in Edith Wharton's day. Russell Page's Pool Garden is a model of classical restraint, a cool oasis, a stone's throw from the bumper-to-bumper traffic. Go on a winter's afternoon, when staff still lower the blinds at dusk, and imagine the carriages drawing up outside. The Cloisters, way up on the northernmost tip of the island, are well worth the trip, and plants depicted in the Unicorn tapestries and other medieval works of art for which this museum is famous have been used in a series of pretty courtyard gardens high above the Hudson River. One is an educational herb garden, another laid out with an orchard and apothecary garden in the manner of a medieval monastery – pleasantly incongruous in this otherwise modern city.

My favourite museum garden, the chic contemporary sculpture garden at the Museum of Modern Art, is sadly not open at the moment due to major building works. But if you're headed over to Queens, where MOMA has been re-located until 2004, you should seize the opportunity to see the Isamu Noguchi Sculpture Garden – a suitably Japanese-inspired monument to the sculptor best-known in the UK for his round paper lampshades. Queens also has one of the most beautiful, but least frequented of the city's botanical gardens, with stunning new perennial borders and a large formal herb garden.

Back in Manhattan, some quiet green enclaves can be found in the most unlikely places. Just a step off Fifth Avenue, at 3 West 53rd Street, is Paley Park, a 15 x 30m (50 x 100ft) model of Sixties landscape design, with robinia trees rising from the cobbled floor, ivy-clad walls, white Harry Bertoia chairs and a 6m (20ft) waterfall on the far wall, which drowns out the city's clamour. Nearby Greenacre Park, at 221 East 51st Street (between 2nd and 3rd Avenues), is similarly modernist in style, with two such water sculptures and brighter seasonal planting. The Downtown equivalent of these chic neighbourhood parks are the colourful community gardens of the Lower East Side. Created on vacant lots from the 1970s onwards, with support from organizations like the Green Guerillas and Green Thumb, these are spirited affairs, where junk sculptures and makeshift shrines to the Madonna rub shoulders with pocket-handkerchief potagers, communal compost heaps and covered stages for parties and poetry readings. Head for 'Alphabet City' (east of 1st Avenue, where the numbers peter out into letters) and check out the '6th and B Garden' (on 6th Street between Avenues B and C), or the lovely Liz Christy Garden on the corner of Bowery and Houston Street, named after the founder of the Community Garden movement. Throughout the city, look out for the many tiny fenced-in 'Viewing Gardens', created as part of ex-mayor Rudi Giuliani's controversial clean-up crusade and maintained by volunteers.

Trudging the streets is the best way to come across some of the city's most stunning green spaces. This is how I happened upon Martha Schwartz's swirling Day-Glo green benches and 1.8m (6ft) grass mounds at Federal Plaza (corner of Worth and Lafayette Streets) – a graphic piece of landscape art that still cuts the mustard with the lunchtime sandwich brigade. The trees on Trump Tower (5th Ave and 56th Street) are as startling as an art installation, as are the blocks of bright tulips down Park Avenue's central reservation in May, and its illuminated Memorial Trees in December. And don't forget the West Village, where the elegant brownstones have well-tended front gardens, and even the street trees have neat, railed-in enclosures to protect them from the unwelcome attentions of dogs.

LATE SUMMER LOVELINESS

I've just counted 23 different plants in flower in my tiny front and back gardens. Though the general impression is one of luxuriant late-summer leafiness, there are morning glories and passion flowers still scrambling up the sunny house wall, nasturtiums, sweetpeas and late-flowering clematis framing the french windows and, out in the front strip, towering black hollyhocks, dark sunflowers, sprays of bronze fennel and 3m (10ft) cardoons with electric violet thistle-heads. For many gardeners, "late summer colour" means the scorching hot reds, oranges and yellows of crocosmias, dahlias and daisy-like rudbeckias and heleniums. While I love their firework flowers, I simply don't have enough sun for most of them. And, rather than concentrate such colours in one "hot border" as people with much larger plots can do, I prefer to eke them out as contrasting accents among the subtler shades that predominate in my garden. Against a foliage backdrop of glossy green acanthus, *Euphorbia mellifera*, bamboos, bronze phormium, *Astelia chathamica* 'Silver Spear' and glaucous grey-green *Macleaya cordata* and *Melianthus major,* even the less assertive flowers show up well.

The real stars of the show this year include *Eucomis bicolor* whose five spikes of milky green blossoms, each immaculately outlined in dark maroon, are crowned with the lime green leafy tufts that earn it the common nick-name of the 'pineapple lily'. I bought this as a young plant four years ago and have been pleased to see it increasing from a single flower spike to three and now five. It dies down completely over the winter and every year, come the end of May, I think I've lost it, but then the first new shoots appear. Bloms (01234 709099) sell it at £5 for three bulbs – its only drawback is a faint smell of rancid mushrooms.

New for me this year is *Nicandra physaloides,* also known as the 'shoo-fly plant' because it is thought to keep away aphids. It's a curious-looking plant, with strong lime green foliage flecked with dark purple, and violet-blue, white-throated bell-shaped blooms. The flowers, however, are not the point. They fade after just one day and quickly transmute into spherical papery green fruit, not unlike those of the Chinese lantern but attractively streaked with the same dark black-purple that marks the stems. I have a few plants rising among a large clump of *Geranium phaeum* 'Samobor', whose purple leaf blotches compliment it rather too perfectly. A few flaming orange nasturtiums or crocosmias would lighten things up; in another, sunnier spot nicandra would make a great companion for black and orange cactus dahlias. It is an annual, and seed is available from Chiltern Seeds (01229 581137), who also sell *N. physaloides* 'Variegata', which has cream-splashed foliage.

These nicandra plants were given to me by my mother as seedlings earlier in the spring. The year before, she'd been given a seed-head by a friend who

had brought it back from France not knowing what it was and asked her to try the seed. My mother was bewildered when the plants first began to form their strange fruit calyxes, and when her descriptions over the phone to me drew a blank (such, I'm afraid, is my expertise), she sensibly took advantage of her Royal Horticultural Society membership and sent a sample to their Garden Advisory Centre, RHS Garden Wisley, Woking, Surrey (01483 224234 – free service for RHS members). Within the week they had written back identifying the plant as nicandra. This seems a good opportunity to recommend this service to readers, who sometimes send me parts of plants which, by the time they arrive on my desk here at home, are a sorry, smelly mess and completely unidentifiable. As regular readers will know, I never claim to be an expert in plant identification and the RHS (membership enquiries 0207 821 3000) is much better equipped to help out with such queries.

15 September 2002

LIGHTING THE TOUCH PAPER OF SPRING

In recent years I have taken to making my annual bulb order with the assistance of several of my godchildren. A few are becoming quite keen on gardening, and they love looking through the coloured catalogues, picking out the flowers they like best. Each one gets a bag of bulbs as a present, which I then help them plant out in pots or in their allocated section of garden. Their parents are pleased, too. As many of the bulb companies offer much cheaper rates for bulk orders of 50 or 100 of each variety, it pays to place their own bulb orders along with mine and make the most of my extravagance. Even with my tiny town garden, I fork out more than many would spend on a fortnight's holiday. But to me it is always well worth it. The annual autumn ritual of unpacking the bulbs and burying them in the soil has become a pivotal point in my year; just as the garden is dying down for the winter, I feel as if I'm lighting the touchpaper of spring. The bulbs are like a slow-burning fuse, smouldering away unseen beneath a blanket of compost or mulch, ready to explode into flower the next year. Planting them is an act of hope; it's also one of the closest things to magic that I know. No wonder it appeals to children.

Last October Oliver, aged 7, and his 5 year-old brother Daniel and I spent a sunny afternoon planting hundreds of daffodils in great swathes under the apple trees in their new garden, lifting up patches of turf and placing the bulbs in holes in the soil below. Daniel was captivated by the idea that these boring onion-like objects could turn into flowers, and used to trek outside, even in the depths of winter, to see if he could spot the first shoots coming through. He also planted lots of alliums in his own little plot, and was vastly proud of his huge starry spheres of *A. cristophii* and dark magenta drumsticks of *A. sphaerocephalon*. This year he knew exactly what he wanted: the 1m (3ft) high violet heads of *A.* 'Globemaster' and the smaller, cornflower-blue blooms of *A. caeruleum*. His mother and I had to lure him away from some of the more garish striped parrot tulips, but I threw in a few *Allium schubertii* for good measure – no one, child nor adult, could fail to be bowled over by its enormous heads of flowers, shooting off like fireworks on long thin pedicels.

Another godchild, Ceidra, and her sister Martha attended a fun workshop called 'The Magic of Potting', which was organized by the Netherlands Flower Bulb Information Centre (0207 915 4776), where they dressed up as wizards and used magic potions to plant up pots of bulbs to bring home. Four-year-old Ceidra was so taken by her new charges that she kept digging them up every day to check they were all right, but she has finally grasped the idea that they need to be left alone in order for nature to get in on the magic, too. As soon as my bulb order arrives, I'll give her some 'Paper White' narcissi to plant up in a clear plastic bowl with just pebbles and water. These are great for impatient gardeners of any age, as the roots start to grow within days, and the fragrant white flowers appear in just five weeks. In a warm room, you can almost see the stems growing at an inch or more a day. De Jaeger (01622 831235) sells them at £17.50 for 25 – I stagger mine through the winter, starting off a new bowl every three weeks or so.

For further inspiration on planting bulbs with children, check out the Netherlands Flower Bulb Information Centre's website, www.flowerbulbs.co.uk/magicofpotting. This has some great ideas, including planting a 'fairy ring' of tête-a-tête narcissi and grape hyacinths beneath the lawn and a 'firework cauldron' of crocuses, tulips and alliums to bloom in succession from March to June.

22 September 2002

UNRULY SPLENDOUR

I love the allotment at this time of year. It is riotously untidy, with the grass paths overgrown and nasturtiums romping among the ripening sweetcorn and courgettes. But it is a fecund and colourful untidiness which is uplifting to look at. Our woven willow bower seems to float on a sea of flowers, and purple morning glories sprawl across its roof. Self-seeded borage and love-in-a-mist make a blue haze among the beans, while the sweetpeas, their leaves and stems a parched and papery tangle, are still putting out a few fragrant blooms. There are the first cobs of corn to harvest, along with glossy green courgettes, crimson-streaked borlotti beans and purple french beans. Best of all, there are the 'Autumn Bliss' raspberries to pick – I refuse to be dismayed by the bindweed flowers flying like white pennants from the corners of the fruit cage.

Occasionally, on the way into the site, I experience pangs of guilt and envy when I pass the immaculate plot belonging to Mustafa, who grows the ingredients for the perfect curry in a neat patchwork of sunken beds and weed-free earth paths. This year he has raised a fine crop of outdoor cucumbers up a framework of lashed timber, and a continuous supply of coriander which, unlike mine, never goes to seed. Nor do his squashes ramp unrestrained through the rest of his plot: they have been trained in straight lines (on carpet, to protect them from slugs), or up a pergola-like structure and along its chicken-wire roof, where they can ripen fast in full sun, while salad greens enjoy the dappled shade below. It is all extremely organized, and I often start making resolutions to become more like Mustafa next year. But then I round the corner into our own double plot, and am greeted by all that unruly splendour.

Aesthetics apart, there are other unexpected advantages to our untidiness. Untrimmed sprays of rosemary, mint and lemon balm release their scent into the warm air whenever we push past. Bees and other beneficial insects forage among the flowers. And the other day I uncovered a bed of shallots I'd completely forgotten about. Pulling up a few handfuls of groundsel and speedwell in a half-hearted attempt to stop them self-seeding, I saw the dried-up tufts of what looked like onion tops clustered just above the soil. Of course! This was where I had planted shallot sets in spring. As I lifted more than 40 heads of five to ten shallots apiece, I reflected on what an obliging and trouble-free crop they are. I don't think I can have done more than a little initial weeding and watering while they quietly got on with it and multiplied. When you add into the equation their reputation as a gourmet vegetable, and the outrageous prices for even non-organic shallots in the shops, it's a wonder we don't grow more of them.

Mr Fothergill's (01638 552512) has shallot sets in six varieties including 'Longor' and 'Mikor' , the long Jersey types with their large elliptical bulbs, and round, pink-tinged 'Red Sun', while The Organic Gardening Catalogue

(01932 253666) has a choice of four, including organically raised sets of 'Delvad' (round, with pinkish flesh) and later, high-yielding 'Sante'. Long-bulbed varieties can be planted out in autumn and most of the round types from January onwards, but 'Sante' must wait till March to prevent it bolting. Plant the sets shallowly in rich soil and forget all about them for five months (though for optimum yields, a little light weeding is recommended). When the green stalks have yellowed off the shallots will be ready for lifting – an easy enough job with a fork. Cure in a dry warm place for a few days and store in net bags before using in everything from risottos to wintry stews. They really are the perfect crop for the lazy gourmet gardener.

29 September 2002

CHICORIES AND RADICCHIO

When I went to Florence aged 16 on a school exchange, I was asked one day to help the ancient grandmother of the family pick salad for lunch. We wandered into the garden, where she immediately bent double and started grubbing up plants from the lawn and flowerbeds, indicating that I should do the same. The resulting bowl of weeds bore no resemblance to salad as I then knew it, and was evidence, I was convinced, of the old woman's senility. And then I tasted it. Dressed in peppery olive oil and balsamic vinegar, the flavours and textures of the different leaves made the most delicious salad I had ever encountered. Some were bitter with crunchy, juicy midribs; others were sweeter and softer with that squeakiness between the teeth of freshly picked leaves. The only ones I recognized were dandelions, but I now know they must have included rocket, lamb's lettuce, various different herbs and many types of chicory and radicchio – all referred to generically by Italians as *"cicorie"*.

We've all become much more sophisticated since the Seventies. A pile of baby leaves of Mediterranean or oriental extraction is now a *de rigueur* accompaniment on any respectable restaurant menu, and many gardeners grow their own. Many of us have tried salad seed mixes – called 'Saladini' by the Organic Gardening Catalogue (01932 253666), 'Misticanza' by Seeds of Italy (020 8930 2516) and 'Italian Salad Collection' by Mr Fothergill (01638 552512) – which are usually a blend of lettuce, endive, chicory and radicchio. But I suspect I'm not the only one to have been confused as to the exact identity of the leaves that surfaced. In the UK we tend to think of chicory as the fat white chicons of the 'Witloof' variety that need to be forced in winter. But to an Italian the term embraces round and rosette-headed types that are eaten unblanched, bitter wild chicories that look and taste like dandelions, fat sweet upright 'Sugarloaf' types, long plants whose thick white stems are the principal delicacy, and a gourmet variety named 'Barba di Frate Cappuccino' after the beards of the Capuchin monks.

Confusingly, the term 'chicory' may also be used for what we call radicchio

– the long or round-leaved plants that grow like lettuces in the early stages and go on to develop delicious crispy red and white hearts. The first time I tried a Mediterranean salad mix, I was mystified by a thick-leafed, red-speckled lettuce growing vigorously among the other seedlings. Tough and leathery on the tongue, its main virtue seemed to be that the slugs didn't like it either. It carried on growing long after the other leaves had given up the ghost, and I let it be all winter. Months later I was thrilled to peer between the large outer leaves and discover the jewel-like red hearts within. We ate radicchio all that winter, smugly aware of its astronomic price in the supermarket.

Chicories have a reputation for bitterness – indeed, that is rather their point. The arrow-head leaves may be too much for some palates, but the round varieties and radicchios are milder, especially when blanched. Round types, such as 'Palla Rossa', are self-blanching, while the upright ones just need their leaves tying up ten days or so before harvest. Seeds of Italy has 28 varieties in its excellent catalogue (www.seedsofitaly.com) including the attractive variegated 'Palla Rossa di Chioggia', a striking black-leaved varia-tion of 'Rossa di Treviso' and a mixed pack of 12 varieties. Many can be sown well into autumn and will grow outside unprotected for a harvest that will last until February or March – the perfect overwintering crop. If they taste too bitter, soak the heads in cold, salty water for 30 minutes, or add a little brown sugar or honey to the dressing. Don't forget that you can also cook chicories and radicchios, as the Venetians do. Stripped of the outer leaves, the hearts can be roasted, or fried in olive oil with pancetta and garlic, or simply sprinkled with oil and seasonings and thrown on the barbecue (larger hearts should be quartered) – their crunchy bitterness, rich in antiox-idants, is perfect with grilled meats.

6 October 2002

NEW TREES FOR OLD

The tree outside our house is dying. A young silver birch planted by the local council only two years ago, its bark has rubbed off right around the trunk and it had shed most of its leaves by midsummer. It's always sad to see a tree in trouble, and I feel especially upset about this one as I helped get our street added to the council's '2000 Trees for the Year 2000' planting project and can still remember the excitement when the trees arrived. 'Our' birch is now leaning precariously across the pavement so that people have to duck to pass by. Yet when I rang the council to ask whether they could arrange a replace-ment, I was told this was impossible. Apparently, too many trees were planted in a hurry, without sufficient provisions for maintenance. Young trees need to be watered and have their stakes checked regularly for up to three years, whereas these poor millennium specimens had only one year's care. And there is no budget for renewing the many trees that have been lost.

A tree officer explained that birches are particularly vulnerable to damage as they tend to rely on their stakes for support and don't develop a sufficiently strong root system. When our tree's stake was removed – many months too late – the bark had already started to rub and the trunk to lean. Once the delicate cambium layer beneath the bark was exposed it was only a matter of time before the tree succumbed. I was told that new trees now get double stakes and longer, looser ties to allow more movement and prevent such problems. Interesting though all this was, it wasn't going to get our tree replaced. I even offered to pay for a new one myself, but was turned down in true bureaucratic style due to problems with insurance. Hmmmm.

Then I remembered Trees for London, a dynamic young charity dedicated to improving London's environment through local tree planting projects. It was founded back in 1989 by four friends, all keen clubbers in their twenties, who used to hold rave parties and use the profits to plant trees in London's less leafy boroughs. Working in partnership with local councils, they helped carry out projects ranging from planting more street trees to transforming neglected land around council estates and creating orchards in school playgrounds. Now a registered charity with the original founders as trustees, Trees for London remains true to its streetwise roots by making its planting days like big outdoor parties with a barbecue and club DJ. Involving young local residents has been vital in ensuring that trees don't fall prey to vandals. Current projects include a new woodland in Morden, planting in streets, neighbourhood parks and housing estates in Stockwell, Whitechapel and the Isle of Dogs, and an ambitious 'Ice Age Tree Trail' charting our native trees in the order they were established in the UK after the ice age.

You can help Trees for London's work by turning up at its volunteer planting days (see www.treesforlondon.org) or contributing to the cost of planting trees. To sponsor a tree costs £15 per year, while a grove of five or more trees costs from £72 and a dedicated tree (a larger specimen with a commemorative plaque in honour of a loved one or marking a special occasion) costs £175. Normally, these dedicated trees have to be allocated to one of Trees for London's official sites, but in the circumstances, their director kindly agreed to let me replace our birch. The new tree should go in later this month – all part of the charity's recently launched campaign for a million new (properly maintained) trees in the capital by the year 2010. For further details contact Trees for London, Prince Consort Lodge, Kennington Park Place, London SE11 4AS (020 7587 1320).

13 October 2002

SQUIRRELLING AWAY FOR WINTER

As we begin tidying the allotment for another winter, there's a harvest festival feeling in the air. The warm autumn weather has meant the beans and courgettes kept cropping for longer, and though the sweetcorn's finally over, we're harvesting our first squashes and jerusalem artichokes. There are chicories and radicchio, and late summer sowings of rocket and lamb's lettuce to jazz up shop-bought salads through the winter, along with cut-and-come-again mizuna and spicy giant red mustard. It seems ages since I last shopped for vegetables, and I'm reluctant to start again.

Luckily, we have our first substantial surfeit of produce to store over winter. We devoted a lot more ground to garlic and potatoes this year, and the shallots were a great success. I've cleared some space in our crowded cellar (nicknamed the 'Futility Room') for two sacks of potatoes – one of the tasty red-skinned 'Roseval', much mentioned in the *River Cafe Cook Book*, and another of 'Pink Fir Apples'. Heavy-duty paper sacks are best for this, tied or folded loosely at the neck – you want to let in a little air but no light, to avoid the tubers turning green and toxic. Some of our garlic is plaited into a long rope that lends a pleasing Gallic air to the kitchen – this is easier than it looks if you leave the long stems and remove the earth-encrusted roots. More garlic and shallots are stored in the small netting sacks in which citrus fruit are sold; hanging them up lets air circulate and prevents rotting. There are also a couple of Kilner jars of dried borlotti beans – our first crop of this decorative Italian legume and a welcome addition to winter soups and stews. Having enjoyed most of the beans fresh when their crimson pods lived up to their name of 'Lingua di fuoco' (tongue of fire), we left some on the plant to ripen, which I then shelled, left to dry completely in an airy place for a day or so, and then stored in airtight jars. The fresh beans also freeze brilliantly.

What with a large batch of runner bean chutney (the best fate for the large leathery pods that get forgotten among the foliage) and lots of stewed black-berry-and-apple, there's scarcely an empty jar in the house. And I'll be needing more for the marrow and ginger jam I plan to make with the glut of marrows that friends are refusing to take off my hands. As I survey all the rich and tawny colours in our cellar I feel as smug as a squirrel with its store of nuts.

Growing my own food is satisfying on so many different fronts. First, I still get a kick out of the fact that I've managed to grow anything at all – it seems nothing short of a miracle that a handful of seed should result in all this bounty in just a few months. Although I don't garden to save money (as my bank manager could testify), there *is* a financial bonus, as unusual organic vegetables such as gourmet potatoes and pink shallots are rare and pricy in the shops. More than anything, I appreciate the fact that my produce is pesticide free, and hasn't been picked unripe, irradiated and flown thousands of miles to get to my door. If vegetables could earn air miles, your average supermarket trolley – celery from Israel, apples from New Zealand, etc – could enjoy free Caribbean holidays for my lifetime.

So, as winter creeps closer and I rely once again on bought fruit and veg to fill the gaps in our larder, I shall be passing over the jet-lagged offerings of the supermarkets in favour of in-season produce from our local farmer's market. It may mean no strawberries till next summer, but they'll taste all the sweeter for the wait.

20 October 2002

PARIS FASHIONS

The last thing I expected to bring back from a recent trip to Paris was planting ideas. One is used to French formal gardens having no flowers at all, or relying on tired old colour-by-numbers combinations of salvias and french marigolds to fill the geometric beds. But something must have got into the French. Time and time again I was captivated by exuberant, almost unruly schemes that breathed fresh life into formal layouts. I was even tempted to try some of the ideas back home – the first time I've been inspired by municipal planting anywhere.

One of the prettiest examples was around the boating lake by the palace in the Jardin du Luxembourg, where the garish bedding schemes I remembered from former years had been replaced by a charming concoction in different pinks and mauves. The gracefully curving beds were edged in triangles of lime and magenta coleus and wax begonias – no change there – but among the inner plantings of pink pelargoniums and fluffy mauve ageratums were stunning aubergine salvias and what I think was *S. farinacea* 'Strata', with its spires of woolly silver buds. What really made it for me, though, were thousands of gauras, whose delicate pink-and-white flowers danced above the rest like a flurry of butterflies in the sunshine. Together with the electric purple pinpoints of *Verbena bonariensis,* with which they were interplanted, they blurred the boundaries of the beds and brought a sense of fun and movement to what would otherwise have been a staid and static scene.

Gaura lindheimeri, a native perennial of Mexico, is a plant that always excites people. It has a long flowering season, with pink buds opening into white flowers – hence the pretty impression of white mixed with pink. Heart-stoppingly beautiful in a clump on its own, it can also singlehandedly enliven a dull mixed border – not for nothing does the name of the genus translate as 'gorgeous'. *Gaura lindheimeri* 'Whirling Butterflies' has faint pink markings on the petals, while *G. lindheimeri* 'Siskiyou Pink' has sugar-pink flowers.

Among the lively streets of the Marais, where we were staying, I came across some other examples of formal gardening gone wild around the edges. The garden of the Musée Carnavalet (main entrance at 23 rue de Sevigny) is a typical formal courtyard that has been transformed by pretty planting. The box-edged beds of the parterre spilled over with pink roses, rich purple salvias and mauve and white osteospermums, their subtle colours offset by silvery onopordums, artemesia and santolina that also sprawled onto the path. There were gauras here, too – not in the same numbers, but just enough to impart that welcome (and distinctively un-

French) air of untidiness. If you don't want to visit the museum, there is free access to the garden through the carriage gates around the corner on the rue des Francs-Bourgeois.

Just over the road from these gates is another hidden gem of a formal garden, behind a library whose entrance is on the rue Pavée. Though the library was closed on my visit, the garden could still be admired from the road, with its late-summer fireworks of scarlet cannas, orange tithonias (Mexican sunflowers), *Nicotiana sylvestris* and bright lime green dill shooting off in all directions. Round the edges of the beds, the glossy, puckered foliage of yellow-veined chard made a redeeming backdrop for frilly French marigolds in lemon and cream. This time, the role of untidy interloper was shared between the dill and the floppy white daises of *Cosmos* 'Purity' – proof once again that formal gardens, like so many other things in life, are much more fun when they loosen up a little.

27 October 2002

SLUGGING IT OUT

Tidying up the allotment the other weekend, I was troubled by the number of slugs I found: small grey field slugs, huge rubbery black slugs and, worst of all, the odious fat brown keel slugs with their frilly orange edges. In late autumn there's obviously not the same danger to crops as in spring, when young seedlings are the slugs' delicacy of choice – indeed, there's an argument that at this time of the year the creatures are our friends, helping to clear decaying matter in which diseases can fester. But it's alway upsetting to find your cossetted pumpkins chomped or your winter greens with more holes than a Swiss cheese plant.

To cheer myself up, I curled up with *The Little Book of Slugs* (Centre for Alternative Technology [CAT], £4.99), edited by Allan Shepherd and Suzanne Galant, a light-hearted but useful new book (from Buy Green by Mail, 01654 705959). Born out of their 'Bug-the-Slug' campaign ("Tough on slime; tough on the causes of slime"), it brings together tips from CAT's 25 years experience of gardening in slug-ridden Wales with hundreds of innovative contributions to their www.ihateslugs.com website. Committed to organic gardening, CAT was keen to gather wisdom that might inspire the average gardener to think twice before scattering those blue metaldehyde pellets on the soil. In spite of a recent rash of press releases from chemical slug pellet manufacturers claiming their products are harmless to birds and animals if correctly used, the Government's annual study 'Pesticide Poisoning of Animals' shows that animals, including cats, dogs, wild birds, hedgehogs and predator beetles, *are* poisoned every year by slug pellets, even when the instructions have been followed correctly. And there has been no conclusive study so far on their effect on beneficial microorganisms in the soil.

Some of the more outlandish suggestions in the book are presented in terms of the "good" (gathering slugs at night and driving them to safety on nearby waste land) to the "bad" (snipping them with scissors, spearing them with a screwdriver or throwing them in the path of passing cars) and the "ugly" (swallowing them whole as a nutritious source of protein). But I found many other (to me) more feasible methods and deterrents, each of which has a keen following. These include introducing predators (from hedgehogs, frogs and toads to nematodes and Indian Runner ducks), making barriers around vulnerable plants (using crushed eggshells, coffee grounds, pine needles, sheep's fleece, troughs of salt water, wood and coal ash, sharp sand, sawdust and even lengths of copper pipe), and creating traps or fake shelters (halved grapefruit skins, large cabbage leaves and old Marmite jars as well as the tried and tested 'slug pubs'). One contributor suggested using milk instead of beer in the containers to tempt hedgehogs to come along and polish off the lot. Another had discovered, the day after a boozy barbecue, that the empty beer cans strewn across the lawn were full of slugs that were unable to escape past the sharp inward openings. Bran is a favourite decoy: slugs gorge on it and it slows them down, enabling you to cherry-pick them the morning after – one contributor claimed to have seen the creatures explode, which I don't think I'd fancy before breakfast.

One of the best ideas comes from CAT's own Peter Harper, who uses a bait of wilted comfrey leaves in the middle of each vegetable bed about a week before his seedlings are planted out in spring. After four or five nights, he says, the pile will be heaving with slugs, which can be picked off by hand. At the end of the week, remove the pile of leaves and any remaining slugs, and add to the compost heap, while making a ring of new comfrey leaves around the periphery of the newly planted-up bed. From then on, he claims, only occasional night-time checks will be necessary, and a fortnightly renewal of the leaves. So there we are: lots of good ideas. I'm going to get bugging those slugs.

3 November 2002

THE HEALING FIELDS

"Our hospital with the blue sky" is what Famida calls the allotments where she has been working for the past five years as part of the Natural Growth Project set up by psychotherapist Jenny Grut. Famida's plot is immaculate, bristling with spinach, beet, cabbages, turnips and the feathery salad leeks and spicy *ter-atisa* cress from her native northern Iraq. For Famida and her husband, Abdul, the land is more than just a means of providing food for their family. It is also a space where they can work through the memories and trauma of their experiences as victims of torture and persecution. Jenny Grut, a psychotherapist working for The Medical Foundation for the Care of Victims of Torture, set up the Natural Growth Project ten years ago as a response to the difficulties her clients at the time were experiencing with conventional one-to-one sessions. Not only were there often language problems; the cramped rooms themselves were reminders of past suffering. Because clients habitually reminisced about their farms and gardens back home and because she was convinced that contact with nature and the metaphors inherent in gardening could be healing, Jenny decided to take her work out of doors. In *The Healing Fields: Working with Psychotherapy and Nature to Rebuild Shattered Lives* (Frances Lincoln, £7.99), a new book she has co-written with writer-in-residence Sonja Linden, the ideas and principles behind the project are interwoven with the clients' own deeply moving stories.

Severely disabled or traumatized clients start off in the Remembrance Garden behind the Project's headquarters in Hampstead, north London. Here, they can grow flowers and herbs that remind them of their native Iran, Afghanistan or Bosnia, plant trees and shrubs for loved ones who have disappeared, and create art works using pebbles and mosaics. The more able travel to two allotment sites on the outskirts of London, where a total of 31 plots is rented from the local council. Here, their struggles with weeds, slugs, unyielding London clay and the British weather can provide a fruitful parallel with the frustrations, hardships – and eventual rewards – of putting down their own roots in an alien culture. On set days of the week Jenny comes to work alongside, picking up clues that may provide subtle material for exploring her clients' mental states. "Digging deep, turning over the soil, exposing weeds, composting waste – there is so much to work with," she says. "Sowing seed is such a sign of hope, particularly for asylum seekers unsure about their future. Sometimes the bananas and peppers people remember from home don't grow so well here, and that itself can help them come to terms with this new environment." Fresh air can help with health problems, while communal lunches and bread baking in a traditional clay oven create a new sense of community. Clients are encouraged to build their own sheds from skip timber – one told me his is nicer than the basement flat he has to live in.

Refugee status is a great leveller. In their former lives, some of the group were farmers, while others held office or academic posts, or employed gardeners at their large houses. Here at the allotments they are all equal – Mr Kader, a big landlord back home in Kurdistan, was given short shrift in the early days when he tried to tell others what to do. Mr Kader suffered incredibly harsh torture, Jenny tells me. Yet today he has brought homemade halva to the lunch to celebrate the arrival of a new grandchild. After four years tending his plot, he has now won respect as an 'elder' of the project and his produce beats his British neighbours to win prizes at the annual allotment show.

As some clients move on and other new faces arrive, the character of Jenny's work changes. She is currently focussed on three younger men, who are digging over plots at the far end of the site. "It will be interesting to work with angry young men," she says. "I felt it was time. Over here they have plenty of space to let rip." I left the allotments weighed down with gifts of turnips, onions, dill seed and *teratisa*. I also left full of feelings – moved and inspired by these seeds of hope growing out of unspeakable suffering. For donations to and information about the Medical Foundation for the Care of Victims of Torture, please phone 020 7813 9999.

10 November 2002

ROSES FOR SMALLER GARDENS

One of the joys in my little town garden this autumn has been the lovely climbing rose 'Madame Alfred Carrière', whose second flush of blooms shows no sign of stopping. The gold-pink blush at the base of the white petals gives it a warm glow that most white roses lack, and the scent is delicious. My only complaint is that the blooms are borne so high on the plant that I have to use a stepladder to pick or dead-head them. But that is my own fault for choosing a rose that's too big for my garden.

Like many gardeners with pretentions towards fashion and good taste, it just *had* to be an 'old' rose when I created this garden six years ago. I wouldn't even look at the grimly-named 'patio roses' and garish hybrid teas. Once I'd fallen for the many charms of 'Madame Alfred Carrière' to clothe my north-facing wall, there was no looking back – even if the small-print said she *did* grow to a height of 6m (20ft). I still don't regret my choice, but looking through Mark Mattock's *Roses for the Smaller Garden* (Quadrille, £14.99), I realize that there *are* other choices for those with less space than style.

Born into a rose-breeding family – his great-great-grandfather founded Mattock's Roses in 1875 – Mr Mattock has none of my 'old' rose prejudices, though he does thankfully steer clear of the modern monstrosities named after soap stars and members of the Royal Family. What he has done in this useful book is gather together from the hundreds of thousands of roses in existence – both old and new – a selection whose compact growth and capacity for repeat-flowering make them suitable for the smaller garden. "In a restricted space, any rose has to earn its keep," he explained when I met him recently at his home in Oxfordshire. "You need a controllable plant that won't take over your garden and that will give a good show of flowers when – and where – you want them." The trouble with old-fashioned climbers in a garden like mine is that they soon get out of hand and top-heavy. Mr Mattock therefore recommends the "patio climbers" (repeat-flowerers most of which were bred in the Forties and Fifties), which grow to 2.4 to 3m (8 to 10ft) high and bear flowers all the way up. 'Warm Welcome' is a rich golden orange with bronzy young foliage, while 'Penny Lane' has clean, crisp flowers of palest apricot. Also stunning is 'Altissimo', which can reach 3.6m (12ft) and has single scarlet blooms.

Less rampant climbers can also be grown successfully in containers – Mr Mattock has a large pot on wheels outside his sitting room window in which the old china rose, *Rosa chinensis* 'Mutabilis', is trained up a wicker wigwam. The wheels mean it can be turned around so the wonderful blooms, which start as dark copper buds and open yellow, before turning orange and then crimson, can be admired from inside the house, too. The rose has been covered in blooms all summer – and after pruning back to the support when it finally finishes flowering, it can be trundled away to make space for winter-flowering bulbs.

Other roses recommended for growing in containers include 'ground cover' roses such as the 'County Series', recent introductions which grow to 1m (3ft) high and wide, and flower continuously from early summer until the autumn frosts. The weight of the trusses of flowers on white 'Kent' and soft rose-pink 'The Fairy' will hang down to cover the rim of a large container, creating a mound of blossom. They can also be grown as standards.

Impressed though I was by these suggestions, I still find the lure of the old shrub roses irresistible. So I was relieved to find some that are eminently suitable for smaller spaces. The 'Portland Roses', which include soft-pink 'Jacques Cartier', deep crimson 'De Rescht' and lilac-tinted 'Comte de Chambord', all have the full blooms and delicious fragrance one expects from old roses combined with a long flowering period and a maximum height of 1.2m (4ft). They may not have sensual opulence of the larger shrub roses, spilling their perfumed blooms with abandon over lawns and borders, but until I have more space to play with, that will have to wait.

17 November 2002

SAFELY GATHERED IN

While the pots in my garden are constantly on the move – as different plants come into flower or lend themselves to certain combinations – autumn sees the greatest upheaval. At this time of year tender plants that have been outside all summer are taken back under cover for winter. Succulents and pelargoniums seem to gain an extra lease of life from their annual summer outing, and look a lot healthier for a spell of fresh air and sunshine. Indeed, many of my plants have grown so much this summer that it's been a job to squeeze them back into their winter quarters.

My study window is now almost filled with the fragrant feathery leaves of the pelargonium 'Attar of Roses' that stood outside the french windows all summer – the low sun illuminates the foliage and the scent surprises me whenever I walk in. Also needing shelter from the frost is the lovely grey-leafed *Pelargonium sidoides,* which has more than doubled its size. I envy gardeners in California and the Mediterranean who can enjoy this pelargonium as a pretty edging for borders all year round. But it is more than welcome on my bedroom windowsill, where those cascades of tiny deepest crimson flowers just keep on coming. One of the prettiest plants I know, *P. sidoides* is available by mail order from Special Plants (01225 891686), which also offers a new dark form with near-black flowers.

One prized plant that had grown too big to bring inside was the datura, still bearing stunning white trumpets in early November. It was tempting to chance it and leave the plant outside but I've already lost a couple of daturas to frost, so I made the painful decision to prune it back to about 0.4m (1½ft) wide and high. My shorn datura now fits happily on its old shelf, while the prunings, cut down to 15cm (6in) and relieved of their larger lower leaves, can be overwintered as cuttings. I have had success with this before, keeping a cluster of stems in a clear jug of water on a windowsill till rootlets form and the new generation of plants can be grown on or given away.

In the shelter of my walled garden, sturdier succulents, such as crassulas and echeverias, can usually butch it out over the winter, though I keep an eye out for the slugs and snails who take up residence beneath the rosettes and riddle the leaves with holes. But aloes, aeoniums and other fragile favourites must come inside, their pots artfully arranged as a "coffee-table garden" on a round aluminium tray with handles. Mulching the surface of the soil with horticultural grit not only looks smart; it also keeps in moisture – though remember that these plants are unused to central heating and may require a little more water in the early days. They also need as much light as possible.

So all is safely gathered in – except for the exotic *Echium pininana* – a native of the Canary Islands – in the front garden. This was given to me as a seedling by a gardening friend last summer and, though it seems to have taken happily to south London soil, it has yet to flower. Next year should be the year, provided I can coax it through any cold snaps this winter. As the plant is in the flowerbed and already more than 1.2m (4ft) high it wasn't   feasible to bring it inside, but I needed to find a way to protect the leaves from scorching. Horticultural fleece (£18.45 for 2.7m [9ft] from The Organic Gardening Catalogue 01932 253666) seemed to be the answer to ensure those towering blue spires of flowers next summer. When a fierce frost was forecast, I set about wrapping the plant in swathes of white, aiming for a Christo-like art installation effect.

Such pretensions were soon deflated, however, by one of my neighbour's children asking if I was making a ghost for Hallowe'en.

24 November 2002

GARDENERS FOR CHARITY

Gardeners are good people: it's official. A friend who works for a homeless people's charity told me that research into the profiles of donors to charities rated gardeners the highest. This fascinating information not only confirmed what I've suspected all along – in 20 years of garden writing I've scarcely come across a nasty gardener. It also makes sense that people who gain pleasure from their own homes and gardens should sympathize with the plight of those who have nothing.

Indeed, there are quite a few excellent UK charities who have specific links with gardening. The most famous, of course, is the National Gardens Scheme. Founded in 1927, the NGS raises money for a range of charities by encouraging private garden owners to open their gardens to the public – this year it celebrated its 75th anniversary by raising more than £2 million in entrance fees, teas, cakes and plant sales. Anyone who, like me, has ever opened their garden for the NGS can testify to the hard work it can be but also the great fun and satisfaction involved. If you think your garden might be up to scratch for 2004, contact your local county organizer via the website www.ngs.org.uk or phone the head office on 01483 211535. Gardens are judged on "quality, character and interest" and should ideally suit a 45 minute visit. Garden owners have the opportunity to name their own charity as the recipient of a proportion of the funds raised; otherwise the money is spread between ten main charities, including Macmillan Cancer Relief, Marie Curie Cancer Care and Help the Hospices.

Among the lesser-known charities supported by the NGS are two more with gardening associations. The Gardeners' Royal Benevolent Society (now re-named 'Perennial' 01372 373962) is one of the country's oldest charities, founded in 1839 by a group of philanthropists that included Charles Dickens. That year, at the annual dinner of Florists, Nurserymen and Gardeners, concern was expressed at the number of gardeners and estate workers who, on losing their tied cottages through old age, ill health or other misfortune, ended up in the workhouses, and the Society was set up to support them. The name may have an odd Victorian ring to it, but nearly two centuries on gardening, is often, still, low-paid and isolated work with little job security. Last year more than 800 people were helped by the Society, which offers its own nursing home and sheltered accommodation, along with a team of caseworkers to advise gardeners of all ages and their families. The Royal Gardeners' Orphan Fund (01707 333663), founded in 1887, provides similar help for the children of deceased gardeners.

A truly twenty-first century charity is Fairbridge (020 7928 1704), which offers challenging outdoor activities and personal develoment programmes to disadvantaged young people in inner cities. Targeting 13–25 year-olds in the roughest urban areas, Fairbridge aims to give course-goers the skills and confidence to succeed in society. In the first 18 months of its Youth Inclusion Project in Salford, crime in the area dropped by a quarter and average school attendance among participants doubled. The charity is supported by the Fairbridge Garden Society in London, which raises money for the charity through garden-related talks, visits and events, and from the profits taken by its own excellent garden centre in Fulham. You can support Fairbridge *and* have a good time by coming along to the annual Fairbridge Garden Society Christmas party in early December at the Fulham Palace Garden Centre, Bishop's Avenue, London SW6 6EE. This year, Penelope Hobhouse, Arabella Lennox-Boyd, Caroline Conran and I will be among those signing our books amid the mulled wine, mince pies and general festive cheer. All proceeds from the evening will go to Fairbridge.

1 December 2002

TREATS FOR THE BIRDS

I was thrilled when the blue tits that nested in our garden in the spring returned this autumn to raise a second brood. Long sunny spells at the tail-end of the summer apparently led more birds than is usual to breed again this year – as did the need to compensate for losses suffered during the earlier heavy rains. Though it's now far too late to attract nesting pairs, it's still worth putting up bird boxes over the winter. Basically, the longer the birds have to get used to the presence of a box, the more likely they are to use it. Mine – a smart wooden house my father made, its pitched roof painted to match our own door – had been fixed to the wall for a good couple of years before the blue tits deigned to use it. Some of the most stylish bird houses around, including two sleek models in iroko hardwood and some brand new handmade bird 'chalets', are available from RK Alliston in south-west London (phone 020 7751 0077 for a mail order brochure). Just remember to place them out of easy reach of cats and squirrels.

Now is also the traditional time to put food out for the birds. Though these days the RSPB and British Trust for Ornithology recommend feeding right through the year, I'd hate the birds to get so hooked on fancy seed mixes that they'd turn up their noses (or beaks) at the perfectly good menu of organic slugs, snails and aphids on offer in my garden all spring and summer. Time was when your average visiting bird had a choice of bacon rind, sunflower seeds or peanuts. But there is now a huge range of seed mixes on the market, each geared to different types of birds and seasons. Did you know, for instance, that thrushes, blackbirds and robins can't cope with the tough outer cases of most seeds and grain? Garden Bird Supplies catalogue (01939 232233) – a mail order company specifically geared to bird feeders and supplies – has a special 'Softbill Mix' among its 15 varieties of loose seed and nuts. Finches, blue tits and sparrows can cope with peanuts, while niger seed, a tiny black oil-rich seed similar to the teasel or thistle, is apparently particularly attractive to goldfinches and siskins – take care where you put it, though, or you could have a forest of thistles on your hands. In fact, niger seed might be a good candidate for mixing with suet or other melted fat and moulding into balls to place in feeders or hang from trees. It's a simple but satisfying task – I've just done a large batch for a refillable terracotta feeder I bought from a garden centre a few years ago. The birds gain extra nutrients from the fat and the seed goes down their throats rather than over your lawn.

If squirrels are a problem in your garden, there are plenty of feeders on the market with outer cages to keep them – and larger bullying birds such as starlings – out. Some suppliers offer a 'Squirrel Baffle' that stops the creatures climbing up a freestanding bird table – but these are expensive, due to a unique 'rocking device' that stops the squirrels in their tracks. But if you like squirrels, you may decide that providing the creatures with their own food is the best way to keep them off your bird table. Again, Garden Bird Supplies has a 'Squirrel Sweetcorn' made from maize flour that should keep them out of trouble.

8 December 2002

AN UNDERGROUND LARDER

We've been enjoying a good crop of jerusalem artichokes this year. Thinning the thicket of spindly plants to just four or five strong seedlings last spring has made for larger tubers that are full of flavour and easier to clean. Jerusalem artichokes are so easy to grow (indeed, they are much harder to eradicate, re-sprouting from the tiniest section of tuber left in the soil), that it is tempting just to leave them to get on with it. But I've found that a little extra attention is rewarded by much better yields – in terms of quality as well as quantity. Leaving 1m (3ft) between the plants and earthing up when new shoots are 30cm (1ft) or so high gives them space to spread, while cutting off the tops at 1.2–1.5m (4–5ft) high results in a mass of lower, branching foliage which not only looks tidier than the usual lanky 3.5m (12ft) stems, but also protects the roots from disturbance in high winds. Now is the time to order jerusalem artichokes for planting between January and March – The Organic Gardening Catalogue (01932 253666) offers 15 tubers of the reliable 'Fuseau' for £4.90.

There is something very heartening about root vegetables that can be left in the ground all winter (in milder areas at least) and lifted and eaten as required

– as if the garden were an underground larder providing warming soups and veggie stews. Salsify and scorzonera are two others of the same family (Asteraceae) that I'm keen to try. They look like whiskery white and black parsnips respectively – but I gather their unappealing appearance is redeemed by their delicate flavours. Salsify is sometimes known as the "vegetable oyster" – though I don't yet know whether this is because it actually tastes of oysters or is simply a nod to its gourmet reputation. Scorzonera is also deemed a great delicacy, and, unlike jerusalem artichokes, is supposed to be good for the digestion. Both are easily raised from seed (and again, the Organic Gardening Catalogue is a good source) sown in spring and thinned to about 30cm (1ft) apart – like most root crops, they do not transplant well. The crucial thing is to prevent the roots forking; this is done by avoiding recently manured soil and keeping disturbance between rows to a minimum.

The roots will be ready for use from November onwards, just when other fresh vegetables are very thin on the ground, and can be dug up as needed. In all but the harshest climates they are better left in the soil than stored inside – indeed, the flavour of salsify is said to be improved by frost, and that of both deteriorates after lifting. Never peel salsify or scorzonera before cooking, as they leach out flavour and nutrients. Instead, scrub hard to remove the whiskery side roots before frying, boiling or steaming, and the skins will slip off easily after cooking. Should any roots remain in the ground all winter, the spring shoots of salsify are apparently tasty, too, while the flower buds of scorzonera can be steamed and added to salads. Eleanour Sinclair Rohde, the renowned vegetable expert who wrote prolifically between the wars, suggests frying the buds and adding to eggs to make an omelette – the flowers open when cooked, which looks very pretty.

Another old root vegetable seldom grown these days is hamburg parsley, said to taste like a cross between celeriac and parsley. Its smooth white carrot-like roots are the main delicacy, though it is so hardy that the top-growth can be used instead of normal parsley right through the coldest winters. Again, the roots will be ready from November onwards and can be grated as a winter salad or added to stews and casseroles. Future Foods (01398 361347) and The Organic Gardening Catalogue have seed for sowing in early spring or July – a second sowing will mature much earlier the following year.

15 December 2002

TOMATILLO TACTICS

Last summer some friends arrived to stay at our rented seaside house with a bulging paper bag full of tomatillos they'd grown on their London allotment. I was most taken by the striking fruits – like green tomatoes, each encased in a papery husk not unlike that of a Chinese Lantern – and even more so after our friends, who are aficionados of all things Mexican, fried them up in a spicy *salsa verde*. The tomatillo is thought to have been domesticated from the wild by the Aztecs in the 14th century, and still forms part of the staple diet in modern day Mexico. It is almost impossible to buy fresh in the UK, however, even in these days of gourmet supermarket veg and farmer's markets. Luckily, as my friends explained, it is incredibly easy to grow oneself from seed.

In spite of its exotic origins, the tomatillo copes well with the average British summer. Not only does it ripen sooner, and in cooler weather than the tomato, to which it is related; it has the added and unfathomable advantage of immunity from potato blight. Like many gardeners, I am becoming increasingly frustrated by seeing our tomato crop ruined by blight, which thrives in these muggy wet summers. This year, from £18-worth of rare, trendy and 'heritage' seed, we harvested a mere handful of tomatoes before the blight struck. Had we known what was going to happen we'd have savoured every mouthful – not even Harrods Food Hall can boast the £4.50 tomato.

The tomatillo is not exactly a substitute for tomatoes – nothing else can come close to the flavoursome juiciness of a home-grown tomato still warm from the sun. But if you grow a few plants as well, you'll not be without the ingredients for home-made salsas and pasta sauces. The flavour of tomatillos is, in fact, quite distinct – fresh and slightly sharp with an almost grassy tang when green, and sweeter once the fruits turn yellow and burst from their papery confines. They are part of the same family (Solanum) as the tomato but belong to a completely different species – Physalis – along with the cape gooseberry and chinese lantern. Green-fruited varieties of *Physalis ixocarpa* are the most commonly grown – Future Foods (01398 361347) lists 'Tomatillo Large Green'; Simpson's Seeds (01985 845004) 'Mexican Green Husk' and The Organic Gardening Catalogue (01932 253666) simply 'Mexican Tomatillo' – which may well all be exactly the same thing. There is also a violet-fruited variety, listed by each of the above. Simpson's also includes the yellow-fruited 'Pineapple', which has a hint of that flavour, and are now offering six plantlets of mixed varieties for £7, in addition to seed.

Seed should be sown in exactly the same way as for tomatoes: under cover in early spring, with the seedlings potted on and planted out in the garden when all risk of frost has passed. Tomatillos like a rich but light soil, but are otherwise unfussy, and require little of the complicated pinching-out and tying-in that tomato-growing involves. The plants can grow to 1.5m (5ft) tall, so some form of staking is essential – and Simpson's Seeds suggests pinching out the leading shoot at 0.6m (2ft) tall and nipping off the laterals after the first leaf after each flower to obtain a bushier plant and bigger, better fruit. The fruit is ready for harvesting when it begins to burst free of the husks, and can be chopped raw into spicy salsas with garlic and coriander, lightly cooked to make *salsa verde* and pasta sauces, or added to vegetables, stews or ratatouille. Future Foods has a boxed 'Salsa Sensation' seed collection, featuring one packet each of the purple tomatillo, two of their heirloom tomatoes, the mild chilli pepper 'Yatsufa' and 'Santo' coriander – all for £6.

22 December 2002

AN ORCHID FOR CHRISTMAS

I like a lot of white flowers around at Christmas – they lighten the place up amid all the holly and ivy, tinsel and glitter that festoons the house at this time of the year. As well as the glass bowls of 'Paper White' narcissi that I grow on pebbles in water every winter, there are potted white cyclamen and amaryllis, and rows of white hyacinths in forcing jars ranged along mantelpieces. For me, these pure white blooms are like moments of stillness among the visual cacophony that is Christmas. Presiding like a queen over a corner of the sitting room this year is a huge white phalaenopsis orchid, whose dazzling 10cm (4in) blooms knock the others into a hat. I originally bought it for someone else, while doing my traditional last-minute present shop at the New Covent Garden Flower Market in Battersea, but became so attached to it I nipped back for another. For Londoners, the Flower Market is a good place to buy orchids and other potted plants at wholesale prices – provided you don't mind getting up early and paying the £3 parking fee.

Orchids have a touch of glamour that gives them the edge over other, more humble houseplants. They make fine presents – and are much easier to care for than their exotic looks suggest. True, many of the warm-growing species do need a lot of mollycoddling – a heated greenhouse or conservatory at the very least. But most of the best-known orchids – including phalaenopsis, cymbidiums and many of the feathery oncidiums and delicately patterned odontoglossums –

will be perfectly happy in the average interior, provided the temperature doesn't fall below 10°C (50°F) at night and 16°C (60°F) by day. If you should be lucky enough to receive an orchid as a gift, keep it in a light spot but out of direct sunlight – a north-facing window sill is fine in summer, and a south-facing spot in winter, or if blinds or thin curtains filter out the rays. Larger orchids, such as cymbidiums, will enjoy a summer holiday in the garden if protected from the ravages of slugs, snails and woodlice.

Your orchid may be planted in an

unattractive plastic pot with a tangle of roots escaping from the top, but on no account let this tempt you to re-pot it in normal compost. Many of the easier orchids are epiphytes, growing without soil in the wild in crevices in rock faces or lodged in the bark of trees. Orchid compost, composed of pine-bark chippings, is very free-draining, as orchids hate to sit in water. Place the pot on a saucer filled with water and porous clay pellets (sold in bags at any good garden centre) so that the base of the pot sits just above the water. This will keep the humidity at the desired level – grouping other smaller plants together on a larger tray of pellets also helps and looks nice, too.

Don't over-water. This is the most common problem among inexperienced orchid-growers, resulting in rapid loss of foliage, rotting roots and eventual death. Orchids like to be moist when growing and drier when dormant in the winter months, when many of them flower. Use orchid feed (available from larger garden centres) every third watering in winter and every other time in spring and summer – but again, don't overdo it or you'll scorch the roots. With phalaenopsis, you can encourage extended flowering by cutting back the stems to a lower node after the first flush of blooms. Re-pot orchids every two or three years, teasing out the old compost from between the roots, discarding any dead roots and trimming back the longest live ones to around 15cm (6in). Place in a pot 5cm (2in) larger than the last, and pack with compost so the base of the new growth is level with the surface. Following these simple principles should ensure that your orchid is around to provide pleasure, beauty – and visual calm – for a good many Christmases to come.

29 December 2002

GOODBYE TO THE ALLOTMENT

We always meet up at the allotment some time between Christmas and New Year – Clarkey, Simon and myself, our two dogs, a Thermos of tea and what-ever we can muster in the way of leftover Christmas cake and mince pies. It's become a matter of pride and tradition to turn up whatever the weather. There is always the pretence of doing some work, like pruning the fruit bushes or planting garlic, which is traditionally done (according to some sources) on New Year's Day. But it's invariably so cold that the ground's too hard to work, and so it turns into an excuse to see each other, and look back on the past season and plan for the year ahead, while our tea sends swirls of steam into the air.

On some occasions we haven't had too much to be pleased about, but this has been a good year at the allotment. With no real extra effort, we've had marvellous crops of potatoes, shallots, courgettes and beans, and the sweet-corn has been the best ever. True, the tomatoes succumbed to blight again, and it may be plain foolish to keep on trying. But the slugs seemed to hold off our lettuce patch for once – thwarted by Seeds of Italy's 'radicchio and chicory mixed pack' (£1.25 for 12 varieties, ring 020 8930 2516) in which milder 'cut-and-come-again' salad leaves are protected by the bitter radicchio, which slugs don't seem to like. If our strawberries could be counted on the fingers of two hands, the raspberries and red-, white- and blackcurrants came so thick and fast that we could hardly keep up with the summer puddings. And – as if we could forget – there was also our triumph at the Lambeth Country Show with our prize-winning round courgettes, French beans and sweetpeas.

This year's winter meeting will feel somewhat different from the others. It may well be my last at the allotment. After what must be the longest house sale in history, my husband and I have finally exchanged contracts on that much-longed-for house by the sea. Actually, it's not so much a house as a shack made from a pair of ancient railway carriages, but it does have a great deal of charm and a large garden to boot. Just down the track from the cottage we were renting the other year, it has a nature reserve next door and just a field of horses between us and the beach. But unlike the old house, which was built on pure shingle, this garden has enough soil for a few gnarled apple trees and some lovely old roses around the door.

Urban gardening won't be left behind entirely. The new house will be mainly for the summer months, so we're not leaving town for good. There's a fair amount of fixing up to do, and the garden is so overgrown I'm not even sure what's in it – I'm told there's a pond, but I've yet to come across it. In the meantime, I'll be making some changes in our London garden, to help it survive my prolonged absences, and I daresay I'll be back at the allotment for a bit until my new garden gets going. After seven long years at the allotment it will be hard to say goodbye. This place has been a lifeline for a Londoner like me – a haven of peace and beauty in the city; a refuge from the builders and work; a place in which to learn by trial and frequent error. It has provided me with endless enjoyment and inspiration – as well as a more or less constant supply of organic fruit and vegetables. And it has deepened a very dear friendship. Gardening in company has been one of the unexpected bonuses of having an allotment, and I've learned a great deal from my friends and fellow plot holders – and had great fun too. As I bid Clarkey and Simon goodbye at the gate, I look back at the familiar ramshackle landscape with great fondness. Though a country garden of my own is a real dream come true, I know I shall miss this place.

Index